Homosexuality, Law and Resistance

Homosexuality, Law and Resistance explores contemporary social theory and developments in the study of sexuality through the analysis of law and its practices. Each chapter explores the power of discourse in law in relation to homosexualities, while simultaneously examining how homosexuals resist and disrupt these legal discourses.

The book includes detailed case narratives of some of the most highly publicised and far-reaching contemporary struggles surrounding homosexuality in law. These include the ban on homosexuals from serving in the armed forces and the reduction of the homosexual age of consent. It also contains case studies focused on the plight of homosexual refugees in asylum and immigrations procedures.

The author also undertakes a sustained critique of what has come to be known as queer theory. This critique addresses the 'textual' and 'abstract' limitations inherent in much queer theory by combining the analysis of discourse and representations in law with a sociological investigation of the complex of practices and counter-practices found in law.

Many of the themes explored in this book will be of interest to students and academics working in the fields of sociology, cultural studies, law, politics, gender studies and sexuality. This timely work will prove a valuable addition to the literature of all these fields.

Derek McGhee is a lecturer in the Department of Sociology and Social Policy at the University of Southampton, United Kingdom. *Homosexuality, Law and Resistance* is his first book, based on his doctoral research on homosexualities in the legal complex. He is currently conducting research on gays and lesbians in 'the family'.

Routledge Research in Gender and Society

Homosexuality, Law and Resistance

Derek McGhee

London and New York

First published 2001
by Routledge
11 New Fetter Lane, London EC4P 4EE

Simultaneously published in the USA and Canada
by Routledge
29 West 35th Street, New York, NY 10001

Routledge is an imprint of the Taylor & Francis Group

© 2001 Derek McGhee

Typeset in Garamond by Taylor & Francis Books Ltd
Printed and bound in Great Britain by TJ International Ltd,
Padstow, Cornwall

British Library Cataloguing in Publication Data
A catalogue record for this book is available from the British Library

Library of Congress Cataloging in Publication Data
McGhee, Derek
Homosexuality, law and resistance/Derek McGhee.
Simultaneously published in the USA and Canada.
Includes bibliographical data and index.
1. Homosexuality–law and legislation–Great Britain. I. Title.
KD4103 .M38   2001
346.4101'3–dc21

ISBN 0–415–24902–3

To my parents John and Jeannette McGhee and my family Andrew and Jem Cullis.

Not all homosexual persons can be identified as such by their appearance and manner for many have no special characteristics. Homosexuals themselves are usually able to recognise each other in various ways, including gestures, smiles and mannerisms, and peculiarities of appearance and habits. In some there is a tendency to self-display in dress and hair-styles and in the use of scent and make-up. In the effeminate type of male there is often a certain softness which is difficult to describe but easy to sense. The voice may be high-pitched and facial hair scanty. On the other hand, many homosexuals are virile and masculine. Homosexuals are often charming and friendly people and many of them are well known to be of artistic temperament.

(British Medical Association, Memorandum of Evidence
submitted to the Wolfenden Committee, November 1955)

Contents

Acknowledgements

The acknowledgements included here span two particular periods in two academic locations. The first is in relation to postgraduate research at the Sociology Department at Lancaster University (1995–9) and the second relates to a lectureship in the Sociology and Social Policy Department at the University of Southampton since January 2000.

Homosexuality, Law and Resistance started out as a PhD thesis, entitled *Passing Resistance*. This thesis resulted in the author being awarded a PhD in 1999 (Lancaster University). In relation to the period of doctoral research I would like to thank Dr Leslie Moran and Professor Scott Lash for their support, criticism, guidance and friendship as my supervisors. I would also like to thank them for working very hard to help attract ESRC funding for this research.

I would like to thank my PhD examiners Dr Elena Loizidou, Professor Jeffrey Weeks and Dr Catherine Reed for their critical and enthusiastic engagement with the project, and their encouragement to publish the thesis as a research monograph.

Many individuals have had various 'involvements' with this research at Lancaster University and at the University of Southampton. I would like to thank the following: Dr Bernard Harris (for making sure my book proposal reached the 'right' desk at Routledge), Professor Carl Stychin, Professor John Urry, Professor Scott Lash, Dr Leslie Moran and Professor Rob Shields for their critical reflections on the 'book proposal'. I would also like to thank 'established' and 'newer' friends and colleagues such as: Dr Ann Cronin, Dr Jonatas Ferreira, Dr Claire Valier, Monica Degen, Dr Celia Lury, Richard Tutton, Dr Catherine Reed, Dr Traute Meyer, Dr Wendy Bottero, Mel Semple, Dr Paul Sweetman, Dr Graham Crow, Dr Susan Halford, Dr Caroline Knowles, Professor Clare Ungerson, Gordon Causer, Professor Rosemary Pringle and Dr Sue Heath.

I would also like to take this opportunity to thank family and friends such as Gwenneth, Leslie and Robert Cullis, and John, Tanya (Oram) and Katy McGhee for their support during the various stages of this research.

I owe the following individuals a great debt of gratitude for providing me with much-needed documents and reports during the research: Squadron

Leader I.D. Williamson, RAF Service Personnel, Ministry of Defence; David Smith, Editor, *Gay Times*; Angela Mason, Director, Stonewall; Simon Russell, of the Refugee Legal Centre and Amnesty International; Malcolm Bryant of Maurice Cohen & Co. Solicitors; and I would especially like to thank Michael Dunne, Lancaster University Law Librarian, for all his assistance in locating and tracing material. Thanks also to Sue Hemmings for her support and encouragement.

Thanks are also due to the team at Routledge Research for all of their support and assistance.

Some parts of this book have been previously published and are re-published here with the permission of the publishers. A version of Chapter 1 appeared under the title of 'Looking and Acting the Part: Gays in the Armed Forces – A Case of Passing Masculinity' in *Feminist Legal Studies* 6(2) (1998): 205–244. A version of Chapter 2 appeared under the title of 'Accessing Homosexuality: Truth, Evidence and the Legal Practices for Determining Refugee Status – The Case of Ioan Vraciu', in *Body & Society* 6(1) (2000): 29–50. A version of Chapter 3 has been accepted for publication under the title of 'Persecution and Social Group Identities: Homosexual Refugees in the 1990s', in the *Journal of Refugee Studies* 14(1) (forthcoming, 2001). A version of Chapter 4 appeared under the title of 'Wolfenden and the Fear of Homosexual Spread: Permeable Boundaries and Legal Defences', in *Studies in Law, Politics & Society* 21 (2000): 65–97.

Introduction

> These discourses have really affected lives; these existences have effectively been risked and lost in these words.
>
> (Foucault 1979b: 79)

This book consists of case studies in which men who have loving and sexual relationships with other men experience specific exclusions and restrictions before the law. In many ways this is a book about knowledge, and how knowledge is deployed and ultimately disrupted in certain legal institutional contexts. The body, identity and discourse, as well as power and resistance, are some of the central themes that will be explored here.

The four case study chapters presented in the book are composed of three legal struggles surrounding homosexuality and law. These are: the analysis of the British armed forces homosexual exclusion policy; an analysis, in the form of two case studies, of refugee determination procedures in the UK in relation to applications for refugee status based on homosexuality; and, finally, an analysis of parliamentary discourses in relation to the age of homosexual consent between 1957, when the Wolfenden Report was published,[1] and 2000 (see chapter synopsis at the end of this introduction for more details).

The purpose of these case studies is not to find out what homosexuality is but rather to explore how law attempts to know homosexuality and homosexuals in order to justify its particular treatment of them.

The focus of this book, on homosexual identities and legal practices, facilitates the intersection of three interrelated sites of analysis. These are: (a) the analysis of the technologies whereby homosexual identities and 'homosexual' behaviour and activities are presented and produced as knowledge within the representational practices of law; (b) the analysis of how these discursive identities and knowledges are deployed in legal practices so as to justify the juridical regulation, control or exclusion of homosexuals; and (c) the analysis of the vulnerability of these discursive justificatory mechanisms. This vulnerability is characterised in the case studies by disruption, infiltration and the de-subjugation of alternative knowledge.

The centrality of homosexual identity to legal practices in this book unsettles the Wolfenden Committee's attempt to separate homosexuality as a condition from homosexual acts. In the Wolfenden Report it was stated that 'homosexuality is a sexual propensity for persons of one's own sex. Homosexuality, then, is a state or condition, and as such does not, and cannot, come within the purview of the Criminal Law' (1957: para 18, 11). According to Moran, the Wolfenden Committee concluded that ' "homosexuality" was not an object of concern of either the law in general or the Criminal Law in particular' (Moran 1996a: 93).

Moran exposes the ambiguity of the Wolfenden Committee's claim that the Criminal Law (and the law in general) should not be interested in homosexuality, as the Committee's use of the phrase 'homosexual offences' inseparably conflates homosexual identity with 'homosexual' acts (Moran 1996a). In the case studies included in this book it will be demonstrated that homosexual identities and homosexuality as a condition are indeed a concern of international refugee law, armed forces policy and the criminal law in relation to the homosexual age of consent.

In terms of identity the book is concerned with surfaces, the performative surfaces of power and the performances of the body – especially the gendered body as surface, as signifier of identity. In the case studies that follow, the dominant interpretations and representations within legal practices are shown to cover the surfaces of events and produce discursive bodies and identities. The case studies demonstrate how male homosexuals in particular, in the practices within legal institutions, become objects which must be produced, fixed and separated out from other (heterosexual, 'normal') men so that they can be subsequently eradicated (excluded, restricted, imprisoned and executed). Lesbians, in some cases, share these experiences of separation and eradication, for example, in the case of the armed forces exclusion policy on (both male and female) homosexuals. On the whole, however, female homosexuals are excluded from the particular criminal legal discursive construction of homosexuals analysed in the various case studies. For example, as is seen in Chapter 4, female homosexuals are not subjected to a higher age of consent than female heterosexuals.[2] Female homosexuals, as yet, also do not feature centrally in the UK's homosexual refugee case law, analysed in Chapters 2 and 3. However, this does not mean that lesbians are excluded from the atrocities which homosexuals of both genders endure in particular countries such as Iran and Romania.

As a result of the relative absence of female homosexuals from the archive of material analysed in this book, an in-depth cross-gender analysis that would include both male and female homosexuals is not fully developed. It would be illegitimate to develop such an analysis from the cases included in this book, as they predominantly focus on the legal practices that produce, exclude and restrict male homosexuals. Issues of female homosexuality, when they arise, are examined in the relevant case studies.

The heteronormativity of law

This book can be described as being part of a wider conversation between socio-legal studies and queer studies, that investigates the production and deployment of sexualised identities in legal and political discourse. Central to this queer socio-legal approach is the concept of heteronormativity. Berlant and Warner define heteronormativity thus:

> By heteronormativity we mean the institutions, structures of under-standing and practical orientations that make heterosexuality seem not only coherent − that is, organised as a sexuality − but also privileged. Its coherence is always provisional, and its privilege can take several (some-times contradictory) forms: unmarked, as the basic idiom of the personal and the social; or marked as a natural state; or projected as an ideal or moral accomplishment.
>
> (Berlant and Warner 1998: 548)

Heteronormativity is therefore the term used to specify the tendency in the contemporary Western sex-gender system to view heterosexual relations as the norm, and all other forms of sexual behaviour as deviations from this norm (Spargo 1999: 73). This book demonstrates the complex ways in which heteronormativity pervades legal institutions and the practices therein. It will be demonstrated that the representations of 'the homosexual' in the legal institutional practices under analysis are deployed in specific relations of power that illuminate a relationship between law, heterosexualities and homosexualities. However, in the case studies included in this book Berlant and Warner's definition of heteronormativity as an unconscious, unmarked and 'invisible, tacit, society-founding rightness' (1998: 548) is shown to understate and to generalise the heteronormative organisation of law. In the case studies included here, the relationship between law and heteronormativity will be shown to be directly expressed and explicit in particular legal practices, rather than being tacitly inferred or indirectly expressed in general as in Berlant and Warner's definition.

In many ways the case studies included in this book are demonstrations, in local legal institutional contexts, of how and in what ways heteronorma-tivity works, in and through legal practices, especially in relation to the law's claims to know homosexuals and homosexualities in relation to partic-ular heterosexualised norms. This is nowhere more apparent than when, in legal practices, homosexual identities are deployed within a justificatory and contrasting discursive couple with normative identities. For example, in the case studies particular homosexual identities are deployed in institutional discourses alongside identities such as the military man, the 'genuine refugee' and the vulnerable adolescent, in order to justify and legitimise the particular institutional and institutionalised treatment of homosexuals. Law here is presented in terms of Ewald's (1990) description of social law, that is 'law which is welded to the power of norms' (Rose and Valverde 1998: 544). This is unlike law as conceptualised as a juridical system of external rules. This is law that 'appears – or claims – to emerge out of the very nature of, that which is governed. Its normativity is predicated upon and justified by its normality: the normal child, the normal family, normal conduct' (Rose and Valverde 1998: 544).

Legal practices are presented here from a critical legal studies conceptualisation that challenges and exposes the myth of the unbiased neutrality and unemotional and detached objectivity of legal practice. The formative statement of the British Critical Legal Studies Conference was as follows: 'the central focus of the critical legal approach is to explore the manner in which legal doctrine, legal education and the practices of legal institutions work to buttress and support a pervasive system of oppressive non-egalitarian relations' (Grigg-Spall and Ireland 1992: ix). Law, according to Ireland and Grigg-Spall, 'generally acts to consolidate and maintain an extensive system of class, gender and racial oppression' (1992: ix); to this must be added the oppression of non-normative sexualities.

The struggles or challenges to the legal restriction and/or exclusion of homosexuals documented in the case studies included in this book throws this assumed neutrality at the heart of liberal legal reasoning into sharp relief. The institutionalisation of the particular and contextualised heteronormative relations of power within the legal practices under analysis in the case studies puts paid to the myth of law as the site of 'objective, unmediated voices by which transcendent, universal truths find their expression' (Williams 1993: 9).

Law is approached here in a particular way. It is not 'law' in general that is under analysis, rather it is local institutions and the practices within what Rose and Valverde describe as the 'legal complex' (1998: 542) that will be analysed in the case studies. Rose and Valverde insist that 'law' should not be viewed as a unitary institution. Rather, 'law' should be viewed as multi-institutional and impure. According to Rose and Valverde

> The intellectual premises and analytic methods of legal studies tend to presuppose that objects and problems form within the workings of law itself. But in order to analyse the ways in which problems form at the intersection of legal and extra-legal discourses, practices and institutions, it is necessary to de-centre law from the outset.
>
> (Rose and Valverde 1998: 545)

The 'law' of *Homosexuality, Law and Resistance* is therefore a de-centred law. Law is presented and approached in this book as the intersection of the legal and the extra-legal in a complex of institutional settings.

Power, discourse and the body in the legal complex

By using the concept 'heteronormativity', the relationship between hetero-sexuality and homosexuality immanent in legal practices is brought to the fore. Within this relationship the constructions and representations of the homosexual, particularly the homosexual body, are implicated in specific regimes of truth and power relations. The concept of performativity is central to this analysis. According to Butler, a performative is that discursive practice that enacts or produces that which it names (Butler 1993a: 13). Therefore, in terms of the naming of homosexuality within heteronorma-tively organised institutional practices, performativity is construed as the power of discourse to produce effects through repetition or reiteration (Butler 1993a: 20). What Butler means here is that power is not power that acts but a reiterative acting that is power (1993a: 9), that is 'power acts as discourse' (Butler 1993b: 17).

Discourse describes how social knowledge is organised in particular ways. Discourse is the concept used to describe how knowledge is institutionalised in social policies and the organisations through which they are carried out. Discourses are thus about relations of power, about organised positions and places in the field of power (Hughes 1998: 159). In Foucauldian theory, discourse is not just another word for speaking, but a historically situated material practice that produces power relations. Discourses are bound up with specific knowledges (Spargo 1999: 73). Discourses exist within, and support, institutions and social groups. In legal institutions the discourses which produce homosexual identities are interdependent with specific juridical effects which restrict or exclude homosexuals. The critical discourse analysis presented in each of the case studies can be described as performing deconstructive readings of reiterated, institutionalised discourses in order to reveal underlying paradoxes and absent presences within them. In this context, critical discourse analysis is akin to Foucault's definition of critique. According to Foucault:

> A critique is not a matter of saying that things are not right as they are. It is a matter of pointing out on what kinds of assumptions, what kinds of familiar, unchallenged, unconsidered modes of thought the practices we accept rest.
>
> (Foucault 1988: 154)

Thus, the case studies included in this book can be described as critiques of the self-evidence of discourses that have become accepted in social and institutional practices. However, this is only one side of the project presented here as these critiques are as much to do with making space for alternative, competing or subjugated knowledges within the legal complex as they are with the analysis of discourse.

Bodies, or, more specifically, representations of the homosexual body, are central to the interdependent relationship of power/knowledge in the legal complex. According to Hyde, 'bodies are, among other things, the ways we represent other people to ourselves' (Hyde 1997: 3). That is, bodies are at least in part 'the linguistic, discursive device for representing that aspect of other people, which is not opaque and inaccessible to us' (Hyde 1997: 3–4). In this book the sensuality (especially 'the visuality') and corporeality of legal institutional practices is a central concern. It is not only the sensuality of legal practice that is emphasised here, but also the emotionality of these institutional practices. For example, in Chapter 1 the irrationality of 'paranoia' is as evident in the justifications for the homosexual exclusion policy in the armed services as this policy's alleged 'rationality' and 'practical' basis. Similarly, in Chapter 4 the justifications for a higher homosexual age of consent are explicitly linked with fear in parliamentary debates, especially the fear of the degenerative forces of homosexuality spreading into the nation's young people, especially the nation's sons.

As described above, in each case study the representation of the homosexual body in legal discourse can be contextualised within a heteronormative power relation characterised by performativity. However, as the case studies will demonstrate, it is also through the body that homosexuals develop tactics for coexisting alongside such discursive productions and the power effects that justify their particular juridical treatment. In this book I demonstrate that it is through the body and the sensory, social scrutiny of bodies by other bodies[3] that homosexuals become, in certain social settings, privatised, self-governing, circumspect subjects of power (Rose 1990; Moran 1996a). What I mean by this is that, through the internalisation of hostility and official sanctions, homosexual men learn how to become unrecognisable socially as homosexuals. They become men who can pass as assumed heterosexuals in some of the most anti-homosexual institutional contexts in contemporary societies.

In the case studies that follow, passing occurs within what Chaney describes as the reciprocity of 'visual power' relations, that is, where ways of seeing are also necessarily ways of being seen' (1996: 103). However, Chaney's descriptions of the reciprocity of sight must be modified here. The term 'reciprocity' connotes a degree of mutual exchange, a degree of equality between participants. As a result, it is unsuitable for the conceptualisation of the asymmetrical power relations between homosexual bodies and the heteronormative gaze – that sentient, diacritical scrutiny of bodies for the signs of homosexuality. The term 'intercorporeality' (Williams and Bendelow 1998: 51) better conceptualises this social sensorial relationship (albeit an ocularcentric one) between homosexuals and the surveillant embodiments of heteronormativity that they encounter in institutional contexts. In these settings, homosexual bodies must attempt to coexist by tactically accommodating to this embodied visual power relation.[4]

These intercorporeal encounters are situated within the heteronormative relations of power which Butler describes as the heterosexual matrix. Butler defines the heterosexual matrix as 'that grid of cultural intelligibility through which bodies, genders, and desires are naturalised' (Butler 1990: 151). The heterosexual matrix is characterised by:

> A hegemonic discursive/epistemic model of gender intelligibility that assumes that for bodies to cohere and make sense there must be a stable sex expressed through a stable gender (masculine expresses male, feminine expresses female) that is oppositionally and hierarchically defined through the compulsory practice of heterosexuality.
>
> (Butler 1990: 151)

The gendered body is crucial to understanding the specific episodes of resistance/survival presented in the case studies. Gender, according to Butler (1989, 1990, 1993a), is the signifier of an underlying sexual orientation; gender is thus a manipulable signifier of sexualities that may or may not correspond to particular gender performances. In the case studies, it is the performance of appropriate varieties of 'heterosexual masculinities' that becomes the tactical means whereby homosexual males can act their bodies, when a situation necessitates it, so as to signify heterosexuality (or deflect attention away from their homosexuality). In the context of social hostility towards homosexuality, homosexuals become aware of the significance of their appearance and behaviour, and thus 'attach overwhelming importance to monitoring their own and other appearances that they can control' (Chaney 1996: 103–4). As a result of this particular focus on the tactical and resistant possibilities of gender, in the case studies that follow, Foucault's reputed over-theorisation of power and under-theorisation of resistance, and also the alleged 'absence of gender in his [Foucault's] work' (Ramazanoglu 1993: 4) are addressed. Foucault has been criticised by feminists for treated the bodily experience of men and women as being the same in relation to the characteristic institutions of modern life (Bartky 1990: 65). These case studies will demonstrate that the bodily experiences between men and within gender (masculinities) differ in relation to the characteristic institutions of modern life too.

The threat of becoming known or recognised as a homosexual, as a 'sexual suspect' is a recurring theme throughout the book, as is the role law plays, in its multi-institutional practices, in promoting self-governing, private homosexualities. Self-protection and privacy are central tensions throughout the book, and are played out in this specific discursive intercorporeal realm.

According to Plummer, the social process of recognising homosexuals is largely dependent on the mediation of certain patterns of socially constructed meanings (Plummer 1975: 179). As a result, what is observed socially is of crucial importance because this is the primary source of intelligibility, especially if the heteronormative sensorial relation is conceived in terms of 'the gaze', as a way of looking based on knowledge of 'the normal' from which abnormalities are distinguishable.

Therefore, it is through the surface of the body, and the discursive coatings applied to bodies, that the homosexual is represented and recognisable in legal discourse. Yet it is also through the body's surface appearance and deportment that homosexuals have the ability tactically to camouflage their difference through a capacity to pass, to remain invisible (Edelman 1994: 4). What this means is that this 'somatisation of power relations involves the imposition of limits upon the body which simultaneously constitute the condition of the possibility of agency' (McNay 1999: 104).

Passing here consists of the homosexual's tactical ability to avoid a marked, stigmatised (and thus recognisable) homosexual identity and instead take on the unmarked trappings and characteristics that signify heterosexual identity. As Goffman explains, 'the normal and the stigmatised are not persons but rather perspectives' (1963: 163). Goffman was aware of the intercorporeality (or what he would refer to as the reciprocal monitoring of one's own body and the bodies of others in co-present encounters)[5] of embodied normative power relations. Goffman was also aware of the possibility of embodied tactics employed by the stigmatised who were attempting to render their stigma socially invisible. Goffman's analysis is especially relevant for individuals with potentially invisible stigmas such as homosexuals. In this conceptualisation Goffman serves as a precursor for much queer theorising surrounding the politics of drag, for example in Butler's work (1989, 1990, 1993a), and the epistemologies of 'the closet' in Sedgwick's work (1991). One could say, following Goffman, that homosexuals, while living as invisible 'insiders' (assumed heterosexuals, or the assumed potential heterosexualities of adolescents) accumulate, through processes of primary and secondary socialisation, both knowledge of how they are treated socially and also how they, as homosexuals, can avoid being recognised and treated as such. Goffman describes this process in the following passage:

> there are two phases in the learning process of the stigmatised person … his learning of the normal point of view and learning that he is disqualified according to it. Presumably a next phase consists of his learning to cope with the way others treat the kind of person he can be shown to be. A still later phase is … learning to pass.
>
> (Goffman 1963: 101)

In order to appreciate both the discursive production and exclusion of homosexuals in legal practices, and the tactics utilised by homosexuals to counteract, and survive within, such power/knowledge regimes, this book necessarily comprises a range of types of analysis. The analysis of institutional technologies, and the discourses and representations deployed within them in legal practices, will occur side by side with the analysis of embodied social tactics.[6] Therefore, the analysis of the legal power to produce 'the homosexual' and homosexualities is presented simultaneously with the homosexual body as a site of agency, survival and disruption. That is:

> An analysis of power, which stresses relationality, makes visible the prolific sites of possible resistance. Our bodies are the medium through which power functions. By virtue of their location within power, our bodies are also effective sites of resistance to power's capillary alignments.
>
> (Cheah and Grosz 1996: 19)

The examples of resistance explored below, through the gendered body tactic of passing as heterosexual and the controlling of identity information (Goffman 1963), result in a rather peculiar reversal in terms of gay liberation strategies and the requirement to be 'out'. In the particular contexts under analysis, 'the closet' is presented as a reclaimed site, following Sedgwick (1991), simultaneously protective and subversive, a site that homosexuals can dip in and out of, when needs be. From this perspective, 'the closet' is, rather controversially, reclaimed as a queer space which allows homosexuals to be 'simultaneously (queer) inside and (straight) outside' (Taylor 1997: 15). As will be demonstrated in the case studies, concepts of the 'public' and the 'private' in this book, especially in Chapters 1 and 4, are produced less as geographical phenomena than as visual and corporeal arrangements of proximity between the bodies of observers and the bodies they scrutinise. That is, 'the public' and 'the private' become here 'lived distinctions' in and around 'bodily behaviour' (Young 1990: 140). Closetedness, in this conceptualisation, thus results from the internalisation of visual, legal and corporeal arrangements. Closetedness is less a permanent state than a contingent, in some cases necessary, form of subterfuge. Passing here becomes synonymous with resistance.

A queer context: contextualising queer theory

Queer theory has been a growing academic movement since the 1980s. It has been described as a new paradigm of cultural studies, which draws on the work of theorists such as Michel Foucault, Jacques Derrida, Jacques Lacan and Roland Barthes (Escoffier 1998: 173). It is not a singular or systematic conceptual or methodological framework, but a collection of intellectual engagements with the relations between sex, gender and sexual desire (Spargo 1990: 9). Queer theory thus describes a diverse range of critical practices and priorities: readings of the representation of same-sex desire in literary texts, films, music, image. Queer theorists also analyse the social and political power relations of sexuality that include critiques of the sex-gender system, studies of transsexual and transgender identification, of sadomasochism and of transgressive desire (Spargo 1999: 9). In this book, it is the analysis of the social, political and legal power relations of sexuality that is the central queer enterprise.

The academic and political movement from gay and lesbian studies to queer theory and politics has been described by Halperin as being a movement from liberation to resistance (Halperin 1995: 26). Much of queer theory can be said to be reacting subversively to heteronormativity within societies and cultural forms. However, allied with this focus is the realisation that, in order to resist the reciprocity of heteronormative effects of power, queers have to alter their 'political' emphasis on sexual identities. According to Seidman:

> central to queer theory is its challenge to what has been the dominant foundational concept of both homophobic and affirmative homosexual theory: the assumption of a unified homosexual identity. I interpret queer theory as contesting this foundation and therefore the very telos of Western homosexual politics.
>
> (Seidman 1997: 92)

The 'revolution' in queer theory and politics, therefore, comes in the form of the view that the affirmation of a homosexual identity, the foundation of gay and lesbian identity politics, is not necessarily a step towards liberation. In fact, queer theorists, following Foucault, view these identity categories as being complicit with disciplinary and regulatory practices (Seidman 1997: 93). As a result, one of the major contributions of queer theory to sexual politics is the conceptualisation of the hazards of political mobilisation from unitary identity categories.

Queer theorists demonstrate that identity categories are normative and therefore exclude certain varieties of homosexualities, bisexuals, the transgendered and the transsexual.[7] Such exclusive identity practices have resulted in the development of sub-genres in queer theory and politics such as coalitionism, a politics beyond foundational identity categories, of new political movements built around inclusion and shared interests rather than exclusion and specificity. Much of this variety of queer theorising is influenced by Laclau and Mouffe's (1985) conceptualisation of the possibility of new social movements linking through chains of articulation. According to Herman (1994), these chains of articulation have the potential for being the mechanisms whereby new social movements can open up, that is, become non-exclusionary, and also facilitate coalitionisation with other political groups. Therefore, queer is synonymous with, not the abandonment of identity categories, but the rethinking of them as open to conflicting meanings and always interlocking with categories of race, gender and class (Nicholson and Seidman 1995: 17).

This work on composite and multiple queer subjectivities, which is concerned with political coalitional mobilisations across categories such as race, gender, class and sexuality, is not fully engaged with in this book.

Coalitional strategies would be unsuitable in the case studies under analysis here, which are concerned principally with the discursive power of law to produce specifically male homosexualities. In the case studies, the examples of resistance that emerge have less to do with queer political mobilisation and organisation than the queerness of legal knowledge itself. Part of the sexual politics documented and demonstrated in the case studies occurs through the process of queering this dominant legal knowledge. According to Grosz, the key to understanding the deconstructionist approach employed by queer theorists (and central to the case studies included in this book) lies in 'the queer' realisation 'that the knowledges that deal with them are also queer' (Grosz 1995: 249).

In the late 1980s and early 1990s, the heterosexual/homosexual binary opposition became the central focus of queer theory. Much of the impetus for this work in and around this binary opposition came from Derrida's observations that these binarisms never coexist peacefully; rather, they consist of 'a violent hierarchy' (Derrida 1981: 41). However, it was not just the violence of the heterosexual/homosexual binary opposition that was the focus of queer analysis, it was also the political potentiality of the interdependency of these terms. Queer theorists such as Sedgwick describe the diacritical arrangement of the heterosexual/homosexual binary opposition in terms of the ontologically valorised heterosexual term depending for its meaning on the simultaneous subsumption and exclusion of the homosexual term (Sedgwick 1991: 9). Butler describes this relationship in terms of the homosexual category's constitutive interrelationship to the heterosexual category (Butler 1993a: xi). Similarly, Diana Fuss describes the homosexual term as 'the indispensable interior exclusion' of the heterosexual term (1991: 3).

The queer response to complicity and entrenchment within the homosexual/heterosexual binary opposition was the academic development of an intolerance towards 'the normal' (Warner 1993, 2000), both the 'normality' of essentialist gay and lesbian identities, and the 'naturalness' and 'normality' of heterosexuality. Queer theory, in contradistinction to gay and lesbian studies, demonstrated the necessity of redirecting academic and political activities away from research and theory focused on gays and lesbians as minorities, to research that focused on the process of gay and lesbian minoritisation in society. The focus of queer theory thus became the attempt to understand how various ways of construing sexual marginality shaped the self-understanding of the culture as a whole (Epstein 1996: 155). Thus, queer studies can be described as 'the study of the knowledge and social practices that organise "society" as a whole by sexualising, heterosexualising or homosexualising culture' (Seidman 1996: 13).

Seidman describes gay and lesbian identity politics as a 'politics of interest … organised around the claims of rights and social, cultural, and political representation by a homosexual subject' (1995: 131). Queer 'identity' politics, on the other hand, is described by Seidman as a 'deconstructive or queer cultural politics of knowledge' (1995: 130). What queer authors actually began to advocate was a politics of positionality or relationality, that is, of supplementarity. The supplement (here homosexual) is that which appears to be an addition to an apparently original term, but on which the supposed original (heterosexual) actually depends (Spargo 1999: 46). Queer politics thus became the politicisation of the supplementarity of homosexuality relative to the alleged originality (and superiority) of heterosexuality. The queer political objective became the problematisation of the discreteness and fixity of the discursively articulated supplementary category in order to decentre 'the heterosexual' category with which it is in a relationship of interdependence. There are many examples within queer theory of a concern with and solution to entrenchment within the heterosexual/homosexual binary. For example, Teresa de Lauretis calls for a queer 'demarginalisation' (de Lauretis 1991: iii); Butler encourages 'insubordination' (Butler 1991); and Cohen suggests that gays and lesbians should become 'ec-centric' (Cohen 1991: 15).

This queer cultural politics of knowledge in and around identity and diacritics has resulted in certain 'late' queer academics,[8] such as Shane Phelan, concluding, 'ultimately, queer theory's target was identity' (1997: 2), that is, textual identities within the heterosexual/homosexual binary opposition, and the subversive politics of unsettling the superiority of the heterosexual term through strategies that trouble if not erase the boundaries between them. This political agenda has inspired several critics, for example Frank Mort describes the queer agenda as tending towards a polarised codification of sex within the heterosexual/homosexual binary opposition that institutes 'a reductionist slight of hand' (1994: 212). For Mort, queer theory thus fails to 'grasp the multiple points of construction of modern sexuality' (1994: 213). Not only is the queer 'agenda' reductive, some critics have also accused it of being alienated from social contexts and institutional practices. These tendencies have resulted in accusations that queer theory and politics has rarely, if ever, moved beyond a stereotypical textual, literary deconstructive analysis (Stein and Plummer 1996: 137).

In Seidman's opinion, following Mort and Stein and Plummer, queer theorists have often surrendered to a narrow culturalism and textualism, and, as a result, 'the "social" is often narrowed into categories of knowledge and culture while the latter is itself often reduced to linguistic discursive binary figures' (Seidman 1995: 139). For Seidman, the queer deconstructionist approach is limited as it remains at the level of the critique of knowledge and the decentring of cultural meanings (1995: 134). Seidman's suggested remedy for this limitation was the 'articulation of a politics of knowledge with an institutional social analysis' (1995: 139). Stein and Plummer also suggested that the textual limitations of queer theory could be overcome by the articulation of textual, discursive queer theory with social analyses which foreground 'how identities are constituted in the cultural practices of everyday life, though mediated by texts' (Stein and Plummer 1996: 138).

What is being strongly advocated here is that deconstructionist queer analysis at the level of discourse and representation should be taken into the analysis of institutionalised practices and politics and the practices of everyday life. This would counteract the dangerous tendency for queer theorists 'to ignore "real" queer life as it is experienced across the world, while they play with the free-floating signifiers of texts' (Stein and Plummer 1996: 137).[9] Along these lines, Judith Butler, one of leading lights of queer theory actually began to put forward some 'late' queer criticisms of her own in an article published in 1999. In this article Butler suggested that 'queer theory might seek to reflect on its own exuberance' and 'utopianism' (1999: 17). Butler's warning to queer theorists is that they should be careful not to deprive themselves of the critical tools they 'need in order to read the trace and phantom of heteronormativity' (1999: 18). What Butler is critiquing here is the exuberant expectation of social transformation that accompanies much of queer theory's deconstructive critique (Seidman 1995: 135). Allied with this is the unlimited politics of difference inherent in queer theory:

> the deconstructive critique of the hetero/homo hierarchical figure is tied to a politics of difference, its goal is to release possibilities for bodily, sexual, and social experiences that are submerged or marginalised by the dominant regime.
>
> (Seidman 1995: 135)

Butler's concern is that, if queer theorists put all their energies into releasing such bodily, sexual and political experiences within the context of social transformation, they could be accused of abstractly theorising their way out of heteronormative power relations. As a result, this 'utopian strain within queer studies' is in danger of becoming disengaged and politically irrelevant, according to Butler, as 'sexuality remains structured by norms that presume a natural heterosexual teleology' (Butler 1999: 19).

As a result of these 'late' queer insights, homosexual and heterosexual identities are approached in this book as being constituted through social practices and as being textually and discursively deployed and mediated in legal institutional practices. This bifurcated appreciation allows an analysis of how identities are discursively produced as well as an appreciation of how identities accommodate to their social worlds. This in turn promotes insights into how social agents are able to disrupt their particular discursive productions in legal practices.

The model of homosexual or gay social identity that is employed in this book can be usefully described as an identity comprised of a process of accommodation to social worlds (Davies 1992: 83). This homosexual identity is the means by which the subordinated identities within the heterosexual matrix survive and cope with their social and legal subordination, which could be experienced in the form of tolerance, eradication, restriction and exclusion. This is certainly not the last word on identity, rather, this is a model of social identity, or dialogic identity (Taylor 1994), signified on the surface of the body in which social agency is exemplified in the self-conscious comportment and presentation of the body's social legibility. This perspective, according to Davies, 'allows far more easily than traditional accounts of self-concept or identity, the possibility of multiple identities, which compete, collude, and compromise in the process of everyday life' (1992: 83). The homosexual or gay identities which emerge in the case studies included in this book are not essential and fixed identities, they are composite, multiple and above all resourceful identities, that are associated with not docile, but rather with accommodating bodies. In terms of the de-subjugation of alternative knowledges, the primary focus of the case studies is not a politics of subversion and de-naturalisation (these problems with queer theory will be reviewed further in the case studies and in the conclusion), rather, the case studies present an analysis of how de-subjugated homosexual identities and alternative knowledges concerning homosexualities consist, in most cases, of a blend of both trouble and accommodation.[10]

Technologies of law

In terms of the approach to the study of legal institutional practices introduced in this book, two established writers, Carol Smart and Leslie Moran, are important influences. Leslie J. Moran's work, especially his 1996 book, *The Homosexual(ity) of Law*, is exemplary of a politics of law not explicitly expressed, yet implicit in the work. This implicit politics within his work is synonymous with his reluctance to extract his analyses from the legal technologies and discourses under examination. By example, Moran demonstrates the necessity of academic engagement with these components of legal practice. Following Foucault, Moran is less concerned with arguments and political affiliations than he is with describing and illustrating practices and technologies within law which produce homosexual acts as synonymous with homosexual identities. His work is less concerned with who homosexuals are and how homosexuals organise or represent themselves politically than with how law represents and produces homosexual identities and homosexual acts within its practices. Moran's work avoids the trademark over-emphasis on transformation and subversion in queer theory. Also, Moran does not become distracted by a politics based on identity trouble. His influence on this book has been mainly in terms of his approach to law as a discursive technology.

Moran's work can also be described as having parallels with Carol Smart's development of feminist approaches to law, or a feminist politics of law. These parallels can be found mainly in the approach to law, and the development of an alternative legal politics in Smart's work, rather than in its feminist content and framework. Smart's work may give some credibility to the particular approach of *Homosexuality, Law and Resistance*, as this book also attempts to develop 'a rather different kind of politics around law' (Smart 1995: 125–6). Smart's instigation of a different kind of legal politics is a result of her urging feminists to ask different questions about law. Like Moran, Smart approaches law as a producer of identities and subjectivities. Law, for both Moran and Smart, should be approached as a technology that brings into being categories of (homo)sexuality (Moran) and gender (Smart). Thus, both Smart and Moran produce a perspective for legal analysis which recognises that it is through these technologies that 'law imagines human relations' (Moran 1996a: 2). Moran describes his approach thus:

> this study seeks to explore the way in which the machinery or tech-nology for producing the truth of sexuality becomes an important part of legal practice, and the way in which legal practice becomes part of the machinery or technology for producing the truth of sexuality.
>
> (Moran 1996a: 11)

Similarly, Smart sees law 'as bringing into being both gendered subject positions as well as (more controversially) subjectivities or identities to which the individual becomes tied or associated' (1995: 192). Both authors are concerned with power, legal technologies and the discourses and repre-sentations deployed therein which produce and deploy both homosexuality (Moran) and sexuality and gender (Smart). Smart, in her 1995 anthology *Law, Crime and Sexuality: Essays in Feminism*, asks the following question: 'How does gender work in law and how does law work to produce gender?' (1995: 191). By asking this question Smart intended to initiate a shift in feminist analysis away from 'law as sexist', 'law as male', 'law as gendered' (1995: 125) to analysing law as a 'technology of gender' (1995: 217). Smart develops this approach in the following passage:

> such an approach understands law as a mechanism for fixing gender differences and constructing femininity and masculinity in oppositional modes. Thus law is no longer analysed as that which acts upon pre-given gendered subjects, rather law is part of the process of the continual reproduction of problematic gender differentiation.
>
> (Smart 1995: 218)

Smart concluded that feminist approaches should not fix or found gender – as law does – in order to resist or theorise about law. Smart's insights are mirrored in the approach to law exemplified in the case studies included in this book; that is, that a queer politics of law should concern itself less with finding out who homosexuals are and how homosexuals should represent themselves, and what forms their resistance should take, and more with how homosexual identity and homosexual bodies and activities are produced in legal practices.

Following Smart and Moran, it is advocated here that a queer politics of law should begin to ask the following questions: how do homosexual and heterosexual identities work in law? and how does law work to produce homosexual and heterosexual identities? However, in *Homosexuality, Law and Resistance* a third component dedicated to 'resistance' is added to these questions. This third component facilitates a complementary analysis that is sensitive and appreciative of the social tactics engaged in by homosexuals who are directly affected by the legal practices, and the trajectory of alternative knowledges of homosexualities which are subjugated and then de-subjugated within the legal events under study. This analytic enterprise, which goes beyond deconstructionist analysis with its goal of textual denaturalisation, can be expressed in the following research questions: (a) how is it that homosexuals are capable of resisting and disrupting their discursive production in legal practice? and (b) how do homosexuals survive or coexist in social environments where their concrete experiences of legal restriction, exclusion or potential eradication are justified by legal technologies that produce them in particular ways in legal discourse?

De-subjugation and co-optation: tracing the trajectory of queer acts

As genealogies,[11] the case studies that follow will unashamedly privilege the absent presences, or more accurately the present absences, the subjugated knowledges, including embodied alternative knowledges, which are read from the documentation (official reports, trial transcriptions, immigration appeal tribunal reports, reports of the European Court and Commission, etc.)[12] under analysis. It is the tracing of the trajectory of such alternative knowledges from their subjugation within dominant discourses to their de-subjugation and potential effect on these dominant discourses, which is a crucial component of the overall approach.

In the case studies it is not queer identities or subject positions which are the privileged site of analysis but how, in specific legal practices, the production of homosexual identities is disrupted by actions, and queer performances. The case studies demonstrate an eagerness to avoid some of the dangers in theoretical approaches, such as queer theory's endemic subversiveness, and the potential hindrance to research this may cause.[13] In this book theory is utilised as a means of further elucidating or interrogating the practices of law (Bottomley and Conaghan 1993: 1) and the counter-practices which would disrupt law's discursive effects. Thus the use or role of theory instituted in this book is imbued in the building, 'little by little', of what Kritzman refers to as 'strategic knowledge' (1988: xiv). Theory is utilised in the case studies for its illuminating and exploratory potential, not for its own sake.

Methodologically the approach advocated here is something more than that of a reader of documents; it is that of a reader cognizant of the discursive operations of the localised legal institutional practices under analysis

(Kritzman 1988: xiv). Rather, this is an attempt to get inside the workings of institutions through what Kritzman describes as a genealogical 'documentary investigation' that will initiate 'new forms of social activism' (1988: xviii). However, this is a particularly delicate form of activism. The de-subjugation of 'knowledges' which are 'other than' the dominant interpretation, which have been exposed within the mix of contending discourses or in gaps and present absences in the dominant discourse, are fragile varieties of knowledge and must be carefully managed. For example, Foucault describes one of the two main risks newly released de-subjugated knowledges run within his genealogical approach in the following passage:

> is it not perhaps the case that these fragments of genealogies are no sooner brought to light, that the particular elements of the knowledge that one seeks to disinter are no sooner accredited and put into circulation, than they run the risk of re-codification, re-colonisation ... in fact, those unitary discourses, which first disqualified and then ignored them when they made their appearance, are, it seems quite ready now to annex them, to take them back within the fold of their own discourse and to invest them with everything this implies in terms of their effects of knowledge and power
>
> (Foucault 1980a: 86)

Thus, it becomes crucial to avoid de-subjugated knowledges 'remaining as they have always been, surrounded by a prudent silence' (Foucault 1980a: 87). Equally, it becomes crucial that these 'insurrections' (Foucault 1980a: 87) are not re-colonised within the dominant discourse under challenge, especially if they have not yet initiated some sort of change.[14] The re-colonisation of de-subjugated knowledges, or what Foucault describes as the co-optation of alternative knowledges is, according to Ross, 'fundamental to the entire position he [Foucault] develops ... that it may be taken to embody the entire answer to the question of political practice' (Ross 1985: 133). It is Foucault's view that the co-optation or re-colonisation of de-subjugated knowledge is inevitable (unless, as he pointed out, it is met by silence). Not only is co-optation inevitable, Foucault welcomes it because 'in assimilating the resistance' he hopes that 'the terms of power change' (Gandal 1986: 122). The case studies that follow are particularly concerned with this movement and disruption of dominant discourses. The 'political programme' of the queer genealogies included in this book can be described as being characterised by the attempt to make room for, or more accurately to demonstrate how room is made for, de-subjugated knowledges within the social and institutional practices under analysis.

According to Philip Barker, each of Foucault's texts should be viewed as a tactic 'that engages with a specific object such as medicine, criminology, psychoanalysis, prisons, sex, the functioning of institutions and so on' (Barker 1993: 67). It is hoped that the presentation of events and cases featured in this book will be themselves tactical, in terms of the effort to disrupt the intolerable and prejudicial representation of homosexuals and homosexualities within the legal complex. Furthermore, on a political or tactical note, the presentation of the events and cases within this book reveals that the most profound, yet modest, response to legal practices is the disruption of commonly held and familiar conceptions. Thus, the approach to the study of 'law' advocated here, where law is presented as a system of practices based on and justified by knowledge in the form of discursive technologies, inseparably conflates reform and 'change' with the disruption of law's power to define and discursively deploy 'the homosexual'.

Queer imperatives

This book is motivated by 'deeply political' (Shiner 1982: 386) ethical imperatives in reaction to the social and political violence perpetuated against homosexuals within society and in the legal complex. It is also an attempt to clear some space for a particular 'political task'. This 'political task' is described by Foucault:

> It seems to me that the real political task in a society such as ours is to criticise the working of institutions which appear to be both neutral and independent; to criticise them in such a manner that the political violence which has always exercised itself obscurely through them will be unmasked, so that one can fight them.
>
> (Foucault 1974: 171)

Homosexuality, Law and Resistance is particularly suitable for this task, as it is aligned within the critical legal studies movement which attempts to expose the power relations within law's claims of neutrality and objectivity. The unmasking and queering of law's heteronormativity in this book is not playful or ludic (Ebert 1995), it is imbued with 'political' imperatives. This book can be described as combining academic 'erudite' knowledge with local, disqualified, low-ranking knowledges in order to produce knowledge that is of tactical use (Foucault 1980a: 82, 83). The queer genealogical enterprise advocated here is therefore an attempt to facilitate, expand or re-problematise the tactical and ethical disruptions achieved by the de-subjugation of certain alternative discourses. The central political enterprise in each of the case studies below is the documentation of the moments when the unthought, unseen and unspoken are released into circulation and take hold of the institutional regimes that attempt to subjugate them. In the following passage, Foucault describes this new intellectual work, that is, the 'new political role for intellectual work' (Gandal 1986: 122), which has as its task the unmasking and deconstructive disruption of dominant discourses within institutional practices in order to lever in change, as giving:

some assistance in wearing away certain self-evidenceness and common places ... to bring it about ... that certain phrases can no longer be spoken so lightly, certain acts no longer, or at least no longer so unhesitantly, performed, to contribute to changing certain things in people's ways of perceiving and doing things, to participate in this difficult displacement of forms of sensibility and thresholds of tolerance – I hardly feel capable of attempting much more than that. If only what I have tried to say might somehow, to some degree, not remain altogether foreign to some such real effects.

(Foucault 1987: 112)

The inspiration and motivation for *Homosexuality, Law and Resistance* is certainly Foucauldian in conceptualisation. This is indeed a 'postmodern politics' that is characterised by multiple intersecting struggles. The political goal that underlies this book is not a utopian end of domination. The book could be described as an example or demonstration of what Beck, following Foucault, describes as 'sub-politicisation' (Beck 1994: 23), within the politics of law. Beck describes sub-politics as the activity of shaping society from below (1994: 23), as a 'rule-altering politics' (1994: 36). The queer genealogical approach demonstrated in the following case studies presents power as being dispersed in a multiplicity of networks and maintains that resistance must be realised through a series of localised strategies (Kritzman 1988: xv).[15] The multi-genealogical research conducted in the case studies included in this book demonstrates that there can be no uniform 'bloc' politics to counter law's power effects on homosexual lives. The analysis within each of the case studies produces different legal institutions as deploying contradictory discursive representations of homosexual identity in order to justify different degrees and examples of subordination and regulation, thus necessitating different contextualised tactical responses.

There is an optimism present in this book, but there is also simultaneously a sobering political modesty in the approach. Both of these attributes are inherited from Foucault (especially in his later interviews). The following passage from Foucault captures such a modest, yet optimistic, ambition, which serves as a suitable end-point for this section of the introduction. According to Foucault:

There's an optimism that consists in saying that things couldn't be better. My optimism would consist rather in saying that so many things can be changed, fragile as they are, bound up more with circumstances than necessities, more arbitrary than self-evident, more a matter of complex, but temporary, historical circumstances than with inevitable anthropological constants.

(Foucault 1988: 156)

Synopsis of chapters

In Chapter 1, 'Military men: queering the homosocial habitus', numerous theoretical insights are employed to illuminate particular institutional practices and developments within the armed services in the UK, the USA (and in Australia) regarding homosexuality. In this chapter, Judith Butler's theoretical insights concerning the gendered body, the heterosexual matrix and performativity, and Eve Kosofsky Sedgwick's commentary on homosociality are explored in an attempt to make sense of the UK's armed forces homosexual exclusion policy. However, in order to engage fully with contemporary developments, especially in the USA (the don't ask, don't tell policy), theorists such as Goffman, Plummer and de Certeau are also enlisted. These theorists help to develop a conceptual framework to explain the homosexual's tactical ability to control identity information and pass as heterosexual. These theorists are utilised to conceptualise the tactical invisibility of the homosexual subject and his or her recognition as such in anti-homosexual environments like the armed forces. This conceptualisation is given added urgency with an analysis of what are described as 'passing policies' under development within the British armed forces. These passing policies can be described as attempting to formalise in policy what is already informally enforced in the armed forces environments, that is, the exclusion of all homosexual connotations and behaviour from service personnel, whether in acts, dress, expression or conversation. This informal structure is described, following Bourdieu and Sedgwick, as a homosocial habitus, an informal structure which is evident in both the findings of the US Rand Corporation Report (Rand Report 1993) as well as in the British Ministry of Defence (MoD) Homosexuality Policy Assessment Team Report (HPAT 1996). In this chapter, the MoD's schemes of perception and schemes of knowledge are presented as colliding and becoming unsettled by the invisible, unremarkable and non-disruptive homosexuals serving compatibly as assumed heterosexuals in the armed services in the USA and the UK. This chapter also includes an analysis of the European Court of Human Rights decision on 27 September 1999, where the UK was found to be in breach of the European Convention on Human Rights and Fundamental Freedoms (1953) by banning homosexuals from serving in the armed forces.

In Chapter 2, 'Authenticity, evasion and the unknowable homosexual', themes such as passing, information control and clandestine homosexuals, that were introduced in Chapter 1, are again the focus of attention. However, in this chapter it will be demonstrated that the capacity of homosexuals for evading recognition by controlling identity information is both the homosexual's source of protection and the source of his or her non-recognition and hence exclusion from legal protection within UK immigration and asylum procedures. This is the first of two chapters dedicated to homosexual refugees. In these two chapters the criminalisation of homosexuals in countries such as Iran, Romania and Cyprus is observed within the context of established European Convention human rights standards. Moreover, these examples of criminalisation are also explored in terms of the inclusion and exclusion of homosexuals from a particular international convention on refugee status: the United Nations Convention of 1951 (UN 1951).

In Chapter 2, a Romanian man's (Ioan Vraciu) application for refugee status based on his membership of a persecuted social group (homosexuals) in Romania is analysed. This case provides the institutional setting for exploring the practices and processes engaged in by immigration officials for authenticating identities. It also provides an excellent point of contrast between two different effects of passing, that is, passing as a technology of survival and compatibility, as in the armed forces, and passing as a technology of anonymity, contributing to the difficulty of proving one's homosexuality. The attempt to authenticate Vraciu as a homosexual illustrates that the knowledges which claim to know homosexuals (and for that matter heterosexuals) are themselves also queer. In this chapter, legal practice is exposed as an idiosyncratic and exclusive discursive practice. Legal knowledge becomes a matter of the control of discourse and orders of discourse, where qualified and disqualified knowing subjects are separated by what Lyotard (1988) describes as a *differend*, a gap in communicability. With only insubstantial evidence available to support Vraciu's self-declaration, it was suggested (by a lawyer representing the Home Office) that he should be medically examined to determine objectively his evasive homosexual identity from traces left on his body from homosexual encounters, especially sodomy. Anal examination is a much disputed, but historically enduring, medical-legal technique for the clinical recognition of (especially) male homosexuals, as a result of their distinctive anal hallmarking. Vraciu avoided this fate however. Instead his sexuality was authenticated through a psychiatric consultation, where his telling of his own sexual biography and experiences were to be converted into psychiatric-medical fact by an exchange of discourse.

What this chapter leaves the reader with is a sense of uncertainty: is Vraciu a homosexual or not? This case opens up a queer space between the knowability and unknowability of sexualities. However, it also fires a warning shot across the bows of queer theory, and the tendency to place such a high premium on troubling the boundaries between heterosexual and homosexual identities. Perhaps the only way homosexuals can find protection, in certain circumstances, for example, in the Immigration Appeal Tribunal, is through being knowable, being recognisable to heteronormatively organised institutional practices. Resistance to exclusion in this chapter becomes a matter of understanding how law works, what law needs to function and knowing when and how best to assist law in order to avoid particular exclusions.

In Chapter 3, 'Persecution and immutable identities: homosexual refugees', the homosexual's capacity to pass and remain unremarkable is again the focus of analysis. However, this ability of homosexuals to be 'invisible' is used to exclude homosexuals from a particular benefit, that of being included as members of a persecuted social group (under the United Nations Convention on Refugees 1951). This exclusion is demonstrated through the exploration of a range of homosexual refugee applications.

The first part of the chapter explores how, in the 1990s, British immigration officials systematically dismissed applications made by male homosexuals on the grounds that they did not resemble traditional, or genuine, refugees. According to immigration officials, genuine refugees are members of persecuted demographically distinctive racial, tribal and clan social groups, who can reproduce themselves biologically. This minority model for recognising refugees is based on the fact that these social groups cannot avoid the persecution they may suffer at the hands of a state. This chapter examines how homosexuals were presented in tribunals as men capable of avoiding their alleged persecution as a result of their ability to pass as heterosexual. They were also presented as men who have the ability to avoid their alleged prosecution-persecution through refraining from practising. Also, homosexuals are described as being unlike 'genuine' refugees as they are incapable of reproducing their 'social group' biologically. In this chapter, homosexual refugees are conceptualised as 'strangers' (Simmel 1950) in their own nation-states. More accurately, these homosexual refugees are described as being 'organic strangers', an amalgamation of distance and nearness; yet, unlike Simmel's description of the stranger, homosexuals are not inorganically appended to the social group, homosexuals are 'of' the group, 'families' and nations that would eradicate them. In this chapter themes such as the intercorporeality of the heteronormative gaze, the sensuality of legal practices, where bodies diacritically scrutinise other bodies for signs of abnormality (in this case, homosexuality), are explored. As are themes such as passing, this time in terms of immigration officials advising 'heterosexual-looking' and '-acting' homosexual applicants that their 'heterosexual' demeanour is unlikely to draw attention to their homosexuality when they are repatriated to countries with records of awesome human rights abuses against homosexuals.

Following on from Chapter 1, using Judith Butler, I describe this conceptualisation of heterosexual-like demeanour in terms of gender as a corporeal act, a cultural sign that signifies an underlying sexuality. The presentation or acting out of heterosexual masculinity is presented in this chapter by immigration officials as an alternative (for avoiding persecution on their return to the country they have fled from) to granting refugee status in the UK.

In the second part of Chapter 3, the exclusion of homosexuals from the protection of refugee status at an international level is explored, including the analysis of various cases ranging from such countries as New Zealand, Canada and the USA. In this chapter the global impact of a particular decision made by the USA Board of Immigration Appeals, in the case of Acosta, a refugee applicant from El Salvador, is explored. In the Acosta case, non-traditional refugee applicants, such as homosexuals, around the world found a gap in the refugee determination process in which their particular experiences of persecution at the hands of the states in question could begin to be recognised. In this chapter it will be described how, in the late 1990s, more and more countries (including the UK) began to include homosexual refugees within their definition of members of a persecuted social group as a direct result of the Acosta decision in the USA. In the Acosta decision, social group immutability is seen to take on a specific form, not as an essential identity, nor as a group afforded special rights alone, but in terms of immutability contextualised within established human rights standards. Within this formulation, immutable characteristics are those that are beyond the power of the individual to change, or are so fundamental to individual identity or conscience that individuals ought not to be required to change them. It is here that a reversal occurs in that the focus (through the vehicle of human rights law) changes from the homosexual's behaviour and practices to the state's behaviour and practices towards homosexuals.

Chapter 4, 'The fear of "homosexual spread": Legislating the Heteronormativity of Protection 1957–2000', extends the theme of homosexuals as organic strangers, as introduced in Chapter 3, this time in the context of homosexuality and age. In this chapter a genealogy of the homosexual age of consent discourses in the English criminal law is analysed within a context of European-wide reform, and the inseparability of the domestic laws of states from the supra-national institutions such as the European Convention on Human Rights and Fundamental Freedoms. The institutional settings of the European Convention (the European Commission and Court) are presented as fundamental sites for the de-subjugation of alternative and competing knowledges, especially in relation to the case narratives included in this book.

In this chapter the necessity of maintaining a higher age of homosexual consent is presented in terms of a particular 'fear' expressed in parliament: the fear of homosexuality spreading into the wider male population. This fear was crystallised in juridical and parliamentary discourse by the Wolfenden Committee, who published their report in 1957. What the Wolfenden Committee achieved on the issue of homosexuality and age was the introduction of two influential discourses. These are (1) the unfixed nature of male adolescent sexuality and (2) a particular chronological immutability when on maturation to a specific age (21 and later 18), a young man's sexuality was assumed to have become immune to 'corruption'. This chapter explores how the Wolfenden Committee decreed that society had a duty to protect young men, through the vehicle of the criminal law (specifically, the higher age of consent), during the particularly vulnerable period of their adolescence. In this chapter, juridical and parliamentary discourse veer between presenting the superiority and 'naturalness' of heterosexuality whilst at the same time presenting heterosexuality as something extremely vulnerable which must be fiercely protected. Thus, in this chapter, the necessity of regulating homosexuality in young people is exposed less as an issue of morality and 'rightness' than as an issue founded upon a particular paranoid fear of homosexuality, especially in males.

The chapter also consists of a narrative of subjugation and de-subjugation, especially in the context of 'the family'. It is demonstrated that it is in the name of 'the family' and the hetero-familial future, in parliamentary discourse, that homosexuality must be regulated and controlled. However, in this analysis homosexuals are also presented as being organic strangers, as inside, yet, in parliamentary discourse, outside of the family. In this chapter I use Freud's description of *heimlich*, that which is familiar yet also secretive and opaque, to describe the disavowal of adolescents who are homosexuals within this particular discursive battle over what is, and is not, of 'the family'. I also analyse how it came to pass that, in a case heard before the European Commission in 1997, a young man, Euan Sutherland, initiated a politics of avowal that released discourses of adolescent homosexuality from subjugation. The Sutherland case thus exposed how the hegemonic discourses of the protection of young men from homosexuality through the higher age of consent actually amounted to the criminalisation of particular young men. The chapter also includes an analysis of the recent Section 28 debates in the House of Lords (February 2000), and the clashes between the House of Lords and the House of Commons in 1998, 1999 and 2000 over the reduction of the homosexual age of consent.

In the conclusion I describe this book in terms of a de-subjugation of the hidden knowledges of homosexual survival and trouble. I describe how queer theory has been utilised and altered in the pursuit of these de-subjugations within institutional practices and counter-practices. I reiterate that the homosexual subject is indeed constituted in legal discourse, as is the homosexual body; however, in the case narratives included in the chapters of this book, I re-present the subject and the body in terms of social agency, resistance, survival and ultimately of trouble. In *Homosexuality, Law and Resistance* some of the central themes of queer studies are critically explored. It is by taking these queer theoretical insights in relation to interiority and de-objectification into specific institutional contexts that the book is able to complexify the simplistic and reductionist functionalism of the diacritical politics in much queer theory. By so doing, the case studies contained in this book present queer theory's subversive and transformational political aspirations as being barren theoretical exuberance, especially in light of just how troublesome the 'accommodational tactics' within the case narratives are revealed to be.

1 Military men

Queering the homosocial habitus

Inarguably, there is a satisfaction in dwelling on the degree to which the power of our enemies over us is implicated, not in their command of knowledge, but precisely in their ignorance.

(Sedgwick 1991: 7)

Introduction

By virtue of section 1(1) of the Sexual Offences Act of 1967, homosexual acts in private between two consenting adults (at the time meaning 21 years or over) ceased to be a criminal offence. However, such acts continued to constitute offences under the Army and Air Force Acts of 1955 and the Naval Discipline Act of 1957 (section 1(5) of the Sexual Offences Act of 1967). Section 1(5) of the 1967 Act was repealed by the Criminal Justice and Public Order Act of 1994 (which also reduced the age of consent to 18 years). However, section 146(4) of the 1994 Act provided that nothing in that section prevented a homosexual act (with or without other acts or circumstances) from constituting a ground for discharging a member of the armed forces.

This chapter focuses on the law and policy that informed the exclusion of homosexuals from the British armed forces. The focus of this case study is on the Ministry of Defence's (MoD's) identity- or status-based homosexual exclusion policy. My analysis of this identity-based exclusion policy primarily focuses on the MoD's machinery for producing discursive homosexual identities as being incompatible with armed service. I trace the trajectory of this production of homosexual incompatibility through various legal sites, for example the institutional practices of the courts, parliamentary debates and reports, and MoD reports. There are two documents that are of central importance to the analysis. These are the 1995–6 House of Commons Select Committee on the Armed Forces Bill Report[1] and the 1996 *Report of the Homosexuality Policy Assessment Team (HPAT)*[2] which resulted from the MoD's internal review of the exclusion policy. These two reports are crucial to this case study since the evidence collated within the HPAT report was quoted as being the decisive factor in the decision by the 1996 House of Commons Select Committee to propose to Parliament that the homosexual exclusion policy in armed forces should be retained. The 1995 judicial review[3] and subsequent 1996 appeal[4] trials are also referred to in the analysis that will follow, as a means of illustrating certain points (although, overall the analysis is concerned with the policy surrounding the ban rather than the legality or 'unreasonableness' of the ban).

The first section of the case study focuses on the MoD's discursive deployment of homosexual identity as being incompatible with armed service. Here, I am especially concerned with demonstrating the MoD's production of the issue as a matter of the consequences of lifting the exclusion policy. This framing of the issue by the HPAT facilitates my analysis of the exclusion policy as a politics of identity, or more accurately a politics of identification. Here the identity politics does not consist of a gay and lesbian challenge to the exclusion policy, but of a politics of identification based on the attempt by the armed forces to defend and protect the bounded heterosexualised identity of the armed forces as an institution. The HPAT and its subsequent report are the primary machinery for producing the idea of the heterosexual purity of the armed forces as being under threat from the infiltration of 'acknowledged' or 'out' homosexuals.

The HPAT's brief was to investigate the hypothetical attitudes and feelings of 'ordinary servicemen and women' towards openly homosexual servicemen and women being allowed to join the armed forces. The MoD intended to present these findings as evidence that 'ordinary' members of the forces would not tolerate 'acknowledged' homosexuals in their platoons and regiments, and that the inclusion of homosexuals would undoubtedly disrupt the trust and cohesion found in such groups. My analysis proceeds to examine the gaps in the MoD's discourse of homosexual incompatibility. These gaps emerge as traces of non-evidence, which expose the existence, and evidence (through a present-absence) of, a wholly 'other' homosexual who is already inside the allegedly pure heterosexual context of the armed forces. In the third section of the chapter I focus on this homosexual, who, despite the MoD's discursive deployments of homosexual incompatibility, seems to be compatible to the armed forces. My analysis in this section employs the insights and concepts of various social theorists, for example, Bourdieu's concept of habitus, Foucault's concept of panopticism (which he borrows from Bentham), Sedgwick's homosociality, Butler's gender as corporeal signification, and also de Certeau's work on tactical forms of resistance. By using the latter concepts and theoretical frameworks I describe the armed forces environment as a homosocial habitus which is regulated by informal structures. I demonstrate that these structures operate at the level of the cultural signification of sexuality in and through the signifier of gender. In this section I describe how it is that a homosexual serviceman[5] can pass as an assumed heterosexual in this armed forces environment by looking and acting the part within this panoptic homosocial habitus. This involves the performance of the appropriate corporeal signification of gender, or more specifically heterosexual masculinities. This performance, then in turn signifies an underlying assumed or actual heterosexual orientation.

The fourth main area of inquiry in this case study is how the tactical passing as assumed heterosexuals by homosexual servicemen within the armed forces homosocial habitus is finding its way into policy. The last section of this chapter explores various examples of what I refer to as passing policies, ranging from the inadequate US 'don't ask, don't tell' policy to the policy proposed by Stonewall to the 1995–6 House of Commons Select Committee on the Armed Forces Bill. Stonewall advocated the implementation of a Uniform Code of Sexual Conduct, and a Code of Guidance (along the lines of the Australian Defence Forces code of guidance). Implicit in Stonewall's policy proposals is a right to privacy that is consistent with the passing of homosexual forces members as non-disruptive assumed heterosexuals. As well as discussing this proposed policy, I also analyse in the postscript to this chapter a policy change, in itself a passing policy, which has been developed from within the MoD as a result of the unfavourable findings of the European Court in 1999.

The final section of this case study is devoted to various policies and policy proposals and designs that refocus and reframe the discursive context of the MoD's homosexuality incompatibility discourse. These 'passing policies' are policies which foreground the informal homosocial structures of armed forces environments (domestic and international) and the body as the place of choreographed 'assumed heterosexual' compatibility.

The trials

In 1995 four applicants – one lesbian, Jeanette Smith, and three gay men, Graeme Grady, Duncan Lustig-Prean and John Beckett,[6] who were administratively discharged from the respective armed forces in which they served – launched a legal challenge to the homosexual exclusion policy by way of a judicial review. During the judicial review the test the courts applied to the case was the Wednesbury test of 'irrationality'. In deciding on this point Lord Justice Simon Brown, in the High Court, held that the policy was not 'irrational' (in the legal sense) at the time it was passed, but he made it very clear that he thought the policy was wrong. The judicial review failed to prove that the ban on homosexuality in the armed forces was 'unreasonable'. This decision was appealed against, in the Court of Appeal, and here it was also held that the policy could not be 'stigmatized as irrational' at the time that it was last reviewed. However, this decision was made partly on the basis that the policy was shortly to be reviewed internally by the MoD (by the HPAT) and by Parliament (in the 1995–6 House of Commons Select Committee for the Armed Forces Bill).

The Homosexuality Policy Assessment Team

The HPAT was established in September 1995 to undertake an internal assessment of the exclusion policy on homosexuality in the armed forces. This internal assessment was recommended when the High Court found in favour of the MoD during the 1995 judicial review of the legality of the MoD's policy of excluding homosexuals from the armed forces (HPAT 1996: 15).

The overall approach of the HPAT was to 'set out to collect and assess all information relevant to the issues of acknowledged homosexuals serving in the British armed forces' (HPAT 1996: 25). The team used a multi-faceted study design in order to collect the attitudes of what they describe as 'ordinary' British forces' members towards the unbarring of 'acknowledged' homosexuals in the armed forces. The qualitative and quantitative data they obtained was collected through attitude surveys, interviews, discussion groups and correspondence. They also used additional information obtained from relevant published material and interviews with experts on the subject, and correspondence was also considered in the overall assessment (HPAT 1996: 25). Between 4 October and 22 November 1995, the HPAT administered a total of 1,711 attitude survey questionnaires (1,710 of which were said to be suitable for analysis). The HPAT's means of gathering their qualitative and quantitative data was as follows:

> For each service, the single service representative within the HPAT identified representative combat, combat support and training units. The HPAT visited each unit or base for a full day, a minimum of 170 personnel was requested to attend a briefing and complete a questionnaire [the attitude survey]. From that pool 18 people were required to take part in one-to-one structured interviews and a further 18 people were requested to attend focus (i.e. discussion) groups.
>
> (HPAT 1996: Annex G)

The overall result of the 1,710 analysable attitude questionnaires was that the policy banning homosexuals from serving in the armed forces should not be changed, and if the ban was to be lifted it would be done against the wishes of those surveyed (HPAT 1996: 45). The findings of the one-to-one interviews and the focus groups were, in summary: that there was an overwhelmingly held view that homosexuality was neither 'normal' nor 'natural'. Other minorities, such as women and ethnic groups, were described as being 'normal' and therefore more compatible to armed service than homosexuals. Lesbianism was more acceptable than male homosexuality; in addition, it was often mentioned that lesbianism did not involve sodomy, which was considered by many to be particularly distasteful; and the results showed that servicewomen were generally more tolerant of homosexuality than servicemen (HPAT 1996: 49).

The findings of the HPAT set the agenda through which this issue of the homosexual exclusion policy was to be approached during the 1995–6 House of Commons Select Committee on the Armed Forces Bill. During the hearings of this decisive Select Committee there was a reiteration of the discursive production of homosexuals as being disruptive to operational effectiveness through their recognisable difference and inability to control their sexual advances towards 'ordinary' servicemen and women. These discursive technologies for justifying the necessity of the homosexual exclusion policy will be discussed in the following sections.

The machinery of exclusion

I Privacy, paranoia and cohesion

One component of the MoD's homosexual incompatibility discourse is the issue of 'privacy' (or lack of privacy) in the armed forces environment. The 'problem' the MoD presented was the lack of 'privacy' in the armed forces, in relation to 'civilian life', for the consummation of homosexual relations. However, allied with this was the concern over non-privacy in the armed forces environment as an issue of the protection and distancing of heterosexuals from sexual objectification by homosexuals in intimate 'residential' situations. In these particular spaces, heterosexuals would be unable to escape and get away from homosexuals. The threat posed by a 'homosexual presence' was presented in terms of the heterosexual's fear of being looked at, and the concern that heterosexuals should be protected from their own temptations in terms of engaging in sexual activities with homosexuals. This need for heterosexual servicemen to escape from homosexuals is presented in the following passage taken from the HPAT's summary of its 'overall findings':

> Homosexuality in civilian life did not bother most servicemen or servicewomen. Focus group participants emphasized that civilians have 'jobs', but they have a 'way of life'. Most civilian jobs were not seen as requiring close physical contact with other people, or involving life-threatening situations dependent upon total trust in a work team. A person's sexuality, therefore, would not, and generally should not, necessarily be of any concern in civilian life. A view expressed in most focus groups was that at the end of a '9 to 5' job, one could usually get away from a homosexual if one wanted to. This was not the case in the armed forces, in many cases, one might have to live with the same people, for 24 hours a day, over extended periods. In ships, in submarines in particular, there is nowhere to get away and 'escape'. Living with homosexuals: sharing accommodation and washing facilities, and the lack of privacy, were of great concern to most participants, although the women tended not to be as worried as the men.
>
> (HPAT 1996: 49)

The nakedness of bodies in showers seemed to be particularly invested with sexual potential by the MoD in the HPAT report. The crux of the matter, according to the MoD, was, if they allowed homosexuals to enlist in the armed forces this would be tantamount to condoning the eroticisation of 'ordinary' heterosexual servicemen by voyeuristic homosexuals.[7] These concerns are articulated in the following passage:

> Heterosexuals ... having to live (and not simply work) in very close, inescapable proximity for unremittingly long periods alongside known homosexuals ... would mean heterosexuals being unable to escape the sexualised gazes of others who might see potential objects of physical desire rather than simply the often naked bodies of comrades. It would often also mean unwillingly colluding in potentially erotic situations through touching, lying alongside or having constantly to brush past homosexuals.
>
> (HPAT 1996: 120)

An allied concern about the presence of acknowledged homosexuals in the armed forces was the suspicion that someone (thought to be, or predominantly heterosexual) could be suspected of 'giving in' to a homosexual's advances. It was thought that this suspicion would become pronounced especially in relation to isolated shared tasks such as: small group detachments; observation posts; sentry duty (which regularly continues for an entire week) and technical jobs in confined spaces (HPAT 1996: 63–4). According to the HPAT, 'an important background concern in all this would be "not what might happen but what would be said to have happened", about which suspicions could reverberate around task or informal groups indefinitely' (HPAT 1996: 64). Therefore, the HPAT report not only produced the incompatibility of homosexual identity to armed service in terms of activities such as voyeurism and the objectification of 'ordinary' servicemen in the hybrid work and residential spaces (Goffman 1962) of the armed forces. The report also presented the potential problem of 'ordinary' servicemen indulging in sexual activities with acknowledged homosexuals, or being suspected of indulging in sexual liaisons during the many opportunities that would arise in military environments and situations.[8]

Homosexual proximity, homosexual voyeurism and heterosexual scopophobia were among the key justificatory mechanisms deployed by the MoD in various settings including the courts, during the Parliamentary Select Committees and especially in the HPAT report in order to retain the homosexual exclusion policy. Central to this variously deployed homosexual incompatibility discourse is the belief that the suspected or actual presence of a homosexual in the forces' setting would damage the cohesion of units and the primary groups therein. This disruption of group cohesion would, in turn, result in a decrease in the operational effectiveness of these groups within the services. Cohesion, according to the HPAT report, is 'a quality that binds together constituent parts thereby providing resilience against dislocation and disruption' (HPAT 1996: 20). Cohesion, according to military theorists, depends on three main factors: interpersonal attraction, interdependence, and shared attitudes and values (Westbrook 1980: 251). The cohesiveness of primary groups within the armed services was extensively studied during the Second World War.[9] In these studies it was found that the close personal ties found in groups serve two principal functions in combat motivation: they set and enforced group standards of behaviour, and they supported and sustained individuals in stresses they would otherwise not be able to withstand (Stoufer *et al.* 1949: 130–1). Rose described the Second World War as 'a war of morale' (Rose 1990: x). Understanding the efficiency of a fighting unit, for psychologists and military strategists, became a matter of analysing the bonds between individuals, the relations between internal mental states and external relations with others (Rose 1990: x). According to Rose, 'solidarity was key here', the spirit of fighting units was largely dependent, not on hatred of enemies, or external discipline or obeying orders and following rules, but on the informal bonds, loyalties and relationships within groups (1990: 48). This morale, this solidarity, according to Rose, was maintained and produced administratively during the Second World War (1990: 52). Individuals who posed a risk or a threat to unit cohesion, and thus the operational efficiency of the group, were to be eliminated by careful selection and allocation (Rose 1990: 52). One could say that the contemporary practice of administratively discharging homosexuals from the armed services is a demonstration of this administrative elimination of individuals deemed to be threatening to unit cohesion. For this reason the MoD has repeatedly defended the ban on homosexuality as being both practically and contextually motivated by an appreciation of the informal structures of groups, rather than being motivated by morality or anti-homosexual prejudice.

By connecting their homosexual incompatibility discourse to the administrative practices for ensuring the solidarity and cohesion of groups since the Second World War, the HPAT report successfully produced homosexual identity as a problematic 'difference'. This was an identity presented as being recognisable in individuals, and therefore an obstacle to homogeneity and the bonding and cohesion essential to operational effectiveness.

II Corrupting and seductive homosexuals

Homosexual incompatibility with armed service was also constructed around the seduction and preying on vulnerable young forces members. According to the HPAT report, over 45 per cent of the Army, 20 per cent of the Royal Navy, and 10 per cent of the Royal Air Force were under 18 years of age (HPAT 1996: 176). All three armed services were described as being in a relationship of *loco parentis* to these young people. The MoD's primary concern relating to young people and homosexuals was not that a vast number of these young people could be homosexual, or perhaps had not fully realised or come to terms with the fact that they might be homosexual by orientation at the time they enlisted. The MoD's concern lay in the potential exploitation of young members of the forces by 'older, more senior, personnel' (HPAT 1996: 176).[10] The MoD's principal mechanism for emphasising the necessity of maintaining the homosexual exclusion policy in this area was presented by the HPAT in the form of the concern that older, more senior service people could potentially have an effect on 'the still malleable sexual orientation of their juniors' (HPAT 1996: 176). However, this discourse not only produced the transitionality and vulnerability of adolescent sexual identity, but also the corruptibility of male (hetero)sexual identities in general. Heterosexuality in the armed forces, it seems, can only exist securely if homosexuality is excluded from its environments. Within this argument, homosexuality is articulated as something one can 'catch', especially when one is in the presence of a homosexual. This malleability of sexual orientation in military discourse testifies to the official fear and acknowledgement that perhaps heterosexuality cannot be left merely to 'nature' itself, 'but must be actively created through an intensely interventionist project of social transformation' (Smith 1990: 49).[11] The latter was evident in the MoD's obsession with the transitionality of youthful male sexuality, which, according to MoD discourse, could only mature to heterosexuality if it occupied a space free of 'influential' homosexuals.

However, it seems that it is not only adolescents who are vulnerable to the seduction of homosexuality. The following 'Naval Scenario' was depicted during the 1985–6 Select Committee on the Armed Forces Bill to illustrate the incompatibility of homosexuality with armed service (in the navy in particular). It seems that the average adult 'able-bodied-seaman' is in an extended sexual transitional period too:

> Can I suggest a Naval Scenario? A ship has been at sea many months and there are a large number of men on board who have not seen a woman for weeks. If you had a homosexual on board he would bring pressure to bear on others who might respond, and in the close-knit circumstances of a warship at sea this could certainly be very detrimental to discipline and good order on board.
>
> (Rear Admiral Brown, HC Paper (1985–6)
> No. 170, para 669, 185)

Thus, male heterosexual masculinity was produced here from within a hydraulic model of sexuality where, if one direction for sexual energy is blocked, it will re-direct itself (Weeks 1989: 9). The homosexual body, in this scenario, is produced as a disruptive site of substitution and temptation to be used in the absence of a female body. The disruption was caused in this 'Naval Scenario' as a result of a homosexual's presence and a heterosexual's sexual activities with, and advances towards, this hypothetical homosexual.

The lifting of the ban against homosexuals serving in the armed forces was also articulated as being potentially damaging to the confidence the services enjoy, and the esteem in which the general public holds them, that is, a general public made up of parents who allow their 'teenage' offspring to volunteer for armed service. The MoD's fear was that parents would not allow their 'children' to enlist in an organisation that would allow their 'children' to associate and be potentially corrupted by homosexuals. This, according to the MoD, might result in decreasing numbers of recruits. Mr Wilkinson MP (the chair of the 1995–6 Select Committee on the Armed Forces Bill) captured these concerns in his speech to the House of Commons in May of 1996. Wilkinson was convinced by the findings of the HPAT that 'young servicemen and servicewomen were significantly more likely than those aged over 25 years to consider that their families would be worried if they had to serve alongside a homosexual of their own sex. 45 per cent of the younger group agreed that their families would be worried' (in HPAT 1996: 147). In the following passage Wilkinson conflated armed forces values with 'family values' as being shared (in their exclusion of homosexuality) and greatly appreciated by both institutions:

> Although these values may appear a bit traditional, for those who serve in the armed forces they are greatly appreciated. They are appreciated also by parents who are perhaps encouraging their children's aspiration to enter the armed services. If parents felt that the forces condoned homosexuality, a large number of them would do their best to resist the recruitment of their children.
>
> (*Hansard*, Commons, 9 May 1996a: col. 489)

Mr Wilkinson's conflation of the alleged core values of 'the family' and the armed forces can be seen as an attempt to re-enact what Stuart Hall (1991) describes as the great stable collectivities of class, race, gender and nation (and by implication heterosexuality: that is, sexual order) – perhaps in an attempt to avoid the possibility of including homosexuality (sexual and gender disorder) in either institution.[12]

'The family', 'the nation' and the defence of the identical values both 'the family' and the armed forces are presented as sharing, according to Mr Wilkinson, are all articulated here in order to legitimise the maintenance of the ban on homosexuals serving in the armed forces. The assumption behind this statement is that 'the homosexual' is always already outside 'the family' and outside 'the forces', and that 'children' even those of 16,

17, 18 and 19 years of age are always already heterosexual, albeit their heterosexuality is fragile. If homosexuals were to be allowed into the armed forces, according to Mr Wilkinson, families would not allow 'their children' to enlist, and as a result the armed forces would not survive without the influx of new recruits. Mr Wilkinson also implied that the shared values of the armed services and 'the family' could hold 'the nation' to ransom: that we 'ought to be wary' as the armed forces 'greatly appreciate' these values and therefore, we (the nation) should not seek 'to impose on the armed forces values that they do not want' (*Hansard*, Commons, 9 May 1996a: col. 489).

III Malignant homosexuality

The production of homosexual identity in MoD discourse, which was crystallised in HPAT's research and report, was constructed around a particular 'technology of homosexual(ity)' (Moran 1996a: 102). Homosexuality was presented as being an immutable characteristic that superordinately organised the existence and social relationships of homosexuals. The following passage from John Wilkinson MP illustrates this:

> It is the view of the forces, and has been the view of successive governments that it would be inappropriate to insist that the forces accept these people [homosexuals]. People's sexuality runs very deep and it affects the way in which people get on with their colleagues. It can prejudice their behaviour in an invidious way.
>
> (cited in Hall 1995: 12)

Thus homosexuality, in the passage above, was constructed as the superordinate organising characteristic of the hypothetical homosexual forces' member. This homosexuality seems, perhaps because of its depth and centrality to 'these people', to be an irrepressible identity, not secret or carefully guarded. Following the above statement Mr Soames MP (then Under Secretary of State for Defence) quoted the former chair of the Joint Chiefs of Staff of the USA armed forces, Colin Powell's, views on homosexuals serving in the armed forces, in order to describe homosexual identity as behaviourally malignant. Paraphrasing Powell, Soames stated that 'unlike race or gender, sexuality is not a benign trait. It is manifested in behaviour' (cited in *Hansard*, Commons, 9 May 1996: col. 508). Thus homosexual identity, from this official perspective, was articulated as an unavoidably invidious, immutable characteristic and therefore behaviourally and socially malignant, and thus incompatible with service in the armed forces. It is important to note here that it was homosexual identity and not homosexual conduct that was the MoD's primary concern. This was described in the following passage from the 1990–1 Select Committee on the Armed Forces Bill:

I will not say that dismissal is automatic in every case of a prosecution under the Service Discipline Acts, but I will say it is almost certain. To explain that, if there was a fairly minor piece of homosexual activity which perhaps grew out of over-intensive horseplay amongst very young men or adolescents, in such a case ... it would not be necessary to dismiss them from the services if it could be categorised as a transient phase rather than an orientation towards homosexuality

(Captain Lyons, HC Paper (1990–1) No. 179, para 622, 88)

These fleeting, same-sex sexual 'fumblings' by adolescents, who were again portrayed as possessing an unfixed, transitory sexuality, were not, it seems, as incompatible or disruptive to the armed service environment as an unacknowledged homosexual's permanent orientation and identity. It was assumed that the same-sex conduct of these otherwise 'heterosexual' adolescents would go away because they were very young and a homosexual identity had not become a fixed immutable characteristic as in 'homosexual' identity in adults.

In many cases it was the admission to, or confession of, being a homosexual that usually (after the initiation of an investigation) led to the administrative discharge of homosexuals. However, it is not the practices of investigation and interrogation that I am interested in here. It is the non-disruptive effect of these homosexual members of the armed forces prior to the discovery of their sexual identity that I am primarily concerned with in this case study. My analysis focuses on the MoD's description of the 'covert homosexual'. This category of homosexual was only one of nine listed possibilities of homosexual identity in the armed forces, and it was this sort of homosexual who, 'by controlling his actions, expressive behaviour or outside conduct', prevented the service authorities from gaining compelling evidence of his existence (HPAT 1996: 91).[13] This variety of 'covert' homosexual exists alongside the MoD's homosexual incompatibility discourse. The 'covert homosexual' was the variety of homosexual most likely to inhabit this environment, rather than the others listed in the HPAT's taxonomy, 'the flamboyant homosexual' or the 'homosexual activist'. Yet covert homosexual identity is a homosexual presence in the armed forces that was excluded from the HPAT's investigations which focused on the implications of a particular homosexual, the 'acknowledged homosexual', being allowed to join the armed forces. Thus, the machinery of the HPAT report attempted to produce the legibility and intelligibility of homosexual incompatibility from a particular 'scheme of knowledge' (Moran 1996a: 102). This delimitation, however, and the production of the issue of homosexuals in the armed forces, were intermittently unsettled by the presence of this covert, non-disruptive homosexual. One such instance of this surfacing of an 'alternative homosexual' to that produced by the MoD and the HPAT report was presented by Lord Justice Brown during the 1995 judicial review:

> There is ... no evidence of any actual adverse effect on discipline, morale and unit cohesiveness with regard to any of the hundreds of individual homosexuals who have been discharged over the years ... the problems perceived by the Ministry of Defence do not occur in practice.
>
> (Lord Justice Simon Brown, *R* v. *MoD* [1995])

What the above passage begins to expose is that perhaps the hypothetical homosexual produced and investigated by the HPAT was divorced from the actual, contextual, existence of members of the forces who are homosexuals. This perspective was exemplified by Angela Mason, chair of the gay and lesbian parliamentary lobbying group, Stonewall, in her statement to the 1995–6 Select Committee:

> It has been, it is and it will always be the case that there are lesbians, gay men and bisexuals serving in the armed forces who are living and sleeping and showering with members of the same sex. Now there really is not the evidence, and it does not emerge from this report [HPAT], that those individuals have done anything or behaved in any way that would give offence or in any sense disrupt the effectiveness of the units in which they serve, in fact, the evidence is the other way. I think the overwhelming majority of those who have been discharged on grounds of their sexual orientation alone, and there are very, very few discharges on grounds of conduct, perhaps one or two a year, they have actually exemplary service records.
>
> (HC Paper (1995–6) No. 143, para 775, 102)

This lack of evidence reveals the trace of a homosexual identity that is absent from the MoD's incompatibility discourse: a sexual identity that is far from 'manifest in behaviour', that is self-managed, controlled and compatible with service in the armed forces through a project of non-disclosure and non-legibility.

Passing compatibility (in 'the homosocial habitus')

When discussing the armed forces, and especially homosexuals in these institutions which, according to the MoD, depend to such a great extent on the successful bonding and trust between it members, it is essential to contextualise one's analysis. This contextualisation facilitates the recognition that the 'specialness' of the armed forces environment, as described by the MoD, is a result of both formal and informal structures that organise and regulate it. In this section, the focus will be on the informal mechanisms whereby the institutionalised dispositions of the armed forces are organised and formed. Bourdieu refers to the informal structures of an institution as its habitus. According to Bourdieu, these informal structures are constitutive of particular types of environments that produce habitus (1977: 82). Bourdieu describes the word 'dispositions' as being particularly well suited to express 'what is covered by the concept habitus'. Here, he defines habitus as a system of dispositions which designate ways of being and habitual states (especially of the body) (1977: 214). The habitus of an environment or institutional setting is constituted in practice and is oriented towards practical functions (1994: 95). The habitus operates as a guarantee for 'correct practice' (Bourdieu 1977: 54), that is, it works to exclude 'improbable practices' (Bourdieu 1994: 97). The concept of the habitus thus facilitates the exploration of 'the incorporation of the social into the body' (McNay 1999: 95), by allowing for the analysis of the 'subtle inculcation of power relations upon the bodies and dispositions of individuals' (McNay 1999: 99). Thus, in the habitus, we can identify an informal homogenisation of dispositions, whereby the members of a group or class become products of dispositions (Bourdieu 1977: 81) by the processes of 'inculcation and appropriation' (1977: 85). Theweleit has similarly described this process. According to Theweleit, the military cadet receives instruction through the practice of transgression and reactive, institutionalised, informal punishment: 'the cadet never receives instructions; he recognizes his mistakes only in the moment of transgression from the reactions of others who already know the score' (Theweleit 1989: 145).

The habitus of the armed forces is thus mastered by a process of what Bourdieu refers to as 'mechanical learning by trial and error' where 'practical mastery is transmitted in practice' (Bourdieu 1977: 87). This environment is undoubtedly associated with the discipline of both mind and body. According to Bourdieu's reading of Goffman's total institutions, institutions such as the armed forces are in the business of creating 'new men' by the processes of de-culturalisation and re-culturalisation (Bourdieu 1977: 94). Bourdieu characterises the intensive training found in the armed forces initial or basic training as follows:

> Treating the body as memory, they entrust to it in abbreviated and practical, i.e. mnemonic form the fundamental principles of arbitrary content of the culture.
>
> (Bourdieu 1977: 94)

According to Foucault's analysis of institutions such as the army barracks in *Discipline and Punish*, there is in discipline a detailed political investment of the body, which also infests and conquers the social body (Foucault 1977a: 139). Discipline, according to Foucault, 'is a political anatomy of detail' (1977a: 139). These details are both the means of control and intelligibility in what Foucault describes as the technology of disciplinary institutions (and societies), that is, surveillance in the form of panoptic technologies. Disciplinary spaces, for Foucault, are invested with an 'infinitely minute web of panoptic techniques' (1977a: 224) in which 'the two elements – distribution and analysis, control and intelligibility – are inextricably bound up' (1977a: 148). However, it is important to view such 'panoptic' relations of power not merely in the form of a seamless wave of surveillant power internalised by passive objects, but rather as an active characteristic of informal institutionalised practices, especially related to the eradication of inappropriate behaviour and dispositions. In this way, the habitus differs from the panopticon and becomes a more nuanced, subtle and appropriate model for analysing a subjective system of internalised structures and 'schemes of perception' (Bourdieu 1977: 86).

It is my contention that, in the armed forces environment, 'appropriate' forms of masculinity become homogenised and habituated through surveillant discipline. Appropriate heterosexualised varieties of masculinity (masculinities which connote heterosexualities), become homogenised in this environment, and are habitually assimilated and internalised by male forces' members. The armed forces environment can be described as a masculine environment, where women are allowed to take a part, and also a heterosexualised environment, where homosexuals are formally banned and informally unwelcome. Many of the young people who join the armed forces may only realise they have a sexual orientation towards members of the same sex when they have already joined up. These people would obviously internalise the anti-homosexual sentiment, which would be reinforced by the training and bonding activities they would endure during their forces career. Thus, it could be argued that the homosexual forces member would soon realise that openness about his or her sexuality, and any disposition that would signify a homosexual identity, would be inappropriate in the forces' habitus and detrimental to him or her achieving close and cohesive relationships with other people in the group. We can ask another question: how is this achieved?

Giving evidence to the 1995–6 Select Committee on the Armed Forces Bill, Angela Mason referred to the 'extraordinary sensitivity' of lesbians and gays in the armed services. This sensitivity can be described as habitus- or context-specific; it is acted out within an intercorporeal relationship in the panoptic habitus between observers and the observed, where the body as surface, and its dispositions, are scrutinised by 'the watchers' and managed by 'the watched'. In order for there to be no evidence of the MoD's perceived hypothetical problems related to a homosexual presence in the armed services, homosexuals who have served and are already serving in the armed services must be managing their socially conceal-able stigmas (Goffman 1963: 93) by passing as heterosexual. Passing, according to Plummer, 'involves the presentation of a public identity out of harmony with a private identity' (Plummer 1975: 189). Passing, in the armed forces setting, would involve the presentation of a habitus-appropriate identity, an identity which avoids what Plummer, following Goffman, describes as the usage of 'stigma symbols', that is, 'all those give-away signs that are typically associated with homosexuality in the popular stereotype' (Plummer 1975: 191). Heterosexual identity is assumed in the armed forces, in the case of men, by the stereotypical assimilation and performance of forces' masculinities. A 'straight-acting' (non-obvious, manly or even 'ordinary') homosexual male can pass as, or be assumed to be, heterosexual, merely by being in the armed services. Thus, being a member of the armed forces can be said to provide the material circumstance whereby 'straight-acting' homosexual forces members may pass and be assumed to be heterosexual.[14] This passing by the performance of habitus-appropriate masculinity, coupled with the material circumstances of actually being in the forces, is demonstrated in the following passages:

> Often, if you do not conform to the common stereotypes and people do not perceive you to be homosexual they perceive you to be heterosexual. Accordingly, you are judged on the basis of stereotypes.
>
> (Mr Cashman, HC Paper (1990–1) No. 179, para 717, 100)

Edmund Hall (a gay ex-soldier) also describes this:

> The more successful a man's military career, the further he moves away from society's stereotypes of limp-wristed effeminate homosexuals ... simply by being a military man he is giving off signals that mark him out as heterosexual.
>
> (Hall 1995: 34)[15]

This signification of an assumed heterosexual identity in homosexual males in the armed forces occurs within the grid of cultural intelligibility called the heterosexual matrix. It is through the heterosexual matrix that bodies, genders and sexualities are naturalised (Butler 1990: 151).[16] As described in the introduction, in this heterosexual matrix, it is assumed that for bodies to cohere and make sense 'there must be a stable sex expressed through a stable gender (masculine expresses male, feminine expresses female) that is, oppositionally and hierarchically defined through the compulsory practice of heterosexuality' (Butler 1990: 151). According to Butler, the cultural intelligibility and signifiability of gender absorbs (biological) sex. However, as discussed above, gender supported by certain material circumstances can absorb and also signify sexuality, but not always coherently. Thus, in the armed forces setting, a homosexual could assimilate or imitate the available forms of masculinity within this setting in order to make a homosexual identity that is rendered improbable by the material circumstance of being in the forces, even more improbable. The aim of gender, according to Butler, is to signify one historical idea (that is, masculinity or femininity) rather than another (Butler 1989: 256). This signification is necessarily corporeal, that is, communicated through a 'vocabulary of action' rather than the claims of reified nouns (Butler 1989: 256). According to Butler, 'one does one's' gender, as 'gender is a corporeal style, a way of acting the body, a way of wearing one's own flesh as a cultural sign' (Butler 1989: 256). Alongside the importance of the malleability of the social intelligibility of sexual identity, it is this drag or imitation of forces' masculinity that facilitates the ability of homosexual males in the armed forces to pass as assumed heterosexuals. Although it must be pointed out that for many homosexual servicemen this may be merely a case of performing the relevant or related variety of masculinity they have always performed. Accommodating to the masculinity appropriate to the variety of masculinities within the armed forces is, therefore, the means of tactically (de Certeau 1984: xix) resisting one's exclusion from armed service on the grounds of sexual identity. This resistance to exclusion is achieved by being a product, and an active user, of the informal structures and sanctions that make up the forces' gender habitus. This tactical ability to pass is facilitated by the unremarkableness (if one so chooses) of one's (homo)sexuality. The simultaneous internalisation and tactical use of power, evident in the homosexual forces' member's ability to pass as heterosexual, is a demonstration of de Certeau's injection of resistant cultural practices into what he sees as the over-theorisation of power (and the under-theorisation of resistance) in Foucault's *Discipline and Punish*.[17] De Certeau calls these resistant cultural practices 'tactics'. Tactics, according to de Certeau, are temporally specific[18] practices which play on, and with, a terrain imposed on them, that is, the tactic is a manoeuvre 'within the enemy's field of vision' (de Certeau 1984: 36–7). Here, visual, surveillant or panoptic power demands a visual response from the relatively powerless by way of camouflage. According to Ahearne, de Certeau's tactical practices are how the relatively powerless survive in 'a field controlled by a stronger force' (Ahearne 1995: 162). The notion that homosexual forces members can use a form of gender or drag in order to pass within the panoptic habitus of the armed forces setting troubles Butler's limitation of drag to males imitating females and females imitating males. The homosexual forces member's imitation of the varieties of masculinity which assure his signification of assumed heterosexuality within the armed forces, incorporates gender imitation within a range of masculinities rather than only between masculine and feminine genders.

The power implicit in the informal structures of the habitus can be said to be related to the potential varieties of resistance to it. According to Fornas, 'resistance means standing up against something or somebody. It therefore presupposes power, to which it constitutes an answer and a reaction' (1995: 59). The resistance to potential exclusion from the armed forces on the grounds of having a homosexual orientation cannot simply be described as a reaction to power, as in Foucault's concept of reverse or counter-discourse (1978: 101). Homosexuals in the armed forces cannot, whilst still being members of the armed forces, proceed to complain about the statutory ban. As a result of this action they would find themselves excluded from the armed forces by administrative discharge. Resistance to exclusion was to be achieved by accommodating to an environment that organises its cohesion and its homogeneity around the expulsion of homosexuals. Homosociality, according to Sedgwick:

> Is a word occasionally used in history and the social sciences, where it describes social bonds between persons of the same sex; it is a neologism, obviously formed by analogy with 'homosexual', and just as obviously meant to be distinguished from 'homosexual'. In fact, it is applied to such activities as 'male bonding', which may, as in our society, be characterised by intense homophobia, fear and hatred of homosexuality.
>
> (Sedgwick 1985: 1)

In the armed forces environment, it is clear that Sedgwick's definition of homosociality can be described as part of the informal structure of this environment, along the lines of Bourdieu's habitus. The informal structuring of the homosocial aspects of the forces' habitus is evident in the attempted separation of two identities that of 'the military man' and 'the homosexual'. The former identity is dependent upon the strict boundary creation and maintenance between the homosocial environment of the armed forces, with its non-sexual same-sex bonds; and the homoeroticism associated with homosexuality (Stychin 1996: 194). The informal homosocial habitus found within the armed forces environment and the explicit formal banning of homosexuals within the armed forces operate as a means of protecting the boundary. Both these formal and informal homosocial mechanisms operate as a means of protecting the boundary of the de(homo)sexualised space of the masculine forces environment under threat from 'that which must be excluded' from this space, 'the homosexual'. This need to protect or maintain the formal and informal means of de(homo)sexualising the armed forces environment was captured in the following evidence from a Royal Navy Lieutenant Commander from the aptly titled 'Problem Area 10 Increased Dislikes and Suspicions: Polarized Relationships' of the HPAT report:

> Friendships (among Royal Navy ratings) become very deep ... friendships can become reasonably physical with horseplay and banter and, I dare say it, affection ... there is no modesty allowed in their lifestyles, nor needed ... there was no stigma and no threat attached to [nakedness] so it was not unnatural or of any importance. Introduce homosexuals and the whole playing field changes ... officers develop healthy friendships and can spend many hours in each other's company

or in each other's cabins … this would be instantly taboo or at the very least questionable, because everyone would have to build artificial barriers against the introduced possibilities … it simply never entered one's thoughts … when a colleague sat on your bunk you did not immediately have to consider whether you ought to jam your door open or call a third party to attend.

(HPAT 1996: 135)

It seems that homosocial masculinity in the armed forces is a fragile entity: 'for a man to be a man's man is separated only by an invisible, carefully blurred, always-already-crossed line from being interested in men' (Sedgwick 1985: 89). Thus, 'the discovery of the homosexual within homosocial institutions threatens to sexualize the whole environment as individuals are eyed with mistrust … everyone is potentially queered, and being a man's man might arouse more than mere suspicion' (Healy 1996: 5). According to Healy, homosexuality functions as the inverse of homosociality, therefore the two can never be present at the same time (1996: 6). As a result, the proscripted and prescripted expression between men results in a homogenisation of the performance and expression of masculinity, which is assimilated to by the male forces members (heterosexual, bisexual, homosexual): intimacy of the homoerotic variety is proscribed whilst a de-sexualised intimacy between men is prescribed.

The homosocial space of masculinity is a space that is threatened and potentially disrupted by the presence, or suspected presence, of homosexuals. From this deduction it would seem that the segregation of the homosexual as a discrete personage, lifestyle, type (Foucault 1978), a distanced obvious stereotype, that which is not 'the military man', has a function, as McIntosh proposed in her essay 'The Homosexual Role' (1968). According to McIntosh, the homosexual's function was to keep the rest of society pure. This function is demonstrated in the MoD's predicted disruption to the 'small space' forces men 'have cleared for themselves' (Sedgwick 1990: 1) when 'the homosexual' enters this space. Perhaps it is less 'the homosexual' as a segregated identity which keeps the homosociality of the masculine armed forces space pure, than the actual informally sanctioned de(homo)sexualising structure operational in this space. Admittedly, the presence of homosexual desire in this de(homo)sexualised space of male intimacy would be potentially disruptive to homosociality. However, it is the social sanctions and barriers to homosexual desire within this habitus that actually maintain the purity of the homosocial space and not the hypothetical homosexual figure. This discursive homosexual figure is a useful symptom of homosociality, which may be called up in order to enforce or shore up definitive barriers of acceptability and to keep men in line. Therefore the disruptive and incompatible homosexual identity deployed by the MoD is less a reified person or type of person who has an inadvertent function of maintaining the purity of the inside (from which he has necessarily been abjected), than an effect of homosocial sanctions. When homosexual desire enters the armed forces, the purity of the space and the necessary intimacy and cohesion fostered by banishing homoeroticism from this space is put in jeopardy.

The compatible homosexual (a present absence)

The MoD's concerns and its reasons for banning homosexuals from serving in the armed forces were described earlier as being based on practical and not moral judgements. Indeed, the HPAT did concentrate on and make judgements with regard to the practicalities of lifting the ban on homosexuals in the armed forces. However, these alleged practical and non-moral investigations, which were collated and reported by the HPAT, were techniques whereby a particularly incompatible homosexual identity, that of the acknowledged homosexual, was investigated. The limitation of the MoD's consideration of homosexuality in the armed forces was the source of a particular exchange in the House of Commons between two MPs, Tony Banks and Nicholas Soames. During the 1996 House of Commons debate on the Armed Forces Bill Mr Soames stated that:

> The current policy of excluding homosexuals from the armed forces is not – I repeat, not – the result of a moral judgment. The prime concern of the armed forces is the maintenance of operational effectiveness and our policy derives from a practical assessment [HPAT] of the implications of homosexual orientation on military life.
>
> (*Hansard*, Commons, 9 May 1996: col. 505)

In reply to this Tony Banks MP directed the following question at Mr Soames:

> Does the Hon. Gentleman accept that there is undoubtedly a considerable number of homosexuals within the armed forces now? He must know that to be a fact. How is that affecting operational efficiency now?
>
> (*Hansard*, Commons, 9 May 1996: col. 506)

Mr Soames's reply to Mr Banks's question actually confirms Banks's suggestion that there are covert homosexuals serving in the armed forces who do not disrupt cohesion or operational effectiveness because they are unrecognised and unrecognisable as homosexuals:

> There may be some homosexual personnel in the armed forces but they choose to keep that to themselves. That is a matter for them ...

[Interruption] ... I will deal with that later.

(Soames, *Hansard*, Commons, 9 May 1996: col. 506)

During this debate Mr Soames never returned to the issue of covert homosexuals who exist in the armed forces non-disruptively. He did, however, urge the members of the House of Commons to heed the 'anti-homosexual' views of the majority of servicemen and women as demonstrated in the HPAT report.

In the parliamentary exchange presented above, Banks managed to unsettle the MoD's discourse of homosexual incompatibility, which was being reproduced by Soames. Banks achieved this by advancing an alternative interpretation reminiscent of a Shakespearean Lear-esque scenario that privileges 'alternative' wisdom/knowledge over the blind stupidity of the fallen-mighty. Banks's question and Soames's reply in the Commons can be seen as an example of making 'the not-seen accessible to sight' (Derrida 1963: 163), or, more accurately, bringing the unspoken and silenced into debate. One could say that Banks's question opened up a gap in the MoD's scheme and 'hold' on knowledge, out of which an unheard and unspoken 'other knowledge' could emerge, however briefly. This de-subjugated knowledge had the capacity to reverse the deployment of 'the homosexual' as incompatible and malignant as articulated by the MoD, to 'the homosexual' as already there and benign, seemingly non-disruptive to operational effectiveness. Although Banks did not present evidence of these compatible homosexuals, Soames's reply did confirm that this alternative homosexual does exist in the armed forces.

Therefore, Banks (with the help of Soames) did present a homosexual presence which was absent in the MoD's deployment of their common-sensical and practical reasons for maintaining the ban. This present absence exceeded the MoD's mechanisms for ensuring the continued exclusion of homosexuals from armed service by 'signal[ling] in the direction of an entirely other' interpretation (Derrida 1982: 65). Banks and Soames, inadvertently in his reply, situated the unthinkable of the MoD's dominant interpretation in competition with their articulated and normalised thinkable (Smith 1994: 233). Banks's question in the Commons contained the requisite deconstructionist split operation of an initial reversal which facilitates a breakthrough (to alterity), towards that which was unthinkable or outside of the dominant interpretation (Gashe 1986: 172–3). Therefore, by exposing the trace of non-evidence as regards the MoD's deployment of the discursive, incompatible homosexual, and the disruption this figure would allegedly cause to the environment of the armed services, Banks presented the unrepresented. He gave expression to the unheard thoughts (Critchley 1992: 15), the resisted knowledge (Thomas 1993: 80) of the MoD's 'closed, comfortable, established system of meaning' (Douzinas and Warrington 1992: 31).

The MoD's deployment of homosexual incompatibility was fixed and crosscut discursively by the 'violence' of two conflated hierarchical binary oppositions, that of heterosexual/homosexual and compatible/incompatible. The 'naturalness' and hence violence of these conflated binary oppositions was maintained by the deployment of the uncontrollable homosexual. 'The homosexual' in this discursive deployment was produced as being the abuser of rank and the seducer of 'the young', never a non-obvious, controlled professional who was compatible with military service. The presence of covert homosexuals within the armed forces was submerged in the MoD's deployment of the acknowledged disruptive and uncontrollable homosexual, presented as the only possible homosexual in the armed forces. The homosexual, according to this interpretation, desired to infiltrate this space and was never acknowledged as being spatially and temporally already within this space. The benign, compatible homosexual in the armed forces environment, who is accommodating himself tactically and non-disruptively to this environment, is a present absence which, when expressed, becomes 'like shrapnel in a discursive battle' (Terry 1991: 57) which rents and rips the surface of the MoD's scheme of knowledge. The covert, non-disruptive, 'assumed heterosexual', homosexual forces' members, who are negated in the MoD's interpretation, leave a trace, like footprints in sand, which disturbs the order of the MoD's surface interpretation. This trace of non-evidence is not a presentation of something identifiable, but is evidence (shrapnel) of something other, which exceeds the dominant interpretation (Lingis 1994: 175).

Passing policies

The HPAT, when visiting and assessing the armed forces of other countries, for example, Canada, Australia, France, Israel and Germany, discovered that even though the formal bans on homosexuals had been lifted in these forces, homosexuals still did not 'come out', they continued to pass.[19] The HPAT concluded from this insight that:

> Since this common pattern of a near complete absence of openly homosexual personnel occurs irrespective of the formal legal frameworks, it is reasonable to assume that it is the informal functioning of actual military systems which is largely incompatible with homosexual self-expression. This is entirely consistent with the pattern of British service personnel's attitudes confirmed by HPAT.
>
> (HPAT 1996: para 75, 53)

From this conclusion, we can deduce that the informal functioning of 'military systems' referred to above is a description of the informal structures I described earlier as the homosocial habitus. From the observations found in the HPAT and the Rand Report, it seems that the homosocial habitus is the informal structure of the armed forces internationally. This is not a particularly British phenomenon.

What the HPAT report confirmed (especially from foreign visits) is that the informal structures in operation in armed forces environments do prevent any form of homosexual expression other than assumed heterosexuality within the armed forces.

The US 'don't ask, don't tell' policy was announced and subsequently enacted by Congress on 19 July 1993 (Jacobson 1996: 39). This policy, which the HPAT describes as a 'sensible compromise', took the focus away from homosexual identity in the US armed forces, and instead concentrated on the propensity to engage in homosexual acts. This policy was and is far from perfect. However, by encouraging enlistees not to reveal their sexuality, whilst also making them aware of official policy, that admitting to a homosexual orientation would result in discharge, this policy 'allows service by gay people provided that they keep their sexual orientation a secret' (Herek 1996: 197). Thus, the don't ask, don't tell policy can, in theory, be seen as a variety of passing policy which attempts to afford some protection to assumed heterosexual, homosexual service members.[20] However, the statutory ban on homosexual orientation remained in this policy, 'since an open admission of such sexual orientation would be regarded as a propensity to engage in such homosexual acts' (HPAT 1996: Annex H6–4). According to Butler the words 'I am homosexual' are not merely understood as being descriptive in this policy but are figured as performing what they describe. The words in this statement not only constitute the speaker as a homosexual, but they also constitute the speech as homosexual conduct (Butler 1997: 107). Therefore, when one declares one's homosexuality under don't ask, don't tell, this does not amount to the mere communication of information about one's sexual preferences and relationships. The 'telling' of one's homosexuality was, according to Butler, 'fabulously misconstrued' as 'I want you sexually' (Butler 1997: 113). The statement becomes under this policy 'solicitous', a claim or declaration that:

> announces availability or desire, the intention to act, the act itself: the verbal vehicle of seduction. In 'effect' a desirous intention is attributed to the statement or the statement is itself invested with the contagious power of the magical word, whereby to hear the utterance is to 'contract' the sexuality to which it refers.
>
> (Butler 1997: 113)

Don't ask, don't tell also attempted to prohibit any corporeal demonstration of a homosexual propensity, especially bodily contact between members of the same sex 'that a reasonable person would understand to demonstrate a propensity or intent to engage in homosexual acts' (HPAT 1996, Annex H6–4). According to Halley, a 'propensity' to engage in homosexual acts was synonymous in this policy with a propensity to 'harm' unit cohesion and thus operational effectiveness (Halley 1996: 183–4). The objective and logic behind this particular passing policy (and the British MoD passing policies I shall discuss below) is the reduction of the potential risk to operational effectiveness due to homosexuality. Following on from Rose's description of the administrative production of solidarity and group cohesion through technologies of selection, allocation and elimination during the Second World War (Rose 1990), the don't ask, don't tell policy, according to Halley, can be described as being a technology whereby:

> Detecting people with a propensity ... [was] ... merely a way of identifying servicemen who are likely to engage in harmful conduct and getting them out of the military before they can actually harm military essences.[21]

> (Halley 1996: 184)

This attempt to control potential 'homosexual harm' was focused on the site of bodies in visual intercorporeal encounters. Within this policy, bodily acts such as gesturing or touching were to be surveyed for homosexual content. A homosexual propensity to act, and 'homosexual' intentions,[22] and thus a homosexual identity was to be recognised and policed by a particular observer, produced in the form of a 'reasonable person'.[23] Examples of behavioural demonstrations that are prohibited were hand-holding and kissing. However, associational activities (Herek 1996: 9) do not of themselves constitute 'credible information' that would provide a basis for the initiation of an investigation (HPAT 1996: Annex H 6–4). These are activities such as friendships with 'known' homosexuals, possessing or reading homosexual publications, visiting gay bars or marching in a gay rights parade in civilian clothes. Another aspect of don't ask, don't tell has been informally termed 'don't pursue', that is, no investigations or inquiries may be conducted solely to determine a service person's sexual orientation. Don't ask, don't tell, therefore, focused on prohibiting visible 'homosexual' conduct/activity and the speech act of 'coming out'.

According to Stychin, the US don't ask, don't tell policy has created a queer space between acts and identities, conducts and orientations (1996: 187). For Stychin, the valorisation of ontonomination as indicative of a propensity to act was problematised by the non-acting celibate self-defined gay person and by the self-defined straight person who engages in homosexual conduct (1996: 187). In this policy identity and conduct became imperfectly linked. This in turn created a gap or a space in which to argue that dismissal on the grounds of identity alone was constitutionally illegitimate. The reason for this was that identity alone does not reliably indicate a propensity to engage in homosexual activity (Stychin 1996: 187). Stychin, in the tradition of queer theory, illustrated how the gap and interruption between status and conduct (identity and sexual activity) created by this policy could be seen as a means of contesting the heterosexual and homosocial constitution of the male military subject (1996: 194). If the discursive 'homosexual' constitutive outsider of male military subjectivity and his homosocial environment began to appear less different, then, according to Stychin, an 'epistemic panic' may be created (1996: 197). 'The military's immunity against the homosexualisation of acts thus is undermined ... [when] the role of "the homosexual" "other" is diminished' (1996: 196).

Stychin here is focusing on 'the homosexual', the discursively deployed identity that was used to immunise and keep the forces' homosocial space pure as well as constituting diacritically the insiders' identities. This focus is at the expense of the informal social sanctions found in the homosocial habitus of the forces environment. Stychin thus reduces and abstracts 'the homosexual' and 'the heterosexual military man' here to discursive binary identities. By exposing the cultural constructedness of the homosexual constitutive outside, Stychin attempts to de-naturalise the inside, the centre. However, this technique over-emphasises the symptom, that is, 'the homosexual', in a rather functionalist manner, and lays too much stress on the power of textual de-naturalisation as a political strategy. By over-emphasising the symptom Stychin overlooks the system in the form of the informal social sanctions within a homosocial setting. Stychin could be accused of placing all his theoretical and political eggs in the one basket by attempting to unsettle heterosexuality by focusing on a diluted and indiscreet homosexual constitutive outside (Butler 1993a) or interior exclusion (Fuss 1991).

The analysis of the British armed forces' homosexual exclusion policy in this case study so far, like Stychin's approach above, is employed in the troubling of the necessary boundaries between heterosexual masculinity and homosexual masculinity. However, my analysis in this case study is concerned with the context and the materiality of the social practices whereby homosexuals comport themselves compatibly with armed service, rather than focusing and culminating my research at the level of discursive binary figures. Thus my approach, in contrast to Stychin's variety of queer legal theory, is an analysis of how homosexuals accommodate to this social environment that they are discursively excluded from, rather than how the interdependency of the heterosexual and homosexual figures within the heterosexual/homosexual binary opposition can be manipulated subversively.

An example of a passing policy which is actually sensitive to the informal structures within the British armed forces environment, was proposed by Stonewall during the 1995–6 Select Committee on the Armed Forces Bill. Stonewall proposed the replacement of the MoD's non-discretionary 'blanket ban' on homosexuals with a uniform code of sexual conduct,[24] under which any disruptive sexual (mis)conduct, whether heterosexual or homosexual, could be dealt with. Stonewall's proposals to the Select Committee, which were influenced by the recommendations made by the Rand Report,[25] focused on inappropriate sexual acts rather than incompatible sexual identities.

According to Angela Mason, the British armed forces should, when introducing such a uniform code of sexual conduct, simultaneously introduce a code of guidance which would be 'based on respect for the individual's privacy' (HC Paper (1995–6) No. 143, para 792, 104). In other words, this code of guidance would protect individuals whether heterosexual, homosexual or bisexual in their private lives outside the armed forces setting. This right to privacy, according to Mason, would inhibit the active investigations and interrogation of homosexuals within the armed forces; it would also prevent the instigation of investigations due to the admission of a homosexual orientation, during contact with forces personnel such as chaplains and counsellors. Stonewall's recommendations to the 1996 Select Committee for the Armed Forces Bill were as follows:

1 An amendment to the Armed Forces Discipline Acts to introduce a statutory code of conduct to deal with inappropriate sexual conduct covering any misconduct whether heterosexual or homosexual.

2 That a Code of Guidance, similar to that used in the Australian Defence Force, be introduced which would deal with issues of privacy and mutual respect for the sensibilities of all parties.

3 That there be a moratorium on all further discharges of lesbians and gay men prior to the introduction of the Code of Guidance.

(HC Paper (1995–6) No. 143, 191)

As with don't ask, don't tell, Stonewall's proposed policy was appreciative of the informal structure of the homosocial habitus within the armed forces environment and of the tactical management of 'sexual identity' information by homosexual and bisexual service members in order to inhabit this environment non-disruptively. By focusing attention on inappropriate conduct (heterosexual, homosexual and bisexual), Stonewall was attempting to protect the many homosexuals with 'exemplary service records' who have been and are being administratively discharged on the grounds of homosexual identity alone. Persons who have acted inappropriately were thus excluded from Stonewall's considerations.

Stonewall's proposed policy to the 1995–6 Select Committee on the Armed Forces Bill also signals a shift in gay and lesbian identity politics, especially within the legal reform movement. Stonewall's proposed policy can be described as a moving away from identity or 'gay' representational rights claims, to a policy that recognises and is designed around the needs of, and actual context in which, gays, lesbians and bisexuals within the armed forces behave. Stonewall's attempt to propose policy which could equalise the treatment of heterosexuals, homosexuals and bisexuals is based on 'a different political model' (de Certeau 1986: 230) from that found in equality-rights discourse. The cultural specificity of invisibility and mutability of identity, which found its affirmation in the performance of genders in an appropriate homogenised style, was a specificity beyond a given, a past, an object of knowledge (de Certeau 1986: 228). This seemingly groundless or objectless specificity was to find its political ground (Godzich 1986: xii) in conditional behavioural practices, and not in a specifically gay rights claim to be included in (and not excluded from) the armed service.

Stonewall's proposed policy introduced at the 1995–6 Select Committee was not implemented in any part; the members of the Select Committee proposed the maintenance of the statutory ban to the Commons, citing the evidence collected and published by the MoD's HPAT report as central to their decision. However, the HPAT report actually included its own 'passing policy' under the title of 'A Possible Code for a No Open Homosexuality Policy' (HPAT 1996: Annex I). This MoD policy, like the don't ask, don't tell policy and Stonewall's proposed policy to the 1995–6 Select Committee, was designed around behavioural practices appropriate in a homosocial setting. However, the HPAT policy initially attempted to formalise in a code of conduct the informal structure of the homosocial habitus in order to ensure the non-disruption of the forces environment by dispositions that might connote a homosexual identity. According to the HPAT report, the attitudes they collected towards homosexuality in the British armed services and in foreign forces was evidence of the practical incompatibility of the presence of open or strongly suspected homosexuals within service life. As a result of this conclusion the HPAT proposed that:

> It is therefore the responsibility of all members of the armed services to avoid conveying the impression to those in their unit or any other part of the services that they are homosexual either by orientation or activity.
>
> (HPAT 1996: Annex I)

The body, and what Butler would describe as its corporeal signification, is being problematised here; the serviceman's body and behaviour in this statement was produced as a surface or a screen from which gendered meanings and underlying sexualities could be read. From the statement above, one could conclude that it was the HPAT's ambition to control the intercorporeal signification between bodies in order to prevent the reading or recognition of homosexual connotations that would cause a disruption to operational effectiveness. However, even though the HPAT report listed nine different types of homosexualities in the armed forces in its taxonomy, with nine different definitions describing the characteristics of each of these homosexual types, they seem to be unable to list a single discretely identifiable homosexual disposition, expression or style of dressing. The HPAT's potential 'Code of No Open Homosexuality' seemed to be located in between taxonomic prowess and epistemic crisis. The epistemic thoroughness of the HPAT's production of the nine discursive varieties of homosexual identities found in the armed forces is simultaneous with an epistemological failure to 'know' and represent homosexuality within armed forces practice in order to proscribe it. This failure is admitted in the HPAT report:

> Due to varying social behaviour in different parts of the UK and abroad and to constantly changing patterns of dress and expression it was not possible to set out precise guidelines or prohibitions. This does not

provide an excuse for failure to comply with the obvious spirit of the regulations.

(HPAT 1996: Annex I)

What the HPAT mean by complying with the 'obvious spirit' of the regulations was:

> Service personnel will conduct themselves in their professional and private lives in a manner which prevents accusations or suspicions of homosexuality which a reasonable person could find convincing.

(HPAT 1996: Annex I)

The HPAT's 'no open homosexuality' policy can be described as being an attempt to introduce a choreography or code of heterosexualised signification through the attempted regulation of the gesturing and speaking body. What this policy initiative hoped to achieve was a delimitation of the corporeal vocabularies (Butler 1989: 256) of armed service members to that which was characteristic of the varieties of the normalised heterosexual masculinity indigenous to the armed forces homosocial habitus. That is, the HPAT's proposed code (and the US don't ask don't tell policy) can be described as attempts to formalise in policy the intercorporeal relationship internalised by homosexuals in the homosocial environment of the armed services. This policy attempted to produce a voyeuristic heteronormativity and self-surveillancing internalisation of this in homosexuals as the means of eradicating the signs, expression and thus the 'threat' of disruption caused by the suspicion of homosexuality. However, in the case of the HPAT's policy proposal, this attempt was confounded by their inability to determine where the line between the acceptable conveyance of a heterosexual identity and the unacceptable connotations of a homosexual identity could and should to be drawn. In behavioural terms, this inability to separate 'the homosexual' from 'the heterosexual' testified not only to a crisis in representation – what is heterosexual manliness – but also a 'crisis in looking' (Simpson 1994). Sinfield, in his foreword to Simpson's book *Male Impersonators*, describes this crisis:

> Lately, gay images no longer seem distinct from straight images. In advertising, the cinema and pop music, gay kinds of appearance, and gay kinds of invitations to look, challenge not only the idea that gay men should be invisible, but also the idea that they are deeply different from straight men.

(Sinfield 1994b: xi)

What seems to be inconceivable to MoD discourse, and was subsequently exposed by Tony Banks and Stonewall, was that homosexuals in the armed forces might not be all that different from their heterosexual colleagues to look at. The HPAT's failure to recognise or indeed proscribe the corporeal characteristics homosexuals are assumed to display was a testament to the inadequacy of the MoD's perspective, which is colonised by a heteronormative and homosocial attempt to make discrete and separable 'the non-normative', the 'non-heterosexual'. By attempting to regulate the norm, the MoD's perspective can be described as being out of touch with the organisation of the space they would protect from homosexuality, as that space, by its own sanctions, eradicates the signs of homosexuality informally.

Furthermore, the scopic crisis related to 'the homosexual' deployed by the MoD is simultaneous with a scopic paradox. The greatest fear as regards homosexuals in the armed forces seems to be scopophobia, the fear of being looked at (I suppose this fear could be more accurately described as homoscopophobia). This homoscopophobia is paradoxical if one considers that the most salient index of homosexuality 'is how men look at other men' (Miller 1991: 131). From this we can assume that homosexuals who look at heterosexuals in the way the MoD fears homosexuals would look at heterosexuals would be retrograde to the successful passing of homosexuals as assumed heterosexuals as:

> homosexuals are not easy to identify, but if they leered at heterosexuals in private places, they would be more noticed by heterosexuals.
>
> (Shawver 1995: 39)

Conclusion

The 'acknowledged homosexual' produced by the MoD and evident in the attitudes of 'ordinary' service members collected by the HPAT, was a politically pervasive figure of incompatibility, which was an integral component in the maintenance of the MoD's statutory ban in 1996. However, I demonstrated that this 'acknowledged homosexual' was a hypothetical mechanism which had been used by the MoD through the technology of their internal review, in the form of the HPAT report, as a technique for justifying the retention of the homosexual exclusion policy. In the light of the MoD's inability to present evidence of the actual disruption caused by the presence of open homosexuals in the armed forces, we can assume that the discursive homosexual identity upon which the machinery for justifying the exclusion policy was based does not exist in reality. I further demonstrate that the presence of covert homosexuals existing non-disruptively in the armed forces was a secret the MoD, and Nicholas Soames, would rather have kept quiet. However, with the development of high-profile policies such as the US's don't ask, don't tell policy and the Australian Defence Force's Code of Sexual Conduct, the subjugation of the presence of covert, non-disruptive homosexual service personnel was made more difficult. The covert homosexual's ability to pass as an assumed heterosexual became part of the HPAT's own evidence which challenged their discursive machinery for maintaining the ban. However, this component of the HPAT's evidence was subjugated in their report. This process of subjugating the existence of covert homosexuals, that is, homosexuals who resembled 'ordinary' military men, is perhaps the MoD's attempt to keep the heterosexualised identity of the armed forces pure, that is, de(homo)sexualised. The MoD, therefore, could be described as reluctantly recognising the existence or the possibility of covert, assumed heterosexual, homosexuals in the armed forces, whilst simultaneously relegating and marginalising this possibility to the very periphery of the HPAT report, appearing as it did on the very last page of the appendices.

The phenomenon of 'covert homosexuals' present in the armed forces is an absence which haunts the MoD's heteronormative discursive production of the assumed incompatibility of homosexuals with armed service. The tactical performance of the assumed heterosexuality of the homosexual service members can be described as using the heterosexual matrix in the form of the informal homosocial habitus against itself. The ocularity and knowability of 'the homosexual' deployed by the MoD's homosexual incompatibility discourse is destabilised by 'assumed heterosexual' homosexual servicemen passing in the homosocial habitus. In this case study, masculinity is indeed de-naturalised, gender becomes a simulation and unanchored from an underlying sexuality, and heterosexuality, especially heterosexual masculinity, is presented as a vulnerable sexual orientation easily tempted to indulge in homosexual activities in certain circumstances and being easily imitated by homosexuals. However, these de-naturalisations and examples of the 'gender trouble' associated with homosexuals being socially indivisible from heterosexuals through their display of heterosexual masculinities is inadvertently perpetuated within a rather accommodationist strategy that is remote from the subversive intentions of many queer authors. Queer theories and practices are simultaneously adopted and modified in the case study above. Most notably, the potential for subversion-trouble in Stychin's queer legal analysis of the US don't ask don't tell policy can be described as being alienated from the potential that an intersection between queer analytic approaches and nuanced, contextualised social analysis might bring. A queer analysis that remains at the level of discourse and textual politics across the heterosexual/homosexual binary opposition can bring valuable insights. However, this may be at the expense of tracing the trajectory into discourse of social activities such as the intercorporeality of passing and the co-optation of such practices into the formulation of actual or proposed policy. Perhaps a queer reading of this area, which may be overly concerned with the subversion and transformation of the social, sexual and legal order which privileges heterosexuality, would have missed the point: that this is not about subversive de-naturalisations, but about the aims of accommodation, inhabitation and remaining in service within the armed forces through corporeal circumspection.

It is important also to stipulate that the procedures of passing which have found their way into what I call the proposed passing policies are procedures which are other than those predicted or expected in a Foucauldian conception of power and resistance. The homosexuals in the armed forces do not, and cannot, within the armed forces environment, react as expected or scripted in a Foucauldian sense. Power in the forces' environment is parasitically circumvented and redeployed because of the reiterative reversibility (and resignifiability) of its discourses and performatives. This is achieved by 'homosexual' agents who simultaneously blend resistance to power with congruency to power in the form of accommodating to power (within a panoptic homosocial habitus) by 'behaving' themselves as assumed heterosexuals as a means of inhabiting and accommodating to a hostile scopic masculinised and heterosexualised institutional environment.

What this case study presents is the tension between the knowable discursively deployed incompatible homosexual identity of MoD discourse, and the existence of compatible or covert homosexuals in the armed forces environment. The irony of the latter is that this variety of homosexual is present in the MoD's own taxonomy of possible 'forces homosexuals'. The covert, non-disruptive homosexual is also present in the evidence collected by the HPAT from the armed forces of foreign countries which have lifted their exclusion policies but have experienced no increase in the numbers of open homosexuals. This tension arises as a result of the MoD trying to maintain firm boundaries which separate homosociality from homosexuality, by separating out homosexuals from military men, and regarding them as irreducibly different from each other. However, what their own evidence and proposed passing policies recognised was that homosexuality could coexist in the body of the 'military man' albeit circumspectly.[26]

This case study introduces the theme whereby homosexuals often exceed the schemes of knowledge which would produce them within policy, legislation and institutional procedures within law. This will be a recurring theme throughout the remaining chapters, especially in relation to visibility and recognisability. For example, in Chapter 2, homosexual anonymity, secrecy and evasiveness will prove to be problematic in the refugee determination process of a Romanian applicant, Ioan Vraciu. Homosexual social invisibility is a theme that runs through Chapters 2, 3 and 4. In Chapter 2, in contrast to this chapter, the capacity of homosexuals to render themselves invisible is deployed by immigration officials as a means whereby homosexuals should be excluded from the refugee status under the definition of a particular persecuted social group.

Postscript: unjustified interference, covert homosexuals and the European Court

The four discharged service personnel – Jeanette Smith, Graeme Grady, Duncan Lustig-Prean and John Beckett – who launched the judicial review in 1995 and the appeal in 1996, subsequently took their complaint regarding their discharges from the armed forces to the European Court of Human Rights in 1999. In a judgment delivered in Strasbourg on 27 September 1999 in the case of *Lustig-Prean and Beckett* v. *United Kingdom*,[27] the European Court unanimously held that there had been a violation of Article 8 of the European Convention on Human Rights. In a second judgment delivered on the same day in the case of *Smith and Grady* v. *United Kingdom*,[28] the court also found a violation of Article 8 together with a violation of Article 13 (right to an effective remedy) of the Convention.

In this postscript I will focus primarily on the court's decision in relation to Article 8,[29] in the case of *Lustig-Prean and Beckett* v. *United Kingdom*.[30] The court's consideration of this issue was concerned, in particular, with the MoD's investigations into the applicants' sexual orientations and the necessity for specific lines of inquiry whilst interviewing the applicants. In this ruling the court noted that the administrative discharges of the four applicants had a profound effect on their careers and prospects. Moreover, the court considered that the investigations conducted into the applicants' sexual orientations, together with their discharge from the armed forces, constituted grave interference with their private lives.

Morale, cohesion and operational effectiveness: the government's case

The government reiterated the MoD's position on the homosexual exclusion policy before the European Court. That is, in *Lustig-Prean and Beckett* v. *United Kingdom*, the government's core argument for excluding homosexuals of both sexes from serving in the armed forces was that they feared homosexuals would have a negative effect on morale, cohesion and ultimately on operational effectiveness. The government relied, in this respect, on the report of the HPAT published in February 1996.

Earlier in this chapter I described the HPAT report as the technology through which this issue of the homosexual exclusion policy was to be approached during the 1995–6 House of Commons Select Committee on the Armed Forces Bill. During the deliberations of this Select Committee there was a reiteration of the discursive production of homosexuals as disruptive and sexually uncontrollable. However, although the European Court acknowledged the complexity of the study undertaken by the HPAT, it stated certain doubts as to the value of the HPAT report. The court listed the following objections to the 'objectivity' and 'reliability' of the HPAT report: (1) the court questioned the independence of the assessment contained in the report given that the report was designed, carried out and completed by MoD civil servants and service personnel; (2) only a very small proportion of the armed forces personnel participated in the assessment; (3)

many of the methods of assessment were not anonymous, and many of the questions in the attitude survey suggested answers in support of the policy (*Lustig-Prean and Beckett* v. *United Kingdom* 1999: para 88). The court found that, in so far as the views of armed forces personnel outlined in the HPAT report could be considered representative, those views were founded solely upon the negative attitudes of heterosexual personnel towards those of homosexual orientation (*Lustig-Prean and Beckett* v. *United Kingdom* 1999: para 89). The court ruled that the HPAT report had merely collected the negative attitudes of armed forces members and that these were as inappropriate as a predisposed bias towards forces members of a different race, origin or colour (*Lustig-Prean and Beckett* v. *United Kingdom* 1999: para 90). The court noted a lack of concrete evidence to support the government's submission as to the anticipated damage to morale and operational effectiveness. The court stipulated that it is open to a state to impose restrictions on an individual's right to respect for his private life where there is a 'real' threat to the armed forces operational effectiveness. However, assertions as to the risk to operational effectiveness must be substantiated by specific examples (*Lustig-Prean and Beckett* v. *United Kingdom* 1999: para 82), and not evidence of anti-homosexual sentiments amongst the members of the armed forces or 'predicted' reductions in operational effectiveness if homosexuals were permitted to serve. The court also considered that it could not ignore widespread legal changes in the domestic laws of contracting European states in favour of the admission of homosexuals into the armed forces of those states. As a result of the government's lack of evidence to support its argument for the exclusion of homosexuals from the armed forces, the court decreed that convincing and weighty reasons had not been offered by the government to justify the discharge of the applicants.

Interference and investigations

The court took special issue with the practice by service investigators of continuing their investigations after the individuals had admitted their homosexuality.[31] The government suggested to the court that the investigations continued in order to verify the admissions of homosexuality, so as to avoid false claims by those seeking an administrative discharge from the armed forces (*Lustig-Prean and Beckett* v. *United Kingdom* 1999: para 73). The court rejected this argument because the individuals concerned wished to remain in the armed forces. Accordingly, the investigations conducted after the individuals had confirmed their homosexuality were also considered unjustified, as the court was not persuaded by the government's argument that medical, security and disciplinary reasons necessitated the investigations. According to the government:

> The investigations were also necessary given certain security concerns (in particular, the risk of blackmail of homosexual personnel), in light of

the greater risk from the AIDS virus in the homosexual community and for disciplinary reasons (homosexual acts might be disciplined in certain cases including, for example, where they result from an abuse of authority).

(*Lustig-Prean and Beckett* v. *United Kingdom* 1999: para 73)

The court noted that the government justified the bulk of the questioning by way of these security, medical and disciplinary reasons; the government did not, however, seek to defend the level of detailed questioning about precise sexual activities to which the applicants were subjected (para 73). This was the issue upon which the court's assessment of the justification of such investigations turned. The court focused in particular on the nature of these unjustified investigations, especially in terms of the prurient questions put to the applicants during interviews, and the search and seizure of intimate possessions and correspondence. The court found that the investigation process in the case of Lustig-Prean and Beckett was of an 'exceptionally intrusive character' (para 84); and that:

certain lines of questioning of both applicants, were, in the court's view, particularly intrusive and offensive and, indeed, the government accepted that they could not defend the level of detailed questioning about precise sexual activities to which Mr Beckett was, at one point, subjected.

(para 84)

Codes of conduct

According to the European Court, the HPAT report included a range of alternative options to the homosexual exclusion policy. These alternative policies included (a) a code of conduct applicable to all (a uniform sexual code of conduct); (b) a policy based on the individual qualities of homosexual personnel, lifting the ban and relying on service personnel reticence; (c) the don't ask, don't tell solution offered by the USA and a 'no open homosexuality' code.[32] However, according to the court, the HPAT report concluded that no policy alternative could be identified which avoided risks for decreasing fighting power and operational effectiveness with the same certainty as the present policy of exclusion (*Lustig-Prean and Beckett* v. *United Kingdom* 1999: para 54). The government presented this issue, of replacing the current homosexual exclusion policy with a code of conduct, as lying 'at the heart of the judgement to be made on this matter' (para 71). The government argued that although many European armed forces had lifted their homosexual exclusion policies, these policy changes had been adopted in those countries too recently to yield any valuable lessons for the UK. This was the point in the proceedings where the government reiterated one of the HPAT's fundamental 'findings': that it was not the conduct of the person, but the knowledge or suspicion of the fact that a person was, or could be, a homosexual that had the potential to cause damage to morale and effectiveness (para 71). Thus, if homosexuals were allowed to serve in the armed forces, this would create the situation where all members of the forces could be suspected of being homosexual, which, according to the HPAT report, would result in paranoia, damaged cohesion and 'polarised relationships'. According to the government, the only solution was a homosexual exclusion policy. This was addressed by the court in the following terms: in so far as negative attitudes to homosexuality are insufficient, of themselves, to justify the policy (para 90), they are equally insufficient to justify the rejection of a proposed alternative (para 95). The European Court accepted that certain difficulties could be anticipated with the change in policy, as was the case with the presence of women and racial minorities in the past. The court found that any potential difficulties regarding including homosexuals in the armed forces would be essentially conduct-based. As such the court recommended that any 'difficulties' could be addressed by a strict code of conduct and disciplinary rules. The usefulness of such codes and rules was not undermined, in the court's view, by the government's suggestion that homosexuality would give rise to problems of a type and intensity that race and gender did not.

The court considered it important to note that part of the British armed forces had already adopted policy to deal with conduct such as racial discrimination and with racial and sexual harassment and bullying (paras 56 and 57). This policy, which was published in the Army's Equal Opportunities Directive 1996,[33] imposed a strict code of conduct on every soldier together with disciplinary rules to deal with any inappropriate behaviour and conduct. According to the court, this dual approach was supplemented with information leaflets and training programmes, wherein the Army emphasised the need for higher standards of personal conduct and for respect for others (para 95). The government, while not rejecting the possibility of replacing the current 'homosexual' policy with a code of conduct, emphasised the need for caution and that this was one of the options to be considered by the next Parliamentary Select Committee in 2001 (para 94).

Covert homosexuals

In a number of places within the pages of this European Court report, a particular homosexual emerged, as noted in the analysis of the various select committee reports and the HPAT Report. Earlier in the chapter I referred to this particular homosexual in the MoD's own lexicon from its taxonomy of potential homosexualities in the armed forces.[34] The 'variety' of homosexual I am referring to here can be found in category vii of this taxonomy: the covert homosexual. According to the court, the government's concern about the presence of open or acknowledged homosexual service personnel serving in the armed forces (which was the entire focus of the HPAT's attitude survey) was an unsubstantiated concern. The court expressed this in the following terms:

> The private lives of the present applicants were indeed private and would have remained so but for the policy.[35] There was, accordingly, no reason to believe that any difficulty would have arisen had it not been for the policy adopted by the government.
>
> (*Lustig-Prean and Beckett* v. *United Kingdom* 1999: para 77)

The court also noted the lack of concrete evidence to substantiate the alleged damage to morale and fighting power that any change in the policy would entail. This exclusion policy has always been haunted by the spectre of non-evidence. In fact, the HPAT report can be described as an attempt to manufacture 'evidence' (evidence of strong prejudice). However, this was a variety of evidence the European Court found relatively easy to discredit (para 92). The government's insistence that alternative policies, including a code of conduct, would be potentially damaging to morale and operational effectiveness was addressed by the court as being confounded by the MoD's inability to provide concrete evidence of 'homosexual disruption'. The court qualified this observation and statement concerning the 'non-evidence' of homosexual disruption as being particularly telling, as the MoD and the government could not present evidence of such disruption from the ranks of the total of 30 officers and 331 persons discharged between 1991 and 1996 (para 60). The court stated that these numbers were not insignificant, yet still the government was unable to provide concrete evidence that homosexuals serving in the armed forces cause a reduction in morale and operational effectiveness. Even if the absence of such evidence can be explained by the consistent application of the policy, as submitted by the government, this was insufficient to demonstrate to the European Court's satisfaction that operational effectiveness problems could be anticipated in the absence of the exclusion policy (para 92).

Postscript conclusion

The MoD, bowing to pressure from the European Court, did not wait until the next Parliamentary Select Committee on the Armed Forces Bill in 2001 to implement a revised policy. Speaking in the House of Commons on 12 January 2000, the Secretary of State for Defence, Geoff Hoon MP, described how the Chief of the Defence Staff was urged to initiate an urgent policy review of the area. This was in direct response to the European Court's decision that the exclusion policy was legally unsustainable. On 13 January 2000, the MoD published the *Armed Forces Code of Social Conduct: Policy*

Statement. This was a uniform code of social conduct that was to apply to all members of the armed forces regardless of their gender, sexual orientation, rank or status.[36]

A passage from Geoff Hoon's speech to the Commons on 12 January 2000 provides a fitting ending to this case study:

> As all personal behaviour will be regulated by the code of conduct with the object of maintaining the operational effectiveness of the three services, there is no longer a reason to deny homosexuals the opportunity of a career in the armed forces. Accordingly, we have decided that it is right that the existing ban should be lifted. As no primary or secondary legislation is required, with effect from today, homosexuality will no longer be a bar to service in Britain's armed forces.
> (http://www.mod.uk/policy/homosexuality/index.html, 15/06/00, 2)

2 Authenticity, evasion and the unknowable homosexual

> In relation to the closet – the relations of the known to the unknown, the explicit and the inexplicit ... have the potential for being peculiarly revealing.
>
> (Sedgwick 1991: 3)

Introduction

The seed of the idea for this case study began as a *nouvelle*, a piece of news, a snippet of real life (Foucault 1979b: 79) found in the margins of 'gay news' in the UK in 1995, in a small article in the magazine *Gay Times*. The narrative that unfolds in this chapter can be described as an obscure man's encounters with 'law'. This is a narrative where 'fragments of discourse ... [are found] trailing the fragments of reality in which they take part' (Foucault 1979b: 79). It is a case synonymous with anal examination, homosexuality and bogus asylum claims. The man at the centre of this case study is one Ioan Vraciu. He is one of those individuals whose life has been rescued from anonymity as a result of his particular encounter with 'law' in the form of refugee determination procedures. Foucault says, of men such as Vraciu:

> From the darkness of night where they would, and still should remain, is an encounter with power: without this collision, doubtless there would no longer be a single word to recall their fleeting passage.
>
> (Foucault 1979b: 79)

What Vraciu's encounter with power provides is an illustration of power:

> power which lies in wait for these lives, which spies on them, which pursues them, which turns its attention, even if only for a moment, to their complaints and their small tumults, which marks them by a blow of its claws.
>
> (Foucault 1979b: 79)

In the following analysis, Vraciu can be said to have sought out power by bringing his application for refugee status to the British Immigration Authorities. What is distinctive about this case is that Mr Vraciu based his application for refugee status[1] on his alleged homosexuality. This application facilitated an analysis of a particular homosexual–legal interaction in immigration and asylum practices whereby the 'truth' of sexuality was to be established.

This case study concerns itself with Mr Vraciu's second Immigration Appeal Tribunal (IAT) and the events surrounding it.

The IAT is the institutional setting in which an appellant's case is heard before a special adjudicator and lawyers from the Home Office. The primary purpose of these tribunals is, first, the authentication of the appellant's claims – to ascertain whether he or she is who and what they say they are; second, tribunals decide if an authenticated appellant can be included within the particular definition of refugee status under which they have made their application, as stipulated in article 1 A (2) of the United Nations Convention Relating to the Status of Refugees 1951. The range of categories under which an application for refugee status can be made is outlined in the following definition:

> Owing to a well founded fear of being persecuted for reasons of race, religion, nationality, membership of a particular social group or political opinion, is outside the country of his nationality and is unable or, owing to such fear, is unwilling to avail himself[2] of the protection of that country; or who, not having a nationality and being outside the country of his former habitual residence as a result of such events, is unable or, owing to such fear, is unwilling to return to it.
>
> (UNHCR 1979, para 34)

The category under which Vraciu made his application was that of membership of a particular social group, that is, of Romanian homosexuals who, finding themselves outside that country, have a well-founded fear of being persecuted if returned there.

The analysis of the Vraciu case which follows will demonstrate that the procedure for determining refugee status, in the case of applications made on the basis of homosexuality, is a matter of sufficient or insufficient evidence. In this tribunal hearing, Vraciu would not or could not furnish the tribunal with satisfactory evidence to support his claim that he was a practising homosexual. This lack of evidence resulted in the initiation of, or suggestion of, specific procedures for the authentication of a homosexual identity for the purposes of law. The Vraciu case can be described as opening up to academic scrutiny how sexuality in the form of intimate pleasure, preferences, practices and desires must be transformed into objective legal knowledge, that is, translated into the 'objective standards' required by law. What this case study facilitates is an analysis of the boundaries between 'the objective' and the 'socially constructed' in legal practice.

Thus, in this case study, the analysis is concerned with the particular practices of law that were initiated as a result of Vraciu's non-presentation of corroborative evidence to support his claim. This 'lack' of evidence can be said to have intensified the tension between the subjective and the objective realms in this case through the attempt to make (or more accurately, unmake) Vraciu's alleged homosexuality in legal practice.

This authentication process exposes the sensuality and corporeality of the legal practices involved in the discovery of the 'legal truth' of Vraciu's alleged homosexuality. Just as homosexuals in military passing policies in Chapter 1 were conceptualised as passing as heterosexual within a visual matrix which comprised heteronormative, diacritical and intercorporeal encounters, the following case study also concerns itself with bodies, and the search for the signs of homosexuality in specific medico-legal encounters. Legal practice in this case becomes a matter of the law attempting to know Vraciu, as a homosexual or as a heterosexual. What this amounts to is a sensorial and corporeal interaction or communion between Vraciu's body and the 'official' listeners, viewers and suggested examiners of it. These practices are, however, unlike the visual primacy of the gendered body as signifier of, or deflector of attention from, an underlying sexuality as presented in Chapter 1. In the Vraciu case, we shall see that legal scrutiny first focused on the anus as a site where the signs of a homosexual identity might be deter-mined. However, legal attention soon turned to the mouth, and the confessional speech-acts it performs in order to manufacture its facts. In this case it is the mouth that becomes the site for the initial stages of a process, an exchange of discourses, whereby the 'truth' of a homosexual identity is produced for the purposes of law. This chapter, in many respects, can be described as a cartography of the trajectory of unauthorised speech into authorised, factual discourse, through the medium of the machinery of psychiatric technique. The tracing of this trajectory of knowledge in the exchange of unauthorised speech for 'psychiatric facts' presentable to law is a means of focusing on how sexualised identities come into being in the social practice of law.

Background[3]

Ioan Vraciu arrived in Britain on a lorry from Calais and claimed asylum in September 1992. Initially the basis of his application was that he was involved in political activities in Romania during the revolution of 1989, and that he had also failed to report for military service in Romania. Vraciu's initial application for refugee status was refused on 11 November 1992. He appealed against this decision and the appeal was heard by the special adjudicator in June 1994 (this was Vraciu's first IAT). During the course of this IAT Vraciu announced, for the first time, that he feared persecution if he returned to Romania because he was a homosexual. He went on to tell the tribunal that his one and only Romanian male lover had been arrested; as a result of this he feared that his own arrest was imminent. He then fled the country. Vraciu's appeal was dismissed on 29 June 1994. Vraciu re-appealed to the tribunal on 26 October 1994 and it was directed that the matter be remitted *de nova*. Vraciu's second IAT was heard on 28 April 1995. It is the report of this particular tribunal that will be the focus of the following analysis.

Technologies of determination

In the Vraciu case, homosexual identity is produced as being a preconceived, fixed and knowable identity. However, in contrast to the MoD's production of homosexuality in Chapter 1, the preconceptions of homosexual identity produced in the Vraciu case are deployed as mechanisms whereby Vraciu could be excluded from being authenticated as having such an identity. In the following section I will analyse what amounts to Vraciu's failure to be determined as being a 'credible homosexual' during his second IAT. The decision that Vraciu was not a homosexual was informed by three factors: (a) he did not mention homosexuality in the initial asylum application process, he only mentioned homosexuality during his first IAT; (b) his unwillingness to corroborate his claim of being a homosexual by naming or presenting his former lover in Romania or his current Romanian lover in the UK to the tribunal; and (c) Vraciu's determination as being an uncredible homosexual was also produced in terms of his (un)homosexual-like behaviour. This behaviour took the form of his alleged disloyalty and insensitivity towards his former lover who had been arrested in Romania, and his (un)homosexual choice of home decoration, especially in the form of wall posters that depicted female nude figures.

Untimely reticence

The timing of Vraciu's declaration that he was a homosexual is one of the primary reasons why his identity, as such, was regarded as 'not credible'. According to the special adjudicator's summation:

> I have considered the evidence before me and I have come to the conclusion that in this regard (homosexuality) the appellant is not credible. My reasons for so finding are that in the first place his claim is one that did not arise until the appellant's appeal was heard for the first time. No mention[4] was made of it in his asylum application, no mention was made of it in his interview and no mention was made of it in his statement accompanying his application.
>
> (special adjudicator, *Vraciu* 1995: 19)

The special adjudicator went on to dispute Vraciu's claims that he was too embarrassed to admit to his homosexuality during the procedures listed above:

> The appellant sought to convince me that he was embarrassed. I do not find this argument convincing. The appellant was interviewed by male interviewers and was interviewed a year after he arrived in this country during which time, if he were a practising homosexual, he had ample opportunity to acquaint himself with the attitude towards homosexuals of the authorities in this country.
>
> (special adjudicator, *Vraciu* 1995: 20)

Simon Russell (Vraciu's legal representative) challenged the special adjudicator's insensitivity to the appellant's explanations of embarrassment. Russell commented that in a country such as Romania, where homosexuality was criminalised, it would be entirely 'normal' for a homosexual to remain reticent about his sexuality even when outside Romania. Russell also pointed out that authorities in the UK were not especially tolerant towards homosexuals. Russell cited the difference in the age of consent between homosexuals and heterosexuals as well as the ban on homosexuals in the armed forces as evidence of Britain's 'legal intolerance' of homosexuals. Russell concluded that the adjudicator's belief that somehow the presence of men at Vraciu's interview should have rendered his self-declaration as a homosexual easier was incorrect; most probably it would have exacerbated Vraciu's embarrassment and fear (Russell, *Vraciu* 1995: 11). The special adjudicator thus read Vraciu's 'silence' as individual pathology rather than as a problem of institutional intimidation. Perhaps in contradiction to the special adjudicator's view of British attitudes towards homosexuality, Vraciu's silence was tempered by the realisation that he had sought asylum in a less tolerant country than he had first thought.

Disloyalty and insensitivity as non-homosexuality

The special adjudicator also decided that Vraciu could not be a homosexual because, according to the adjudicator's 'professional' experience, homosexuals were 'gentle and sensitive people', who seem to display an essential, recognisable characteristic, that is, loyalty to their partners. This is evident in the following statement:

> In the course of my professional life I have been consulted by and have advised a number of clients who were homosexual. I have always found them to be gentle and sensitive people (adjectives that I would not apply to the rather strident leaders of the various homosexual and militant groups). In my experience it is almost inconceivable that a young

man who has developed a lasting relationship with another young man and indeed who has had only the one homosexual relationship would after a relationship which has lasted two years or so, be prepared to leave his lover in the lurch knowing that person has been arrested by the authorities, would face trial and be imprisoned. Such action in its callousness, is almost inconceivable in such circumstances.

(special adjudicator, *Vraciu* 1995: 21)

Of particular importance in the special adjudicator's statement above is the discursive technique he is employing in order to produce Vraciu's non-homosexuality, or Vraciu's inconceivable homosexual identity. That is, the special adjudicator constructed the inconceivableness of Vraciu's homosexual identity simultaneously with the production of a 'genuine' variety of homosexuality that he claimed to know, and which was knowable through his experience. The special adjudicator thus instituted a dividing practice whereby authentic and inauthentic homosexuals could be differentiated, based on an appreciation of the levels of commitment and loyalty expressed between male same-sex couples. Vraciu, in the eyes of the special adjudicator, failed this test. However, the special adjudicator's presentation of Vraciu as an inconceivable homosexual portrayed an ignorance or selectivity with regards to the actual circumstances and context of Vraciu's behaviour in relation to his ex-lover who remains in prison in Romania. For example, any enquiries made by Vraciu to the police about his lover's arrest, according to Mr Russell, might have implicated the appellant and led to his own arrest.

Non-corroboration and attempting to pass as heterosexual

Vraciu's failure to have his claim of being a homosexual corroborated by supporting evidence also added to his failure to be determined as being a credible homosexual. Alexandra Pond (a lawyer representing the Home Office at Vraciu's second IAT) summarised the lack of evidence that might have supported Vraciu's claim of being a practising homosexual during the tribunal. She declared:

He has failed to give the identity of his boyfriend in Romania and believes that the boyfriend was arrested before he left Romania and has made no effort whatever to find out about him. This is the only sexual partner the appellant has had in Romania. He maintains he has continued his homosexual activities in this country and has had a steady partner since 1994. It was the first mention of such a relationship and this partner has not been called to give any supporting evidence. He does not belong to any homosexual group or club. There has been no authentication of his alleged status. If he fled from Romania because he was a homosexual, nobody in Romania, other than his one lover there, knew of his position. The *Daily Mail* article and photograph depicts his room in this country as being lined with pictures of nude women. With such evidence against him, why does he not produce evidence of his homosexuality and in particular the person with whom he has had a relationship since1994 and who is in this country?

(Pond, *Vraciu* 1995: 13)

Vraciu's homosexuality remained a matter of self-declaration throughout both his IATs. From Pond's statement above, we can see that Vraciu's claims that he was a homosexual were unsupported by any other corroborative evidence. In fact Vraciu's attempts to protect the identities of his lover in Romania and a current lover in Britain[5] actually harmed his attempt to have his alleged homosexual identity deemed credible before the IAT. Vraciu's tactics for his own survival and the safety of his lovers' identities, consisted in him living a careful and secretive life. This covert lifestyle also translated into his non-membership of homosexual clubs or groups.

Factors such as the covert nature of Vraciu's lifestyle, the limited number of his confidants, the care he took over not publicising his homosexual relationships and his own homosexual identity resulted in an unfavourable determination before the tribunal on the grounds of insufficient evidence. Pond mentioned two more aspects of the Vraciu case that troubled her – his blatant publicity attempts in the form of talking to journalists from the *Daily Mail* and *Gay Times*, and the confusing issue of why an alleged homosexual would hang pictures of nude women on the walls of his residence. In a similar fashion to the special adjudicator, Pond presented her idea of a 'genuine' homosexual to the tribunal in order to emphasise Vraciu's divergence from such an identity. Pond's interpretation of the existence of these posters on the walls of Vraciu's residence was that he was a man trying to pass himself off as homosexual in order to be granted refugee status. What Pond did not consider was that perhaps by putting these posters depicting female nudes up on his walls, Vraciu was displaying a habitual tactic, a tactic used by homosexuals in Romania for the purposes of displacing suspicions of their sexuality. Vraciu admitted to this during the tribunal – that he was indeed hoping to deflect attention or suspicion away from his homosexuality by placing such posters on his wall. This was confirmed by the special adjudicator: 'he put posters on the wall so that people would not know that he was homosexual' (special adjudicator, *Vraciu* 1995: 6). Pond's production of Vraciu's non-homosexual identity from his choice of female and not male naked figures depicted on his posters was another attempt during the tribunal to deploy a knowable homosexual, who was unlike the appellant. Vraciu's alleged homosexual identity was presented as inconceivable in the light of what homosexuals are thought to be and do.

Pond's statement, above, produced her criteria, as a Home Office lawyer, for the authentication of homosexuals in such cases. Pond's suggestions, in contrast to the special adjudicator's, were less focused on the subjective assessment of a homosexual orientation and identity. Pond's approach concentrated on the lack of corroborative evidence, especially potential and available supporting evidence in the form of the presentation of Vraciu's existing partner, with whom he had been having a relationship in Britain for a year prior to the tribunal. Pond's statement demonstrated the vulnerability of Vraciu's unsupported self-declaration of being a homosexual. This was achieved by exposing what is essential for applications for refugee status based on homosexuality, that is, the connection of a particular identity – who or what applicants say or think they are – to evidence or facts which prove or support such a claim.

As will be discussed below, Vraciu and his legal representative, Simon Russell, thought that a self-declaration of being a homosexual was evidence enough for the purposes of a refugee application – that the adjudicator would accept this declaration and proceed to the matter at hand; specifically, whether homosexuals in Romania constitute a particular social group with a well-founded fear of being persecuted as defined by the 1951 UN Convention. The by-product of Vraciu's experiences before the tribunal was that homosexuals were actually deemed to be a social group in the form of a separate and differentially treated 'legal class' in Romania and in the UK during Vraciu's second IAT. This will be explored in full in the next chapter. However, it was determined during this same appeal hearing that Vraciu himself was not a 'credible' homosexual, and therefore his appeal was dismissed.

The control of discourse

On reading Vraciu's IAT report one discovers that there are two types of knowledge which are in circulation during the tribunal, and both of these claim to know homosexuality and homosexuals. There is the self-knowledge of homosexual identity as advocated by Vraciu and Russell, and there is the legal technology for producing a homosexual identity. The key 'rule' to the game of truth that was played out between these two forms of knowledge is the recognition that there is an order of, or, more accurately, an economy of, knowledge in operation during the Vraciu case. The key distinction between the 'legal' and 'extra-legal' knowledge of homosexual identity in this case is premised on the fact that within legal practice, legal knowledge is the 'valued' and authorised form of knowledge. During Vraciu's second IAT, it was Pond who introduced this distinction and presented the legal technology of knowledge based on the attempt, for the purposes of law, to connect evidence (factual or corroborative) with a self-declaration of homosexual identity.

In this case study the disjunction between these two knowledges of homosexual identity is of central importance. Legal practice will be shown to be 'an idiosyncratic practice that seeks systematically to appropriate, privilege and secure a specific and limited set of meanings, accents and connotations by means of displacing and rejecting alternative and competing meanings' (Moran 1996a: 11). It will be further illustrated that this control of 'legal' meaning imposes limits upon those authorised to speak. This posed a particular problem for Vraciu and Russell as they based the former's legal claim for the particular benefit of refugee status on Vraciu's speech-act, his self-declaration of being a homosexual. However, Vraciu's speech-act of self-declaration was rejected by the tribunal as uncredible identity information because it was unconnected to appropriate evidence. Thus, we have the problem with Vraciu's application and performance during his second IAT. Vraciu's self-definition had no legal authority and, therefore, was vulnerable to systematic disqualification. What the Vraciu case opens up to academic scrutiny is the realisation that the person who alleges that he is a homosexual cannot be the author of his own identity before the law – he or she remains an object, whose legal identity must be made for him or her by an authorised knower and speaker of it.

The exclusion of Vraciu's self-knowledge from legal discourse is a demonstration of the institutional process, which maintains 'official discourses' and 'official users' of these discourses. These procedures determine the condition of the application of discourses and impose a certain number of rules on the individuals who hold them, thereby not permitting everyone to have access to them (Foucault 1981: 61). According to Foucault, this system ensures that 'none shall enter the order of discourse if he does not satisfy certain requirements or if he is not, from the outset, qualified to do so' (Foucault 1981: 61–2). This organisation of knowledge, this control of discourse (Foucault 1981: 61) is a mechanism of exclusivity whereby legal discourse, in order to perpetuate its status as an 'authorised discourse' (Goodrich 1990: 187), must control meaning. Smart describes this aspect of law in terms of the law's power, whereby law disqualifies other knowledges by refuting and disregarding them (Smart 1989: 162) in order to set 'itself outside the social order' (Smart 1989: 11).[6] Goodrich describes the mechanisms of this discursive control as legal interdiscourse, which is 'the interdiscursive appropriation of meaning which attempts to exclude from the ambit of legal authority the possibility of alternative meanings and other discourses' (Goodrich 1990: 183).

Interdiscourse is described as the means by which legal discourse and language maintain their dominance over, between and among other non-legal discourses, utterances and speaking subjects (Goodrich 1990: 188). This control of discourse is supported by the intradiscursive institutional procedures of legal practice, which Foucault gathers together 'under the name of ritual' (Foucault 1981: 62). Intradiscursive mechanisms of exclusivity, conceived as ritualistic devices by Foucault, act to 'define the qualification which must be possessed by individuals who speak ... [they define] the gestures, behaviour, circumstances, and the whole set of signs which must accompany discourse' (Foucault 1981: 62). Discourses, including legal discourse, 'can scarcely be dissociated from this deployment of a ritual which determines both the particular properties and the stipulated roles of the speaking subjects' (Foucault 1981: 62). Vraciu's IAT can be described as a legal ritual in that it was given the specific institutional name of immigration appeal tribunal. The tribunal as ritual also required the presence of specific institutional figures, such as a special adjudicator, representatives of the Home Office, an applicant-appellant, his legal representative and a translator, etc. However, what is of interest here is not the institutional rituals which support the exclusivity and authority of law, but the interdiscursivity of legal practice, the mechanisms which control who can speak and what can be spoken of: the mechanisms in legal practice 'which function to preserve or produce discourses, but in order to make them circulate in a closed space' (Foucault 1981: 62).

Interdiscursivity thus creates and maintains a disjunction between varieties of speaking subjects in legal practice, between authorised speaking subjects and unauthorised and disqualified speaking subjects. The disqualification of Vraciu's self-declaration of being a homosexual throws into relief the interdiscursivity and exclusivity of the legal meaning making process.

Law is hierarchical but not insulated, legal discourse may be a closed space but access is not denied to all other knowledges, disciplines and discourses. Law invites, indeed solicits other 'expert' authoritative, and therefore authorised, discourses into its discursive economy. What is produced here is a politics of truth predicated on penetrating the 'closed space' of interdiscursively appropriate authoritative discourse. The legal 'truth' of Vraciu's sexuality was not his property in the space of law. The legal 'truth' of Vraciu's homosexuality, if it was going to gain access to legal discourse, needed 'to be made' accessible to the closed space of legal discourse. Vraciu was therefore going to have to engage someone authorised to know and speak of his sexuality on his behalf.

Davies describes the disjunction between knowledges and speakers as a 'hierarchical *differend*' at work within legal practice (1996: 62). Davies uses Lyotard's concept of the *differend* as a useful conceptual tool for understanding the institutionalisation of language games within legal practice. According to Davies's reading of Lyotard, it is the institutionalisation of legal language games which results in an incommensurability arising between parties when they were not speaking, or were prevented from speaking, the same language (Davies 1996: 41).

The frustration caused to legal practice in the Vraciu case consisted of legal practice being prevented from creating the facts that it would proceed to interpret. Vraciu attempted to present his homosexuality based only on his self-knowledge, thereby obstructing law from first establishing the facts of his sexuality from the evidence available. Legally, Vraciu's self-knowledge and evidence expressed in the form of his self-confession remained unacquainted with legal discourse, as there was no presentable or interdiscursively appropriate evidence. Thus, a *differend* arose as the knowledge circulated by Vraciu was not signifiable or significant in the institutionalised interdiscusive legal setting. Lyotard describes a situation of *differend* in the following passage:

> In the *differend*, something 'asks' to be put into phrases, and suffers from the wrong of not being able to be put into phrases right away. This is when the human beings who thought they could use language as an instrument of communication learn through the feeling of pain which accompanies silence ... that they are summoned by language, not to augment to their profit the quantity of information communicable through existing idioms.
>
> (Lyotard 1988: 13)

One could say that Vraciu's words, his confessional speech-acts, were presented in the form of hearsay, or what Heidegger describes as *Gerede* or 'idle chat' (in Haldar 1996: 127). Hearsay is deemed in law as inadmissible information based on what was heard to be said, or even seen to be done by another, that is, statements made by another who is not available for cross-examination or who is absent from the proceedings. These statements cannot be tendered as evidence of any fact stated (Haldar 1996: 126). Hearsay, as we can see from this definition, is based on an absent subject. One can say that Mr Vraciu's self-knowledge and definitions of his own homosexuality are the 'idle chatter' or the unauthorised speech-acts of an absent subject, or, more accurately, a subject yet to be made for legal purposes. According to Haldar:

> The voice of hearsay is an unauthenticated, and therefore inauthentic, voice; as we have already noted this is what Heidegger would have called idle chat or *Gerede*. *Gerede* is empty, rootless and restless. It bewilders any attempt at critical inquiry and remains ignorant of its cognates ... hearsay resists belonging to a subject.
>
> (Haldar 1996: 131–2)

Although hearsay doctrine focuses on the physical absence of a subject from the legal setting, one could say that Vraciu's knowledge about his own homosexuality was conceived as inauthentic knowledge from a yet to be subjectified object, for the legal purposes of determining the evidence of his credibility. From these insights law can be described as 'knowing' only through reification and appropriation, where:

Concrete individuals are turned into legal subjects, unique and change-able characteristics are subsumed under (ideal) types and roles, singular and contingent events are metamorphosed into model 'facts' and scenes in impoverished narratives constructed according to the limited imagination of evidence and procedure.

(Douzinas and Warrington 1994: 230–1)

In legal practice the meaning of homosexuality was to be fixed and the homosexual who was to be successfully authenticated as such would become the 'reified produce ... of meanings conceived as things' (Goodrich 1990: 189). Vraciu and his legal representative, it seems, tried to by-pass a crucial step in legal practices when a claim is being made on the basis of a particular identity. The appellant or claimant cannot name himself, cannot determine his own identity; the 'truth' of his identity must to be made for him by law.

In the following section it will be discussed how it was suggested, and how it actually occurred, subsequent to his second IAT, that Vraciu's disputed homosexual identity was to be produced as 'fact' by medical and psychiatric technologies of examination and confession.

Penetrating Vraciu's homosexuality

The Wolfenden Committee defined homosexuality as a sexual propensity for persons of one's own sex (Wolfenden Report 1957: para 18, 11). This definition was accompanied in the Wolfenden Report by 'some criteria for its recognition' (para 19), that is:

As in other psychological fields, an inference that the propensity exists may be derived from either subjective or objective data, that is, either from what is felt or from what is done by the persons concerned.[7]

(Wolfenden 1957: para 19, 11)

The Wolfenden Committee's definition and criteria for the recognition of homosexuality consist of a carefully worded conflation of desire and attraction, conduct and practices, which are allegedly coexistent in the condition of 'homosexuality'. Homosexuality as a sexual identity is produced in the criteria for its recognition in the Wolfenden Report as a propensity (to act with, to act upon, to be attracted to) members of the same sex. Within this formulation of homosexual identity conceived as a propensity, a homosexual is a man or woman who could be identified through the examination of the characteristics (objective and subjective) related to his sexual tendency. The Wolfenden criteria for the recognition of a homosexual propensity, and thus a homosexual identity, are particularly located within the disciplines of psychology and psychiatry. Within these disciplines the 'truth' of a homosexual identity was to be produced through techniques that incited the audible speech-acts of homosexuals who must speak of their objective and subjective propensities. This incitement to tell was complemented by psychiatric and psychological techniques of listening, recording and diagnosing a homosexual identity from the information the 'patient-offender' was incited to provide. Thus, the Wolfenden Committee's criteria introduced an intercorporeal relationship whereby the homosexual was recognisable primarily through his telling, and, more importantly, through the act of listening to him. One can describe these techniques for the recognition of homosexuals as mechanisms for bringing underlying truths to light. Haldar refers to such techniques as 'practices of truth' (1991: 176). Haldar's conception of these legal practices of 'truth', is premised upon a Heideggerian notion of truth as opening or unconcealment, a conception of 'truth' which depends upon the visionary qualities of light (1991: 176) That is, practices of truth unconceal 'truth', they allow 'truths' to come forth and present themselves in their own light (1991: 176). Practices of truth are, therefore, specific techniques based on sensory cognition,[8] located in specific institutional settings such as court rooms, tribunals and medical clinics (as well as psychiatric consulting rooms or offices). All these institutional settings can be described as spaces where bodies and the sensual capacities of other bodies meet in an attempt to discover, or, more accurately, facilitate the revelation of 'truth'. In these institutional settings there is a communion, albeit asymmetrical, where a body is expected to be the receptacle of truths while other 'living individuals' (Foucault 1973: xv) use specific techniques (physical examination, confession or cross-examination) in order to assist the surfacing of 'truth'. According to Haldar, in law, the examination of evidence is a practice of truth, whereby 'facts' that would otherwise be concealed could be revealed, and these emergent 'facts' could be made to confess (1991: 176).

In the Vraciu case, the tribunal did not follow the Wolfenden Committee's recommendations for the authentication of homosexual identity by psychiatric investigation. Instead, it was suggested by Pond (representing the Home Office), that Vraciu's body should be subjected to another practice of truth – medical examination – in order to determine the truth of Vraciu's sexual identity. This episode was brought to the attention of a House of Commons Standing Committee on the Asylum and Immigration Bill by Mr Alton MP:

> In the past, the Home Office has ... insisted that homosexuals are not distinguished by any outward activity, but only by private acts. Mr Vraciu's application for asylum did not succeed. During a subsequent hearing, a Home Office lawyer, Alexandra Pond, cast doubt on his claims and apparently requested that doctors should test Mr Vraciu to determine his sexuality. Her arguments were accepted.
> (*Hansard*, Commons, Standing Committee D: 18 January 1996: col. 202)

In the quotation above, Mr Alton captures the reasoning found in the Vraciu tribunal panel: that the panel desired the facts of Vraciu's alleged homosexual identity to speak for themselves, to be made in authorised discourse. Vraciu's homosexuality could not be authenticated from his appearance or 'outward activity',[9] nor from his unauthorised self-knowledge of his own sexual identity. Homosexual identity, therefore, according to Pond, with the agreement of the tribunal, was to be read from the signs of private sexual acts left on Vraciu's body. This production of a homosexual identity from sexual acts contradicts the MoD's creation of a gap between homosexual identity and homosexual acts as discussed in Chapter 1,[10] and diverges from the suggested criteria for the recognition of a homosexual propensity suggested by the Wolfenden Committee.

It was the hallmarks of scar tissue and the evidence of the (mis)use of the body especially surrounding the anus and rectal tissue that became the focus of attention. The assumption was that it is the anus that is the corporeal site where medical practices of truth could bring to light the signs of an authentic or inauthentic homosexual identity. The reasoning behind this suggested practice of truth reduced homosexual identity and the diversity of homosexualities to one act, sodomy. Homosexual identity was reduced to the sign of the act of sodomy with the anus being presented as the reified and 'overdetermined cultural localisation of male homoerotic desire' (Fuss 1995: 84). The legal objective behind the suggested examination of the male anus and rectum was the production of the sexual identity of the man concerned. Thus, the object of the medical examinations of 'homosexual' bodies was not merely to identify an act itself but also to identify the signs or symptoms of an identity. According to Moran, homosexual identities are produced through the act (for example, sodomy) and installed behind the act in order to be named as its cause and essence (Moran 1996a: 106). The signs of sodomy were therefore to be read as 'a manifestation of homosexuality' (Bersani 1987: 197).

The suggested examination or 'testing' of Vraciu's 'anal privacy'[11] by doctors in order to authenticate his unsupported claim that he was a homosexual can be described as 'both a ritual of power and an acquisition of knowledge ... [which] ... permits both surveillance and a normative judgement' (Shiner 1982: 394). This medical practice was to compare diacritically 'the normal' anus with the 'abnormal' anus, the 'normal' anus being an organ that had not been subjected to the 'trauma' (or pleasure) of sodomitical genital intercourse with other men. The 'abnormal' anus was therefore an organ that would allegedly be identifiable by visual and corporeal traces of anal-genital trauma caused by sodomitical encounters between men. These characteristic 'symptoms of abnormality', readable by the medical gaze, were to be taken as the signs of the truth of homosexuality, just as the male medical eye, according to Irigaray, investigates 'the object' woman by penetrating her interior 'with speculative intent' in search of her truth (Irigaray 1985: 144). The anus, in the Vraciu case, joins the vagina, as Hyde describes it, as 'a searchable space' (1997: 172). Vraciu's anus became, with the official request for its examination, a 'searchable absence deriving its identity from relations with other people' (Hyde 1997: 172).

The construction of homosexuality in the Vraciu case and the construction of heterosexuality in, for example, rape trials, through the presentation of the vaginal or anal bodily cavity's relation to a man's penis or men's penises can both be described as being phallocentrically organised (Smart 1989: 28). Both the anus in the Vraciu case and the vagina in heterosexual rape trials are presented as the passive receptacles that must be examined in order to ascertain the occurrence of male-to-male penetration or male-to-female penetration of anuses and vaginas, respectively. That is, male homosexuality and female sexuality are presented in legal discourse and practices in terms of their passivity and receptivity to an active and penetrating 'heterosexualised' male anatomy and sexuality. As a result the proof of sexual relations between males, and between males and females, is examinable in the form of the residual fluids, pubic hairs and lacerations and tears left in and at the site of these corporeal cavities as a result of their penetration by a penis or penises. What is exposed by these medico-legal techniques is that sexualities and genital activities across genders and between genders are comprehensible to law through a very limited framework: 'through reference to hierarchical bi-polarities (notably those of active/passive, hetero/homo[sex] and man/woman)' (Collier 1998b: 31) wherein ' "active" sexuality has been historically linked to the hierarchical, phallic and heterosexist polarities of the masculine gender' (Collier 1998b: 31). Homosexual identity was to be derived from the signs and symptoms of relations with other men (who through their 'activeness' seem to be excluded from the category, homosexual). Thus we encounter a rather curious heterosexualization of certain 'homosexual' sexual practices between men.

According to Foucault, the symptom as sign does not offer anything to knowledge, but merely forms the basis for recognition (Foucault 1973: 90):

> The signifier (sign and symptom) would be entirely transparent for the signified, which would appear, without concealment or residue, in its most pristine reality, and that the essence of the signified ... would be entirely exhausted in the intelligible syntax of the signifier.
>
> (Foucault 1973: 91)

Thus a man suspected of being or claiming to be homosexual was to be examined not for 'homosexuality', which is a condition, status or identity, but for alleged signs or symptoms of a homosexual identity. These symptoms of homosexuality were to be diagnosed through medical examination. In such encounters the medical gaze (and, as will be discussed below, the psychiatric ear) are 'always receptive to the deviant' (Foucault 1973: 89); they are ways of looking and listening which are 'in some sense diacritical' (Foucault 1973: 23). This relationship between the truth and 'legal proof' (Weeks 1989: 101) of a homosexual identity inferred from the medical interpretation of the corporeal signs of the anal penetration of one man by another man has had a relatively long history.[12] The logic of this medico-legal or forensic focus on the anus was historically (and is presently in the 1990s) based on the belief that 'sodomy brought certain changes in the appearance of the rectum' (Karlen 1971: 186) which are observable by medically trained eyes. According to Karlen:

> The two most quoted writers on the subject just after the mid-nineteenth century were the leading medico-legal experts of Germany and France, the doctors: Casper and Tardieu. Both were chiefly concerned with whether the disgusting breed of pederasts could be physically identified for courts and whether they should be held legally responsible for their acts.
>
> (Karlen 1971: 185)[13]

According to Karlen, Tardieu, in his book *Crimes Against Morals from the Viewpoint of Forensic Medicine* (1857) portrays homosexuals as degraded monsters, not only morally but physically different from other men. According to Karlen's reading of Tardieu, the pederast: 'has a slender under-developed penis with a small glans, tapering from root to tip like a dog's'. Of particular note was Tardieu's theory in relation to the pathological characteristics of the homosexual anus, that is, according to Tardieu, even before sodomy took place, the homosexual's rectum was smooth and lacked radial folds (Karlen 1971: 186). Johann-Ludwig Casper took an innovative view of homosexuality, not only describing love and passion between homosexuals, but also pointing out that homosexuality and sodomy were not synonymous, and that many homosexuals never experience anal intercourse (in Karlen 1971: 186). Despite this, the medical examination of the anus for signs of homosexuality remains, as demonstrated by Pond's suggested method for authenticating Vraciu's homosexual identity, a 'reasoned' request in law.[14]

However, a physical examination of Vraciu's body for signs that he was, and had in the past (especially in Romania), been a practising homosexual was avoided. Simon Russell introduced the emphasis on homosexuality as not being sufficiently determinable by medical examination to the tribunal. In an attempt to challenge the consensus, led by Pond, that homosexuals can be authenticated through medical examination, Russell described homosexuality as being a 'psychological manifestation'. The special adjudicator recorded Russell's statement as follows:

With regard to the question of whether or not the appellant is a homosexual, Mr Russell submits that no medical evidence can be put forward
to prove this. According to Mr Russell 'this is a psychological manifestation and there is no known medical test for determining it ... [and
that] ... [we] must rely on the appellant's evidence and [we] should
believe him.

(special adjudicator, *Vraciu* 1995: 15)

Instead of the penetration and examination of his body for the truth or
falsity of homosexuality,[15] Vraciu chose to have the truth of his alleged
sexual identity brought to light by psychiatric probing and extraction. This
practice of truth switched attention from one of Vraciu's orifices to another –
from his anus to his mouth – as well as changing the organ of medico-legal
power/knowledge – from the doctor's eye to the psychiatrist's ear.

In a telephone conversation I had with Mr Russell (of the Refugee Legal
Centre, on 8 May 1997) concerning Vraciu's case, he re-emphasised what
was stated above in the adjudicator's report: that is, 'declaring one's homosexuality should be enough'. However, Vraciu's self-declaration proved to be
'not enough' to persuade the special adjudicator of Vraciu's homosexual
identity. According to a document produced by the Refugee Legal Centre,
after Vraciu's second appeal had been dismissed, Vraciu and his legal representatives conceded to the Wolfenden Committee's criteria for the
recognition of a homosexual propensity. Vraciu voluntarily underwent an
independent psychiatric evaluation to prove that he was a homosexual. The
report produced by this psychiatrist stated that in the psychiatrist's opinion
the appellant, Vraciu, was a homosexual. As a result leave was requested
from the immigration tribunal to introduce this scientific factual evidence
to corroborate Vraciu's previously discredited evidence of his homosexual
identity (Refugee Legal Centre, Document no. HX/70517/94, no. 6166, p.
6/11).[16] By utilising a psychiatrist's authoritative authentication of Vraciu's
sexual identity, Russell and Vraciu discovered the order of discourse, the
economy and a hierarchy of discursive value before the law when it comes to
the knowledge of sexual identity. Psychiatric discourse was used by Vraciu
and his representatives as a practice of truth which could both connect
Vraciu's unauthorised 'truth' and transform these fragments of biography
into both a psychiatric authentication of his sexuality as well as evidence of
it for tribunal purposes. What is interesting is that Vraciu's mode of giving
evidence, from his second IAT to his meeting with the psychiatrist, had not
significantly altered. Vraciu was still speaking and telling of his relationships and sexual activities, outlining what he felt and what he did with
other men, as recorded in the IAT reports.[17] However, importantly, to whom
Vraciu told these biographical details had changed, as had the setting of his
telling.

Instead of penetrating Vraciu's anal privacy for the traces of his sexual
biography, psychiatric techniques initiated a practice of truth which was

'dependent on the presence of another's mouth to do its work' (Bartowski 1988: 44). Vraciu's mouth, and the speech that was produced by it, became the source of the psychiatric encounter that would transform his confessional 'raw' chatter into a factual product for the purposes of law.

The exchange of discourse: a practice of truth

The psychiatric mechanism of confession can be conceptualised in terms of a technique whereby one variety of knowledge is connected to another. The psychiatric consultation is therefore the means of transforming the unautho-rised speech-acts of a subject excluded from speaking in the closed space of legal interdiscursiveness into the 'truth' of authorised discourse which could enter this space. Foucault refers to this process as 'the exchange of discourses' (Foucault 1978: 144). In this process, details relating to one's sexual biog-raphy in the form of feelings, attractions, practices, memories of things done and activities fantasised about, must be spoken to, and heard by, what Foucault (1978) describes as 'a master of truth'. The 'exchange of discourses' is demonstrated in the following passage where Foucault describes the two-part process of turning the 'idle chatter' of unauthorised discourse into scientific 'fact' (in the form of sexological discourse) in the nineteenth century:

> If one had to confess, this was not merely because the person to whom one confessed had the power to forgive, console, and direct, but because the work of producing the truth was obliged to pass through this rela-tionship if it was to be scientifically validated. The truth did not reside solely in the subject who, by confessing, would reveal it wholly formed. It was constituted in two stages: present but incomplete, blind to itself, in the one who spoke, it could only reach completion in the one who assimilated and recorded it. It was the latter's function to verify this obscure truth: the revelation of confession had to be coupled with the decipherment of what is said. The one who listened was not simply the forgiving master, the judge who condemned or acquitted; he was the master of truth. His was a hermeneutic function ... by no longer making sexuality a test, but rather a sign, and by making sexuality something to be interpreted, the nineteenth century gave itself the possibility of causing the procedures of confession to operate within the regular formation of a scientific discourse.
>
> (Foucault 1978: 66–7)

Thus, in Vraciu's encounter with the independent psychiatrist, the psychia-trist became the authorised hearer who was to exchange Vraciu's confessed secrets for a psychiatric interpretation of their significance, their 'truth'.

In a similar fashion the role of psychiatry in the production of the facts of a homosexual identity in the cases of self-confessed homosexuals in the armed forces was described by Moran (1996a). Moran's analysis was based on the Admiralty Examination Handbook, which was submitted to the Wolfenden Committee. This handbook described the procedural techniques whereby a military psychiatrist was to transform a self-confession of homosexuality into fact. For example, in the case of the 'self-confessed' homosexual, Admiralty orders recommend the employment of a psychiatrist 'as an officer in the fact-finding examination' from which a sexual biography was to be produced (Moran 1996a: 107). Moran draws our attention to the fact that the self-confessed homosexual is not recognised simply on the basis of his own declaration. The interpretative procedures of the psychiatric examination were the machinery whereby the authenticity of the homosexual identity of a self-confessed homosexual was produced. That is, 'admiralty orders draw attention to the fact that the authenticity of identity is not so much an effect of self-identification but an effect of the machinery of examination, produced through the scrutiny of specialists and subject to their endorsement' (Moran 1996a: 107).

Vraciu's psychiatric encounter was the setting for a three-part exchange of discourse. Vraciu put his fragments of sexual biography into words in response to the psychiatrist-specific examination for the purposes of producing analysable data. From within the unstructured biographical mess that would pass across Vraciu's lips, the psychiatrist would discern the facts of Vraciu's homosexuality, and these 'facts' could be presented to law in the form of an authorised psychiatric pronouncement of homosexuality or non-homosexuality.

In order for the independent psychiatrist to diagnose Vraciu's homosexuality, one can only assume, in the absence of the actual report, that the psychiatrist was armed with a prior knowledge of 'characteristic homosexuality' – that is, of a range of factors, for example, a typology of objective and subjective details, which could be considered to denote a homosexual propensity[18] – just as in a medical examination of the anus, where the signs and symptoms of homosexual acts might be connected to a homosexual identity through specific ways of looking and touching-feeling for the presence of corporeal abnormalities. A psychiatric consultation to determine sexuality is a specific way of listening to, and inciting, talk from which symptoms can be diagnosed through signs. Perhaps the psychiatrist listens for biographical abnormalities just as the doctor looks and feels for corporeal abnormalities within what Foucault describes as the plurisensorial, perceptual configuration of the medical gaze, which consists of touch and hearing in addition to sight (Foucault 1973: 164). In both these technologies of power – the medical examination and the psychiatric confession – the determination of homosexuality was to come from a dominant sexualised ontology at the centre of medico-legal practice: that is, from a heteronormative perspective. It was from this perspective that Vraciu was to be examined, and listened to, for signs or symptoms which would signify sexual 'abnormality'. Thus, at the centre of both these techniques of interpretation there is a dividing practice where the 'official knower' has the power to see and hear the patient's or appellant's 'abnormality' in contradistinction to the norm they embody, and hence proceed to examine from.

Legal closets

One could say that Vraciu may have found himself in a rather precarious position 'in between' two sets of legal systmes that could be described as demanding or initiating contradictory effects. The attempt to render homosexuality and homosexual activities invisible to the hostile Romanian authorities was to be substituted for the 'full' disclosure of the details and circumstances of his alleged homosexuality as demanded by British asylum and immigration officials. Part of the reason why Vraciu might not have made the smooth transition from contextual secrecy in Romania to openness during his asylum and refugee procedures in the UK, might have been the result of his precarious positioning in between these two legal systems. It was not impossible that Vraciu could have been sent back to Romania, where his admission during the tribunals of being a practising homosexual might have been more easily believed by those authorities. Another factor that should also be considered is that the Romanian and the British criminal legislation might be more closely connected in their approach to 'the problem of homosexuality' than one might think. Having fled Romania, a country noted for its hostility towards homosexuals, Vraciu found himself by his own design seeking asylum in a country such as Britain where hostility towards homosexuality is not absent, but merely insulated in liberal toleration. The treatment of homosexuality in the English Criminal Law can be said to be similar in intent to that of the Romanian penal code, in that the control, regulation and eradication of homosexuality can be said to motivate both legal regimes. The difference between the Romanian and the UK penal codes can be found in the degree of regulation and eradication. The Romanian penal code with Article 200[19] can be described as an attempt to completely eradicate homosexuality both publicly and privately from within Romania's borders. In the UK, the English Criminal Law in the form of the Sexual Offences Act of 1967 (as will be discussed in Chapters 3 and 4), concentrates on the eradication of homosexuality in its 'public' manifestation while simultaneously delimiting a circumstantial realm of legal 'privacy' for homosexuals to act in. Thus criminal law, in its Romanian and English forms, may be partly responsible for the reluctance and fear exhibited by Vraciu during the various stages of his asylum and refugee procedures. Silence, secrecy and privacy is what both these criminal legal systems demand of homosexuals. As a result it could be concluded that Vraciu's reluctance to provide information to the IAT was symptomatic of this relationship between law and the self-eradication of homosexuals.

However, Vraciu's reluctance, privacy and tactical circumspection were also symptomatic of a homosexual man who, as a member of a despised and persecuted social group, was trying to accommodate to the hostile social and legal environments he found himself in, in both Romania and in the UK.

The situation of refugee applicants who are reluctant to co-operate with the immigration procedures set out by their host country, as a result of a fear and mistrust of authority, was noted in the United Nations High Commissioner for Refugees (UNHCR) *Handbook* (1979). The latter contains guidelines that display a degree of sensitivity towards applicants' fears of authorities in their own country and in their host country:

> a person who, because of his experiences, was in fear of the authorities in his own country may still feel apprehensive vis-à-vis any authority. He may therefore be afraid to speak freely and give a full and accurate account of his case.
>
> (UNHCR 1979: para 198)

However, this sensitivity must be balanced around the greater ambitions of the immigration and asylum procedures, which are to establish the facts of the application. According to the UNHCR handbook: 'it is a general legal principle that the burden of proof lies on the person submitting a claim' (1979: para 196):

> The relevant facts of the individual case will have to be furnished in the first place by the applicant himself. It will then be up to the person charged with determining his status (the examiner) to assess the validity of any evidence and the credibility of the applicant's statements.
>
> (UNHCR 1979: para 195)

When it came to presenting evidence which could support his claim that he was a homosexual, Vraciu could be described as finding himself within 'an excruciating system of double binds' (Sedgwick 1991: 70). The act of offering information in the form of supplying the names of past and present lovers could be seen as both Vraciu's means of escaping imprisonment in Romania by gaining refugee status in Britain and as his potential self-incrimination if returned to Romania. By providing the evidence required to potentially satisfy the IAT, Vraciu would also be providing a means of his self-incrimination – not only his own but also that of his lover (because there was no guarantee that his application for asylum would be successful, and his lover's [in Britain] identity might also have been made public, which would cause difficulty if they wanted to return to Romania). Perhaps the precariousness of his situation prevented Vraciu from connecting his subjective evidence in the form of his self-knowledge with the corroborative evidence demanded by law. In fact, the best possible evidence that Vraciu could have presented to the tribunal would have been his own arrest by Romanian police because of his 'homosexual activities'. Mr Russell, during

Vraciu's second tribunal, actually produced a Romanian police warrant for the arrest of a Romanian homosexual in order to support Vraciu's claim of having a 'well-founded fear of being persecuted' in that country as a result of his homosexuality. The problem with this demonstration was that merely providing an example of Romanian legal hostility towards homosexuals did not connect Vraciu's subjective claim of being a homosexual to these occurrences.

Apart from Vraciu's precarious position in between the demands and prohibitions of two legal institutions, there was the problem of translating his intimate and private sexual feelings and practices into the facts required by 'law'. Vraciu did 'furnish' the IAT with what he considered to be the facts of his application: (a) that he was a practising homosexual in Romania and had continued to be so in Britain since his arrival; (b) that he feared arrest by the Romanian authorities because of his homosexuality and that his former lover's arrest in Romania supported the well-foundedness of his fear of returning to that country. The problem with these 'facts' was that none of them were grounded in or supported by other presentable facts that could be interpreted by law. Even if Vraciu could have proved by documentation that a man who he claimed to be his ex-lover in Romania had been arrested and imprisoned for reasons related to homosexuality, Vraciu's alleged relationship with this man would also need to be convincingly proved. According to Vraciu, the nature of the Romanian authorities' hostility towards homosexuality resulted in this 'relationship' with his former lover in Romania being known only to themselves. Therefore the only person who was actually potentially capable of furnishing Vraciu's IAT with documented, corroborative supporting evidence of his homosexuality and his well-founded fear of returning to Romania was this former lover, who remained, at the time of Vraciu's second tribunal, in prison. However, Vraciu refused to name his former lover who was allegedly arrested and imprisoned in Romania, even when pressed to do so by the special adjudicator. As a result, there was no means of connecting Vraciu's impenetrable 'privacy' to evidence which would have supported his claim that he was a practising homosexual, that is, to evidence that could be produced by legal interpretation as the fact of a homosexual identity.

There is also the possibility that what appeared to be obstruction and unwillingness to co-operate on the part of Vraciu during the IAT may have been misunderstood. Perhaps Vraciu's personal understanding of the gravity of his self-naming rendered all the other details demanded by the adjudicator less important. Vraciu's understanding of his speech-act: 'I am homosexual' was tempered with his knowledge that he was gambling with the possibility that the outcome could result, if he was returned to Romania, in five years of brutality and possibly rape within a Romanian prison (according to an Amnesty International report).[20] Vraciu's admission of his homosexuality was, in light of the latter, a monumental speech-act. Indeed, it was an 'utterance that initiated a set of consequences' (Butler

1997: 17), and, if he was to be returned to Romania, the consequences would indeed be dire. Silence and reluctance to present what could be kept private and secret (his lovers' identities) could not, in the IAT setting, be read as a measure of the applicant's fear of persecution. However, this same persecution was to be assessed in this legal institutional setting from the facts presented.

The process for ascertaining and evaluating the facts of an applicant's refugee status claim leaves little or no space for an applicant's privacy, reticence, information control or unwillingness to participate in the legal examination of their personal details.[21] These procedures do not entertain or facilitate the translation of subjective biographical details such as fear, feeling threatened or the experience of a sense that one's life was in danger into the objective facts demanded for the purposes of law (Douzinas and Warrington 1994: 222). There is indeed a brutal degree of scrutiny and intrusion, especially into asylum-seekers' circumstances where sexuality is the basis of the claim (and especially where no corroborative evidence is possible or available, and this process has been perpetuated by this academic scrutiny of the case). Vraciu's case is a testament to an IAT's unwillingness to leave any stone unturned. However, within all this legal scrutiny there is an identifiable defiance on the part of Vraciu, even though his case can be described as not going very well (if two IAT dismissals are a measure of his success). Despite these failures Vraciu would not compromise, he would not give the IAT what they wanted, which was to know everything. The only power Vraciu had during these legal proceedings before the IAT was his speech-acts of self-declaration and of silence and his attempt to control and select the information/evidence that was to be offered for consideration. Vraciu's reticence can be described as an activity of 'making' certain details 'public' and 'making' other details 'private' (Fornas 1995: 91).

Vraciu took serious risks and, it could be said, gambled with his own 'liberty' when he chose to actively inhibit the disclosure of his two (long-term) lovers' identities in the presentation of his evidence. The disclosure of these men's identities, it seems, was avoided at all costs, even when his Romanian lover who was resident in Britain could have given evidence before the IAT *in camera*. This degree of loyalty is almost 'inconceivable' (to turn the special adjudicator's description back on itself) if one considers that the presentation of this lover in Britain to the tribunal might have been deemed as credible evidence of Vraciu's homosexual identity. The risk Vraciu took in order not to identify his lovers was indeed considerable if one considers that this defiance of not 'assisting the examiner in full' (UNHCR 1979: para 205) was one of the contributing factors which led to the dismissal of his application.

There is another explanation for this reticence and reluctance, of course, that is, that Vraciu had in fact fabricated his claim based on homosexuality, and had lied about the existence of his former lover in Romania and his present lover in Britain. Apart from his validation by an independent psychiatrist, Vraciu did not present any other factual evidence or corroborative evidence which proved his homosexuality during these procedures.

The Vraciu case shows us that before the law, homosexual self-definition is valueless, unless it is connected to supporting evidence. Homosexuality, in the final instance, is rendered credible in legal practice by connecting the appellant's evidence to exterior, corroborative evidence or factual evidence. That is, by connecting an applicant's claims to supporting evidence such as membership of 'homosexual' organisations or from the statements of people who might have had some sort of sexual contact or relationship with an applicant. Or, as in this case, by a psychiatric-legal designation of identity, by the exchange of an unauthorised discourse for an authorised, authoritative discourse which could penetrate and be heard in the closed space of legal interdiscursivity.

Throughout his asylum and refugee application process Vraciu seemed to try to maintain a meticulous control over his personal details. Even his psychiatric assessment and eventual authentication as homosexual were protected by the ethical confidentiality of the psychiatrist–patient relationship, resembling 'the clos(et)ed space of the confessional' (Bartkowski 1988: 45) – that is, 'clos(et)ed' relative to the publicity of a IAT hearing and the special adjudicator's report of it. We could conclude that Vraciu's primary motivation during his asylum and refugee process was 'keeping private', keeping the law out of his personal life, at all costs, even the cost of having his application for refugee status dismissed.

One could say that Vraciu exhibited a similar accommodational sexual identity as that found in the homosexuals in the armed forces who were passing as assumed heterosexuals in the analysis in Chapter 1. However, in the armed forces, homosexuals who conducted themselves with discretion had this behaviour supported and complemented by passing policies (and proposed policies). In the Vraciu case, homosexual tactics of privatisation and information control were not supported or encouraged by any policy initiatives or procedures. In fact, the opposite was the case. Homosexuals who attempted to remain private and who controlled information about their sexual orientations were seen as engaging in inappropriate behaviour, as full disclosure of all details of a homosexual's life, love, lovers and sexual activities was required. One can say that, for opposite reasons, the varieties of passing policies (and proposed passing policies) described in Chapter 1, and the legal problems encountered in the Vraciu case, are both concerned with the problematics of connecting evidence of a homosexual 'propensity' to a homosexual identity. The US 'don't ask, don't tell' policy and the British MoD's 'No Open Homosexuality Policy' can be described as attempting to educate servicemen and servicewomen to exclude behaviours and activities from their social and corporeal repertoire that could be construed as connoting a homosexual identity. The aim of these policies was the non-exclusion of service personnel who behaved with circumspection. Yet, in Vraciu's tribunal, the opposite was the case. Vraciu had been at pains to dissociate himself from the behaviours or associational activities which could identify him socially (and for the purposes of law) as a homosexual. Vraciu, like a responsible homosexual serviceman or servicewoman in the armed forces, comported himself with circumspection. In refugee law and military passing policies, covert homosexuals are treated differentially: one is supported and included in policy the other is disqualified and excluded.

Conclusion

Vraciu's refusal to allow his claim of being a practising homosexual to be supported by other evidence as well as his belief (which was shared by his lawyer) that his self-declaration of homosexuality should be enough, revealed a great deal about 'legal knowledge' in relation to homosexuality. Legal knowledge of homosexuality is not actually knowledge about homosexuality itself, but about the evidence to which a claim of being a homosexual by an applicant can be connected. The knowledge that is crucial for the purpose of law as regards homosexuality originates outside the homosexual. Thus homosexual identity is to be produced by diagnostic techniques which act upon it in medical-legal encounters. Homosexuals before the law do not own their own identities.

What emerges in this legal scenario is a particular politics of truth consisting in a difference between 'just' knowing, an almost a 'commonsensical' knowing, as in Vraciu's self-knowledge of his own sexual orientation, and the legal activity of actually determining or making homosexual identity from the 'facts' available. During Vraciu's IAT there was a discernible epistemological tension between these two methods of determining, in this case, an authentic homosexual identity. The 'knowability' of homosexuality is central to this case study; however, the determination of homosexuality from the facts available was problematic in this legal setting. It was almost as if a gap or a gash was cut into the hegemonic seamlessness of the social intelligibility of sexualities. Vraciu's case demonstrates that the epistemological certainty of how homosexuality and homosexual identity, and hence heterosexuality and heterosexual identity, is knowable in legal practice is unstable and uncertain. For example, legally, Vraciu, a self-declared homosexual, was categorised as an uncredible homosexual by the tribunal and was therefore produced legally as a heterosexual. In trying to know the facts of Vraciu's homosexuality, 'the law' disturbed the certainty of the knowability of sexualities, or, more accurately, how sexualities can be proven to exist in law. According to Vraciu, he was 'just' homosexual, that was all the evidence he was prepared to provide. The only actual means by which Vraciu's homosexuality was authenticated was by a private consultation with an independent psychiatrist, who interpreted and validated what Vraciu had been saying all along, that he was homosexual. So it seems homosexuals are knowable, homosexuality is recognisable in, and to, law, but the means of knowing this homosexuality, in Vraciu's case, could only occur in the 'clos(et)ed' setting of a psychiatrist's office. The result is that how law knows homosexuality, and what law knows about the determination of homosexuality, is, it seems from this case, inaccessible knowledge. What is opened up in this 'not very open and shut case' is a breach in amongst the opinions, certainties and common senses that proclaim to 'know' homosexuality. In between the multiple layers of epistemologies of 'knowable' homosexuality found in Vraciu's case, for example: the corporeal evidence of 'it'; the common-sensical or social knowledge of 'it'; the discursive deployment of 'it'; Vraciu's self-knowledge of 'it'; and the psychiatric interpretation of 'it'. Perhaps the only certainty is that, in this case, homosexuality is unknowable yet knowable.

Vraciu's homosexuality opens a fissure in the social and legal fabric of sexuality. This discontinuity signifies subversive 'queer' potentials; however, it also signifies powerlessness and misrecognition. In between the dialectic of needing to be recognisable (gay minoritarianism) and wanting to dismantle and subvert recognisability and the discrete categories of sexualities (queer theory and politics), some homosexuals stand 'before the law' attempting to be recognised by the law, for the purposes (and benefits) of law. Their lives and liberty may depend on 'the facts' of their homosexuality being admissible to, and recognisable in law. Cases such as Vraciu's have important resonances for a queer studies and politics of law. The Vraciu case demonstrates the importance, if not necessity, of the understanding of the technologies of law, the mechanisms whereby law functions and produces knowledge. Further, this case demonstrates how power effects are reciprocal to these legal machineries and technologies of knowledge. The Vraciu case also highlights the need for both legal academics and legal practitioners to engage intimately with legal practices, in order to fully understand how law operates within its local institutions. By so doing, lawyers, academics and activists could mobilise to efficiently and tactically counter potential power-effects that impact on the lives of men who have intimate relations with other men.[22] It is of little use assuming that 'stating one's sexuality should be enough' without really discovering what these institutions demand.

This case not only exposes certain practices of the law, but also the vulnerability of 'the homosexual' who wishes to be recognised for what he 'is, or thinks he is' before the law in order to seek legal protection. In Chapter 3, I continue my analysis of the plight of homosexual refugees in the UK and analyse the Vraciu case alongside other contemporary homosexual refugee cases throughout the 1990s. My particular focus in Chapter 3 will be on the technologies established in this particular procedure of determining refugee status. My emphasis will be on how the conceptualisation of 'the refugee' within these technologies has worked to exclude non-traditional minority groups such as homosexuals from being determined as being members of a particular social group with a well-founded fear of being persecuted. In Chapter 3, therefore, the focus is more on the procedures involved in determining whether homosexuals can be classified as a social group in terms of the 1951 UN Convention definition.

3 Persecution and immutable identities

Homosexual refugees

Much of the impetus for the development of international human rights law as it exists today emerged in reaction to the atrocities committed during the Second World War. Like Jews, Gypsies, and the disabled, lesbians and gay men were targeted for extermination by the Nazis. As many as one hundred thousand men were identified as homosexuals and transported to concentration camps. Wearing the pink triangle ... these men were amongst the millions shot, hanged, gassed, worked or starved to death in the camps. ... Despite this clear indication of their vulnerability to human rights abuses, gay men and lesbians were not specifically included in the framework for international human rights protection when the United Nations drew up the Universal Declaration of Human Rights after the war's end.

(Amnesty International 1997: 7, 8)

Introduction

In the previous chapter I concentrated on the legal practices within the IAT setting, especially issues surrounding the admissibility of evidence, the control of discourse, and who, in legal proceedings, has the authority to define a homosexual identity. In this chapter, I analyse the recent case law of applications for refugee status based on a homosexual identity[1] made in the UK, including the detailed analysis of the case of Mr S,[2] an Iranian homosexual refugee applicant. My analysis will focus on both Mr S's IAT reports during 1995 and 1996 as well as additional material collated in preparation for the Court of Appeal.[3] Unlike Vraciu in Chapter 2, Mr S's homosexual identity was accepted as being credible during his first IAT hearing because his self-declaration of being a practising homosexual was accompanied by corroborative evidence. Mr S's determination as a 'credible homosexual' resulted in arguments before the IAT focusing in greater detail (compared to the Vraciu case) on the question of whether homosexuals could be included in the 1951 UN Convention on Refugees' definition of members of a particular social group.[4] The other IATs that I will refer to prior to my analysis of Mr S's case are Mr Vraciu's tribunal report and the case of another Iranian, Mr Golchin.[5] (I will also briefly discuss the case of a Cypriot homosexual, Mr Binbasi.)

British case law in this area is characterised by two divergent decisions, which are found in the Golchin (1991) and Vraciu (1995) cases. In the Golchin case homosexuals were conceptualised as being unlike particular social groups within the Convention definition, such as tribal or religious minorities. However, in the Vraciu case, homosexuals were defined as being members of a particular social group both in Romania and in the UK as a result of their membership of a distinctively treated group of people in both countries. In the S case, the Golchin and Vraciu decisions come into direct conflict, and as a result this case was referred to a higher court (the Court of Appeal).

In this chapter I shall demonstrate that what is known, thought and said about refugee status applicants and their alleged persecution and social group membership in the IAT reports analysed here is organised around a particular discursive identity, that of 'the genuine refugee'. Before turning to the specific focus of this analysis – homosexuality – it is essential to contextualise this exposition within the framework of restrictionism and deterrence found in the UK's immigration policy throughout the 1990s. Particular legislation, for example the Immigration Appeals Act 1993 and the Asylum and Immigration Act 1996 have been described in the following terms:

> the reality of current UK asylum policy is that humanitarian protection is not deemed to be as great a priority as tight border controls and the deterrence of asylum seekers.
>
> (Stevens 1998: 32)

Subsequent legislation, such as the Immigration and Asylum Act 1999, has added to the litigious culture of 'fast-track' efficiency and discouragement, that is, 'fairer, faster and firmer' immigration and asylum procedures (Immigration and Nationality Directorate 2000: 1). This legislation has increasingly brought the binary opposition of genuine/bogus to the forefront of immigration and asylum procedures (as well as media coverage). 'The homosexual' is an exemplary member of a persecuted social group caught up in this particular binary opposition within the 'culture of disbelief' (Harvey 1998: 215) prevalent in UK immigration and asylum procedures.

This case study is thus an analysis of how 'social knowledges' about homosexuals and refugees, as well as prosecution and persecution, in relation to the 1951 Convention 'social group' definition, are organised in particular ways. However, this is only half the story as this analysis is also concerned with examining how it is that dominant discourses and practices within immigration and asylum procedures can be disrupted and troubled by alternative discourses and counter-practices.

In this institutional setting, genuine refugees are conceived as being members of traditional minority groups. Within this regime of truth there are two main problematic discourses which exclude homosexuals in the UK cases (especially the Golchin case) from the social group category: a discourse of biological procreation and a discourse of the distinctiveness of the social group's social and cultural difference. The result of this conceptualisation was that homosexual refugee applicants in the UK, up to 1998 when refugee status was granted to a Romanian man, Sorin Mihai, endured non-protection under the UN Convention on Refugees (1951) despite evidence of human rights abuses in their countries of origin. In 1999, however, in the case of *R v. IAT ex parte Shah*,[6] it was decided that homosexuals from some countries, depending on the state of the evidence, could qualify as members of a particular social group.

In this chapter I describe how it has come to pass that the institutional practices for determining refugee status in terms of social group membership has undergone a critical re-examination by academics and practitioners of International Refugee Law in recent years. This re-examination is characterised by a shift in emphasis from what an applicant 'is' to a perspective that also assesses the evidence in relation to the treatment of certain groups by the states in question. Thus, a state's official treatment, including the legal treatment, of certain groups, from this perspective, is compared with the legal and human rights standards in the host country and those of the supra-national legal bodies of which the host country is a signatory (for example, the European Convention on Human Rights). In this perspective shifting human rights standards play a leading role. In fact, universal human rights become the medium through which two legal regimes, refugee law and human rights law, have become connected and have yielded 'progressive results' (Harvey 1998: 216). These 'progressive results' are synonymous with non-traditional refugee applicants (such as homosexuals) resisting their exclusion from being defined as members of a Convention social group. In this chapter, such resistance is described in terms of the establishment of a nexus between who the claimant is or what he believes, and the risk of serious harm she/he faces (which is inconsistent with established human rights standards) in his or her country of origin.

The 1951 Convention definition of social group

The category in question, membership of a particular social group, is a contentious area in refugee law. It is unclear who the intended beneficiaries of this provision are. It is also unclear whether the provision was merely a means of making the other four categories (race, religion, nationality, political opinion) illustrative examples of social groups, or was intended to include additional discrete bases of persecution (Gagliardi 1988: 269). According to Tuitt, the membership-of-a-particular-social-group criterion was introduced as a means of including non-traditional refugees and non-traditional forms or circumstances of persecution alongside the other four traditional definitions (1996: 38). This sentiment is shared by Helton: 'the "social group" category was meant to be a catch-all which could include all bases for, and types of, persecution which an imaginative despot might conjure up' (Helton 1983: 45). Hathaway, however, dismisses such humanitarian perspectives of the membership-of-a-social-group criterion being an all-encompassing residual category. According to Hathaway, 'their purpose was anything but the creation of a regime to address new, future injustices ... the Convention was designed simply as a means of identifying and protecting refugees from known forms of harm' (1991: 159). The importance of the particular social group definition, disputed as it is, is that this provision is the only available site of entry for non-traditional refugee applicants who do not fall under the other criteria in Article 1 A (2) of the Convention (1951).

Homosexual refugee cases (UK)

The contention surrounding who or what the 1951 UN Convention's 'particular social group' provision should include actually works to exclude homosexual refugee applicants. Among the recent British cases, the decision which best demonstrates the interpretation of the 'particular social group' provision to the disadvantage of non-traditional groups such as homosexuals, is found in the Golchin case. This case exemplifies what Tuitt describes as one of the main functions of refugee law: the construction of an official or formal identity of 'the refugee' which is also the formal or official means of deciding who is and is not a genuine refugee (Tuitt 1996: 14).

In the Golchin case there are two main discursive mechanisms which work to exclude homosexuals from refugee status as members of a particular social group. These are the discourses of biological procreation and of the visibility of 'social and cultural difference'. In the Golchin case, these mechanisms operate within a particular discursive regime, wherein 'social groups' are required to have characteristics of a historical and cultural nature. Thus applications for social group status were compared against the model of a traditional minority group and the stereotype of the 'genuine refugee'. This comparison was disadvantageous to homosexuals, as this statement from the Golchin tribunal demonstrates: 'we think that there is a close approximation of social group to minority group as the term is used in the convention. Both terms, we think, require characteristics of an historical and cultural nature which homosexuals as a class cannot claim' (*Golchin* 1991: 7).

Substituting the concept of minority group for that of social group, in the Golchin tribunal, is an example of a discursive technique which excludes so-called 'non-traditional' social groups, such as homosexuals, from being intelligible and therefore protected under this definition. In the Golchin case, the 'historical element' consistent with the equating of social group with minority group was the capability and capacity for 'affiliating succeeding generations' (*Golchin* 1991: 8). This, according to the tribunal, is a characteristic absent in homosexuals 'as a class'.

By foregrounding minority group as opposed to social group, the tribunal managed to produce an exclusionary regime of truth (Foucault 1980a: 132), wherein 'non-traditional' social groups were subjected to systematic exclusion. The Golchin tribunal even went so far as to produce homosexuals as members of a social group, or, in their terminology, a 'class', but only as a further mechanism for demonstrating the dissimilarity of the homosexual class from a 'genuine' minority group. This was achieved by the tribunal constructing the individual homosexual's member-ship of a 'homosexual class' as being of a purely voluntary nature, and maintaining that such associations usually remain socially inconspicuous. Thus, homosexuals were produced by the tribunal as belonging to a social class whose members exhibited a degree of choice as to whether they asso-ciated with each other. Moreover, according to the tribunal, homosexuals also had a choice as to whether they publicised their 'difference' or not. 'Genuine refugees' and traditional minority groups did not enjoy these characteristics and choices, according to the members of the Golchin tribunal.

A similar regime of truth, that also approached the determination of refugee status through the prism of 'true minorities' and 'genuine refugees', was present in another IAT, in 1989, of a homosexual Turkish Cypriot, Zia Mehmet Binbasi. During this tribunal hearing it was decided that in order for Mr Binbasi to avoid prosecution to the point of persecu-tion for engaging in homosexual activities, he should be advised to 'refrain' from engaging in such activities upon his return to Cyprus (Tuitt 1996: 37):

> it is clear that in Cyprus there is no discrimination against homosexuals who are not active ... so for there to be a well founded fear of being persecuted, the social group would have to be restricted to active homo-sexuals.
>
> (*Binbasi* 1989: 559, in Tuitt 1996: 37)

Homosexual self-control and social invisibility were deployed in the Binbasi tribunal as a mechanism for excluding homosexuals from persecuted social group status. In the Golchin and Binbasi tribunals homosexual iden-tity and membership of a homosexual class were produced as being avoidable or self-inflicted. This was contrasted by the tribunal with the 'genuine' and unavoidable persecution experienced by those social groups which the particular social group definition was allegedly written into the Convention of 1951 in order to protect. By circulating the discourses of avoidable and unavoidable persecution in the Golchin and Binbasi cases, the tribunals also initiated mechanisms for assessing the members of 'social groups' that deserved and did not deserve the protection of refugee law. As a result, homosexuals could be produced as a social group, simultaneously with the production of homosexuals as a group being undeserving recipients of the determination (and protection) of the Convention social group status, as homosexuals could be described as being the authors of their own persecution. In the Golchin case it was stated that if the appellant had the 'choice' of being included in or excluded from a persecuted 'class', he should exercise it to exclude himself. The adjudicator concluded that an appellant could not 'claim asylum if he exercised his choice otherwise' (*Golchin* 1991: 9).

Thus, in the Golchin and Binbasi cases, the question of social group status became a matter of comparing the characteristics and activities of homosexuals and a homosexual class with what the tribunal produced as the characteristics of 'true' minority groups. This comparison worked to exclude consideration of the behaviour of the state in question towards homosexuals in general.

In the Golchin case, the appellant claimed that if he were sent back to Iran he would be identified as a homosexual and that this could result in his execution. The special adjudicator's judgment on the matter of homosexual visibility in relation to Mr Golchin's fears, was as follows:

> I find that proposition an unacceptable one. I am not saying that homosexuals cannot make themselves known, but I do not accept that they must of necessity do so in all cases merely by virtue of being homosexual. There is no evidence that the appellant is one who of necessity may be so identified.
>
> (special adjudicator, *Golchin* 1991: 9)

The special adjudicator was referring in this passage to Mr Golchin's 'physical demeanour', more specifically to Golchin's demeanour as being, in his opinion, unlike or socially unrecognisable as that of a homosexual. Goffman describes demeanour as being conveyed through 'deportment, dress, and bearing' (Goffman 1967: 77). Thus, demeanour is conveyed through and on the surface of 'the body, its presentation and its movement'. It is also through the sensory bodies (of others) that this 'quality' can be assessed and appreciated. Thus, Golchin's gender, the way he acted his body, the way he presented himself socially is, in the adjudicator's opinion, unlikely to designate or make known a homosexual orientation. Gender here, its recognition and what it signifies, is reminiscent of Judith Butler's description of gender as a 'vocabulary of action' (Butler 1989: 256). As already touched on in Chapter 1, according to Butler, 'gender is a corporeal style, a way of acting the body, a way of wearing one's own flesh as a cultural sign' (1989: 256) – a sign, a signifier of an underlying biological sex and a discernible sexuality (heterosexuality or homosexuality). In the Golchin case, the special adjudicator's description, from his own sensory scrutiny of Mr Golchin's inconspicuous 'homosexual difference', of his 'unhomosexual' physical demeanour, was a means of further producing Golchin's homosexuality as being particularly suitable for him to exercise his choice of remaining invisible. As a result, the special adjudicator further distanced Golchin's claims and fears from those of the 'genuine' social group member implied in the discourse. The production of 'invisible' homosexuality perpetuates the continued social eradication of the expression, public visibility and even the practice of homosexuality in the countries concerned. Of course, this social invisibility is further exaggerated in lesbian women. For example, an Amnesty International report published in 1996 concerning the treatment of homosexuals and lesbians in Romania stated:

> the absence of any signs of lesbian life in Romania are conspicuous. Romania is the only country in Europe (and one of a select few in the world) with legislation against consensual lesbian sex. Publicly self-identified lesbians are virtually non-existent ... the invisibility of lesbians combined with the low status of women makes the possibility of creating a social space comparable to the gay men's cruising area [for lesbians] unthinkable.
>
> (Amnesty International 1996: 4)

The differential social control of women, and differential access to public spaces are allied problems that compound lesbian invisibility, along with the lack of freedom of movement (and thus flight) available to women in general. This explains, in part, the absence of lesbian asylum claimants in the UK (and hence the absence of analysis of 'lesbian' refugee cases in this chapter).

The special adjudicator's statement in relation to Mr Golchin's gender or demeanour demonstrates a sensory (intercorporeal) relationship between the tribunal panel and Golchin. The suggestion here was that the gendered body could be employed as an instrument for the purpose of avoiding persecution. However, simultaneously, the gendered body became the mechanism whereby the tribunal demonstrated further justification of why homosexuals did not deserve to be included in the social group definition. On this basis the homosexuals in the Golchin and Binbasi cases were presented as men in societies, who, unlike members of perceivably different minority groups – for example, tribes, families, religious groups, linguistic communities – were different and strange, yet also similar and part of the group. Golchin's and Binbasi's homosexual difference, and the ability they allegedly exhibited of passing as heterosexuals, resulted in them being produced as both strangers in the Simmelian sense, and as non-strangers.

Just as strangeness is otherness 'anticipated and tolerated only at a distance' (Bauman 1988: 9), homosexuals are simultaneously produced in the Golchin and Binsbasi cases as being strange and having the ability to deflect attention away from their strangeness. As a result homosexuals were produced in the tribunal as being unlike perceivably and unavoidably 'different' minority groups ('real' strangers). According to Simmel, it is the 'synthesis of nearness and distance which constitutes the formal position of the stranger' (1950: 404); the stranger, 'like the poor and like sundry "inner enemies", is an element of the group itself' (1950: 402). The homosexual's strangeness is a queer type of strangeness. According to Simmel, 'in the case of the person who is a stranger to the country, the city, the race, etc. ... this uncommon element is once more nothing individual, but merely the strangeness of origin, which is or could be common to many strangers' (1950: 407). Thus, in Simmel's formulation, the stranger originates from a background, a tribe, a religious community or even a foreign country, and this is the uncommon element which characterises his difference relative to the dominant group. According to Simmel, strangers are both 'inorganically appended' to a group, that is, they display characteristics which are other than the norm of the dominant group, and yet the stranger is, or becomes, 'an organic member of the group' (1950: 408). Homosexuals can be described as organic strangers, who do originate from the 'inner circle', the 'native group', the 'in-group' (Bauman 1988: 9, 19). The uncommon element homosexuals display is not a matter of where they originate from, but what they deviate from, that is, heterosexuality. The homosexual's strangeness, therefore, originates from his or her non-heterosexuality or deviation from the norm of heterosexuality (whether permanently or inter-mittently) in heteronormatively organised societies. In such societies heterosexuality is the 'normal', 'natural' and expected sexual activity that is fused with the cultural and religious traditions of marriage, familial procre-ation, gender role expectations, national identity and the national future. In the Golchin and Binbasi cases, homosexuals were produced as both other and same: they were capable of hiding their otherness and their sameness could be assumed. This production perpetuates the continued social eradica-tion of the expression, public visibility and even the practice of homosexuality in the countries concerned.[7] As well as this, the production of homosexuals in the Golchin and Binbasi cases also resulted in the exclusion of homosexuals from the benefit of refugee status based on the social group definition organised through discourses of true minorities and genuine refugees. Thus homosexuals in the Binbasi and Golchin cases endured a double exclusion from protection, nationally and internationally: in the national criminal law (in the countries in question) and in international refugee law in the UK.

Thus, in the Golchin case, the officially constructed refugee identity that emerges is one that focuses on expected characteristics of ethnic minority groups. This conceptualisation neglects the interaction of state authorities with certain groups, groups with a socially (and legally) ascribed status such as homosexuals. There was, simultaneous with this non-problematisation of matters related to Golchin's and Binbasi's alleged legal persecution as homo-sexuals, an acceptance of the legal (and penal) systems and their legal treatment of homosexual activities in the countries in question. These regimes include, relative to the UK, harsher sentences, as well as corporal and capital punishments in relation to homosexuality and homosexual acts.

Academics such as Goodwin-Gill, Grahl-Madsen and Hathaway have attempted to initiate a reconceptualisation, a de-reification of the 1951 Convention social group category as it has habitually been conceived in determination procedures around the world. The work done by these academics has paid particular attention to the exclusive conceptualisations of 'social groups' in terms of traditional minority groups in refugee determination procedures. These authors have been engaged in the project of shifting attention away from the applicant's social or minority group characteristics in these determination procedures and instead focusing on the state in question's interaction with this alleged social group. For example, Goodwin-Gill advocated the inclusion of the reaction of other groups to the putative social group as being just as strong an indicator of social group status as minoritarian characteristics:

> In determining whether a particular group of people constitutes a 'social group' within the meaning of the Convention, attention should therefore be given to the presence of uniting factors such as ethnic, cultural, and linguistic origin; education; family background; economic activity; shared values, outlook, and aspirations. Also relevant are the attitude to the putative social group of other groups in the same society and, in particular, the treatment accorded to it by the state authorities. The importance, and therefore the identity, of a social group may well be in direct proportion to the notice taken of it by others, particularly the authorities and the state.
>
> (Goodwin-Gill 1983: 30)

In the passage above, Goodwin-Gill was attempting to expand the Convention social group category as it has been narrowly interpreted and produced in refugee determining procedures in order to address the exclusionary nature of this conceptualisation in terms of minority groups only. Thus Goodwin-Gill attempted to unsettle and open up the interpretation and production of the Convention social group category to include both traditional minority groups and other non-traditional groups who nevertheless endure considerable state oppression and discrimination. Goodwin-Gill's ambition was to increase the range of factors that could and should be taken into account when a host country assesses an application for refugee status based on the Convention social group category. Goodwin-Gill's attempted reformulation of the social group definitions was an endeavour to move away from the uncritical and abstracted determination of what characteristics are constitutive of membership of a particular social group. Simultaneous with this, Goodwin-Gill suggested that the criteria for assessing what constituted a well-founded fear of persecution should be modified to include evidence of a state's practices and treatment of the members of certain groups.

Grahl-Madsen also attempted to initiate a reconceptualisation of the Convention social group determination process away from the narrowness and exclusivity of the minority group substitution. Grahl-Madsen tried to achieve this by suggesting that Convention social group determination procedures should include in their assessment the 'behaviour of the persecutors': 'it is the behaviour of the persecutors that determines what persons shall be considered refugees in a legal sense' (Grahl-Madsen 1966: 175).

Grahl-Madsen attempted to further tether the Convention social group category to state treatment of social groups or classes by qualifying the meaning of the term 'persecution' for refugee determination purposes. According to Grahl-Madsen's formulation, persecution might as a rule only be attached to acts or circumstances for which the state or the government (or, in appropriate cases, the ruling party) were responsible. Thus episodes of persecution for Convention purposes should be characterised as acts committed by the state (or the government) or organs at its disposal, or behaviour tolerated by the state that left the victims virtually unprotected by the agencies of the state (Grahl-Madsen 1966: 189). Following on from this, Hathaway put forward a definition of persecution for the purposes of refugee determination as being evident when there was a demonstrative breach in a state's basic obligation: the protection of its nationals (1991: 104). Hathaway elaborates on this in the following passage:

> The intention of the drafters [of the 1951 Convention] ... was not to protect persons against any and all forms of even serious harm, but was rather to restrict refugee recognition to situations in which there was a risk of a type of injury that would be inconsistent with the basic duty of protection owed by the state to its own population. As a holistic reading of the refugee definition demonstrates, the drafters were not concerned to respond to certain forms of harm *per se*, but were rather motivated to intervene only where the maltreatment anticipated was demonstrative of a breakdown of national protection.
>
> (Hathaway 1991: 104)

According to Hathaway, and of particular significance to homosexual social group applicants, legal prosecution can be determined as being persecution because both the content and implementation of the criminal law are within the control of the state. The reason for this, according to Hathaway, is that it is possible for a state or government with persecutory intent to use the criminal law as a means of oppressing social groups (1991: 170). State persecutory intent may take the form of the existence of discriminatory and oppressive criminal laws and the corresponding severity of the recommended punishments for 'homosexual offences'. Hathaway devised a test for persecutory intent in terms of criminal prosecution. According to Hathaway, if the nature of the criminal offence and its prosecution and punishment are 'politically neutral in substance and application, then it cannot serve as the basis for a claim to refugee status' (Hathaway 1991: 170).

Grahl-Madsen offered a rule of thumb relevant to members of social groups who face a well-founded fear of imprisonment or execution for committing homosexual acts. In deciding whether a person belongs to a particular social group with a well-founded fear of being persecuted, 'it is generally agreed that a threat to life or freedom on one of the grounds in the Convention will always be persecution' (Grahl-Masden 1966: 193). Grahl-Madsen puts 'the return' of the applicant to his country of origin, as well as the behaviour or the persecutory intent of the authorities in that country, at the forefront of his suggested method for the determination of refugee status. The United Nations High Commissioner for Refugee's (UNHCR) guidelines (1979) for the determination of refugee status include a component for the assessment of whether legal prosecution and punishment in the country in question can be determined as persecutory in intent. According to the guidelines, the status of the prosecution and punishment an applicant is likely to face is measurable. The persecutory intent of legal prosecution and punishment, and thus the breakdown in a state's obligation to protect its nationals is, according to the guidelines, to be established by comparing the country of origin's laws against those of the host or asylum country in that area. Not only this, international legal instruments such as the European Convention on Human Rights should also be employed as a yardstick for assessing persecutory intent:

> Due to the obvious difficulty involved in evaluating the laws of another country, national authorities may frequently have to take decisions by using their own national legislation as a yardstick. Moreover, recourse may usefully be had to the principles set out in the various international Covenants on Human Rights.
>
> (UNHCR 1979: para 60)

In this formulation, the treatment of homosexuals in Cyprus and Iran, respectively, in the Binbasi and Golchin cases discussed above, would have been found to be inconsistent with legal standards in the UK and with European Convention human rights standards. Both the English criminal law and the mechanisms of the European Convention (the European Court and Commission) have provided privacy for homosexual consenting adults with the implementation of the Sexual Offences Act of 1967 and in the *Dudgeon* v. *United Kingdom* (1981) decision before the European Court. In Cyprus and Iran this legal protection or space of legal indifference is absent. If laws relating to homosexuality in the UK and within the case law of the European Convention on Human Rights were compared with homosexual legislation in Cyprus, Iran and Romania the latter states would be found to deviate from established standards of practice, thus displaying a measurable persecutory intent towards members of the particular social group or class of homosexuals.

In the Golchin and Binbasi cases there was no problematisation of the laws of the countries in question. The applicants were advised to conduct themselves in a fashion so as to accommodate to the legal hostility directed towards homosexuals and thus to avoid prosecution to the point of persecution in Iran and Cyprus.

During the Vraciu tribunal, however, the legal situation for homosexuals in Romania was actually raised by the special adjudicator. However, the legal situation was mainly 'trivialised', despite reports by such groups as Amnesty International (1996, 1997) who documented the excessiveness of the Romanian state's official treatment of homosexuals. The special adjudicator in the Vraciu case described his view of the situation in Romania for homosexuals in the following statement:

> The position would seem to be not dissimilar to that which prevailed in this country prior to the Wolfenden Report where at that time homosexual acts were illegal even between consenting adults but prosecutions were few and far between. It does seem to me that at present ... [in Romania] unless two consenting adults flaunt their homosexual activities in such a manner as to cause a public scandal, little, if any, action is taken with regard to homosexual acts between adults committed in private.
>
> (special adjudicator, *Vraciu* 1995: 24)

It was decided that because Vraciu's homosexuality was 'entirely clandestine' (special adjudicator, *Vraciu* 1995: 24) in Romania, he could be returned to that country. The logic of this decision was that if Vraciu continued to conduct himself with discretion on his return to Romania, there would 'be no reasonable likelihood of persecution' (special adjudicator, *Vraciu* 1995: 25). As in the Golchin and Binbasi decisions, the remedy for the claims made by a homosexual concerning his fears of being persecuted in the Vraciu case was that the applicant should comport himself with discretion.

However, the special adjudicator in the Vraciu case proceeded to determine whether the Romanian authority's prosecution of homosexuals amounted to persecution. In the adjudicator's opinion this was not the case because if Vraciu had been arrested in Romania he would have received a 'fair trial and if found guilty under the present law, be liable to imprisonment of between 1 and 5 years' (*Vraciu* 1995: 25). In this assessment we see another similarity between the Vraciu and Golchin cases, that is, the 'acceptance' of the legal treatment of homosexuals within the appellants' countries of origin. Homosexuals were presented in these tribunals as criminals, deserving criminalisation and imprisonment for activities that in the UK have been decriminalised since 1967. However, the special adjudicator in the Vraciu case proceeded to inadvertently produce homosexuals in Romania as belonging to a 'legal class', in order to show that Vraciu's claim was uncredible as a result of his presentation of insufficient evidence of his membership of this homosexual 'legal class'. I refer to the special adjudicator's production of homosexuals as being members of a particular persecuted social group in Romania as 'inadvertent' because it was his intention to disqualify Vraciu's claim on the basis of the 'general' rather than 'personal' prosecution of homosexuals:

> On the basis of the documents put before me by Mr Russell [Vraciu's legal representative] it would appear that prosecutions that have taken place, mainly prior to 1994, have been of a fairly general nature against homosexuals as a whole and not selecting any particular individuals or group of individuals.
>
> (special adjudicator, *Vraciu* 1995: 25)

The generalised prosecution/persecution of all homosexuals in Romania was exactly the grounds on which Vraciu was making his application for refugee status, especially in relation to the general non-differentiated excessiveness of the prosecution and punishment of homosexuals relative to the UK's legal standards and European Convention human rights standards. It was because of this generalised and excessive treatment of homosexuals that Vraciu had a 'well founded fear of being persecuted' on being returned to Romania. The outcome of this tribunal hearing was that Mr Vraciu was determined as being an uncredible or inauthentic homosexual as a result of a lack of evidence to support his self-declaration that he was a homosexual. However, during this tribunal homosexuals were recognised as being members of a particular social group who suffer distinctive prosecutions and punishments in both Romania and the UK. This is demonstrated in the following passage from Vraciu's tribunal:

> It would seem to us to be unarguable that in the society in the United Kingdom ... homosexuals are treated differently according to the criminal law, there is a great discussion as to the advisability of homosexuals in the armed forces. There is no doubt that there is both an external and internal recognition of those who are sexually oriented in such a way as to form a 'group' so identified by that characteristic. It seems to us ... that it cannot be argued that in Romania homosexuality is not recognised as a characteristic putting the person into a special category.
>
> (special adjudicator, *Vraciu* 1995: 14)

Even though Vraciu's application was unsuccessful, this determination that homosexuals were members of a distinctively recognised and defined social group in Romania (and in the UK) initiated a case law tradition in 'homosexual' refugee determination procedures which was inconsistent with the approach found in Golchin (and Binbasi).

In the next section, the case of an Iranian homosexual man, Mr S, will be the focus of analysis. The importance of the S case to this exposition, especially Mr S's 1996 IAT, is that this case is the site where both the Golchin and the Vraciu decisions on the inclusion or exclusion of homosexual refugee applicants from the Convention social group category were present and in contention.

Background material

Mr S was born on 31 March 1968 in Iran. He came to Britain on 21 February 1993 after being given leave to enter for six months as a visitor. In June 1993 S applied for asylum in Britain. Initially S based his appeal on his support of the Mojahedin (an Iranian political organisation) in Iran. S stated that he had been a supporter of the Mojahedin from his time at high school and had been involved with the distribution of leaflets and attended meetings. As a result of his involvement with the Mojahedin, S claimed that during September 1988 he had been arrested and detained for seven weeks; he was beaten and kept in solitary confinement for three weeks of this sentence. Following his release S claimed to have reduced his Mojahedin activities until 1992 when he was involved in a dispute between himself and a lecturer at his university over the introduction of a compulsory subject based on the last will and testament of Khomeini into the curriculum. This dispute, according to S, resulted in him being supported by other students and caused a riot at the university. On his arrival in the UK, the Home Office interviewed S on 9 February 1994; his application for asylum was refused in June 1994. On 6 March 1995, S made his homosexual orientation known to the British authorities. S's first tribunal was heard on 6 October 1995, his second on 20 March 1996. In both these hearings S's homosexual status and persecution as such in Iran were the basis of his appeals. On 16 April 1996 he was given leave to appeal, again with his homosexual status as the basis of his appeal.

S's experience before his tribunals (1995, 1996) can be contrasted with Vraciu's experience because, unlike that of Vraciu, S's homosexual status was determined as being credible during his tribunals. S's authentication as being a homosexual was the result of S and his legal representatives playing the legal game of truth with an understanding of the processes whereby law produces knowledge from the facts it uncovers from the evidence provided. Instead of basing his application on a self-declaration of being homosexual, as in the Vraciu case, S and his legal representatives provided the tribunal with corroborative evidence of the applicant's homosexual identity. The inclusion of these examples of corroborative evidence in S's case resulted in him avoiding Vraciu's fate of having his 'unsupported' self-declarations of homosexuality being determined as being uncredible. S's supporting evidence was presented to the tribunal in four forms: that of, (a) a witness, (b) membership of a 'homosexual' organisation, (c) letters and correspondence, and (d) an injunction obtained by S addressed to his former male partner.

Although S's supporting evidence was subsequently attacked during the

1995 IAT by Mr Horner, a lawyer for the Home Office, the special adjudicator's decision on the appellant's sexuality was as follows:

> Any decision must necessarily be based on the facts of the particular case, but from the appellant's own evidence, the evidence of his friend Mr Vakil and the injunction proceedings in which he engaged in Brentford County Court, I consider that there is, but only to the lower standard required in this case, a reasonable likelihood that he is a practising homosexual.
> (*Secretary of State for the Home Department* v. *'S'* (75394) (1995, unreported)

Discord: the Golchin and Vraciu decisions

S's 1996 tribunal was heard by Mr Brown (Justice of the Peace), Mr Cadogan (Justice of the Peace) and the Chairman Mr Whitaker, the latter being the legally qualified member of the tribunal (Russell 1998: 136). During the tribunal both Brown and Cadogan cited Golchin, and the discursive mechanism of substituting minority group for social group, in the Golchin tradition, as the means of determining the 'truth' of an application based on the Convention social group category. Mr Cadogan's opinion was based on an unfavourable comparison between 'homosexuals' and other 'real' social groups such as the members of 'a caste or a clan group' (Cadogan, in *Secretary of State for the Home Department* v. *'S'* (75394) (1995). Brown's opinion was very similar to that of Cadogan above, and also firmly in the Golchin tradition:

> for my part, I believe that homosexuals are not a social group, unlike caste or clan groups, homosexuality being purely voluntary. In my opinion, it is not possible to endorse such people as a social group. I feel my opinion is reinforced in the light of the decisions in *Golchin*, which I agree with.
> (Brown in *Secretary of State for the Home Department* v. *'S'* (75394) (1995)

The outcome of this tribunal was that the Chairman, Mr Whitaker, dismissed the appeal, the result being that the case would be heard in a higher court (the Court of Appeal). The reason for this was that the Chairman differed from both Brown and Cadogan regarding the possibility of Mr S being

> prosecuted to the point of persecution for his homosexuality were he to return to Iran; and whether homosexuals could be included in the definition of a social group within the 1951 Convention.
> (Whitaker, *Secretary of State for the Home Department* v. *'S'* (75394) (1995)

Whitaker's dismissal of the appeal was based on the decision in *Vraciu*

(1995), cited above, in which homosexual social group membership was established as a result of homosexuals being treated as a distinctive 'social group' in both the UK and Romanian criminal law. Whitaker's foregrounding of the prevailing legal situation in Iran was in contradistinction to his colleagues' explicit disengagement from the considerations of the law of other countries. Neither Brown nor Cadogan regarded prosecution for homosexual activities to be persecution; prosecution was regarded as dependent purely on the law of Iran. Brown stated the following regarding the Iranian state's official treatment of homosexuals:

> I am not in a position to criticise a government's criminal laws or the penalties imposed for their breach but it is rather difficult to extend prosecutions for criminal acts into a Convention reason for asylum.
> (Brown, *Secretary of State for the Home Department* v. *'S'* (75394) (1995)

In Brown's statement we find an acceptance of the Iranian legal and penal system as regards homosexual activities. The practice of homosexual activities, which in the UK are legal in certain circumstances (age, consent, number of participants, privacy), since the passing into law of the Sexual Offences Act of 1967, became in Brown's statement non-controversially 'criminal acts'.

It is important to note that Whitaker's decision was influenced by paragraph 60 of the UNHCR guidelines (1979) for determining refugee status by suggesting that legal standards established in the UK and in the European Convention in relation to 'homosexual activities' should be compared with those of Iran. As a result of this, Whitaker furnished the means whereby S's well-founded fear of being persecuted if returned to Iran could be connected to the persecutory intent of the Iranian criminalisation and punishment of homosexuals. This was achieved by Whitaker's demonstration that the Iranian state's treatment of homosexuals constituted an objective and comparable breakdown of its obligation to protect its nationals. According to Whitaker:

> I consider that there is no doubt that the enforcement against him of any of the Iranian penalties available for homosexuality [including public flogging and execution] would fall well within the realm of persecution. By British standards these penalties are unnecessarily repressive and extreme and, were one to apply the standard set by the European Convention of Human Rights, totally disproportionate to the legitimate aim pursued, i.e. of defining the boundaries of, and seeking to control within socially acceptable limits, homosexual behaviour
> (Whitaker, *Secretary of State for the Home Department* v. *'S'* (75394) (1995)

Whitaker thus advocated a method or a perspective for determining social group status that was in line with a shift away from determinations based on the comparison of a social group's characteristics with those of a preconceived traditional minority group. Whitaker's attempt to introduce a shift in the UK's refugee determination procedures regarding homosexuals concurred with the published opinions of authors working in the area of international refugee law such as Goodwin-Gill, Grahl-Madsen and Hathaway. Whitaker's attempted reconceptualisation was also consistent with discernible shifts in international refugee law and practice in the USA and decisions over refugees in Commonwealth nations such as New Zealand and Canada (which will be discussed below).

Developments in international refugee and human rights law

Whitaker's reconceptualisation had already been implemented in the proce-dures for the determination of refugee status under Article 1 A (2) of the Convention Relating to Refugees (1951) in countries such as the USA, Canada and New Zealand. This was a shift from determining refugee appli-cants from their socially 'knowable' characteristics to a perspective which was sensitive to the treatment of certain groups by other groups, usually a 'minority' by the 'majority' within the country of origin. This shift also challenged the opinion demonstrated in the Golchin case, that homosexuals were responsible for their own otherness, that they were 'unremarkable' strangers (Simmel 1950) who were in control of their own persecution. This view was contrary to human rights standards established in *Dudgeon* v. *United Kingdom* before the European Court of Human Rights. In the Dudgeon case the 'direct effect' of laws which outlawed homosexual acts between males was recognised on the lives of that 'particular class of person' (*Dudgeon* v. *United Kingdom*). In Dudgeon (and subsequently in the *Norris* v. *Ireland* and *Modinos* v. *Cyprus* cases) the legality and right to non-interference by a government in circumstantial (in private, with one other adult, over the age of consent) homosexual activities was upheld. Thus governments that criminalised all varieties of homosexual acts between men can be described as not meeting the standards of the European Convention on Human Rights and Fundamental Freedoms. Human rights case law has established homo-sexuals as individuals who should, in specific circumstances, be protected from state interference in their discreet and private lives.

The origin of this intersection of international refugee law with human rights law for the determination of a particular persecuted social group status emerged in a judgment made by the United States Board of Immigration Appeals in *A Matter of Acosta* (1985). In this case, Mr Acosta, a taxi-driver from El Salvador, was unsuccessful in his application to be considered a member of a persecuted social group. Acosta's claim was based on the persecution he had suffered at the hands of anti-government guer-rillas in El Salvador as a result of his membership of a taxi cooperative. Acosta and his colleagues had resisted the anti-government guerrillas'

request for them to join in a work stoppage that had resulted in assaults and
even loss of lives (Gagliardi 1988: 273). Acosta's application was refused
because this taxi co-operative was not deemed a 'particular social group',
even though the fear Mr Acosta had experienced was thought to be 'well-
founded'. The *Acosta* decision made by the US Board of Immigration
Appeals as to what should constitute a social group for Convention (1951)
purposes was as follows:

> We find the well-established doctrine of *ejusdem generis*, meaning liter-
> ally, 'of the same kind', to be most helpful in construing the phrase
> 'membership of in a particular social group'. That doctrine holds that
> general words used in an enumeration with specific words should be
> construed in a manner consistent with the specific words. ... The other
> grounds of persecution ... listed in association with 'membership in a
> particular social group' are persecution on account of 'race', 'religion',
> 'nationality', and 'political opinion'. Each of these grounds describes
> persecution aimed at an immutable characteristic: a characteristic that is
> either beyond the power of an individual to change or is so fundamental
> to individual identity or conscience that it ought not to be required to
> be changed. ... Thus, the other four grounds of persecution enumerated
> ... restrict refugee status to individuals who are either unable by their
> own actions, or as a matter of conscience should not be required, to
> avoid persecution. Applying the doctrine of *ejusdem generis*, we interpret
> the phrase 'persecution on account of membership of a particular social
> group' to mean persecution that is directed toward an individual who is
> a member of a group of persons all of whom share common, immutable
> characteristics. The shared characteristics might be an innate one such as
> sex, colour, or kinship ties, or in some circumstances it might be a
> shared past experience such as a former military leadership or land
> ownership. The particular kind of group characteristic that will qualify
> under this construction remains to be determined case-by-case.
> However, whatever the common characteristic that defines the group, it
> must be one that the members of the group either cannot change, or
> should not be required to change because it is fundamental to their
> individual identities or conscience. Only when this is the case does the
> mere fact of group membership become something comparable to the
> other four grounds of persecution.
>
> (*Matter of Acosta*, cited in Hathaway 1991: 160)

Hathaway summarised the parameters of social group membership
introduced by the *Acosta* decision as follows: (1) groups defined by an
innate, unalterable characteristic; (2) groups defined by their past temporary or voluntary status, since their history or experience is not within
their current power to change; (3) existing groups defined by volition, so
long as the purpose of the association is so fundamental to their human

dignity that they ought not to be required to abandon it (1991: 161). According to Hathaway, 'excluded, therefore, are groups defined by a characteristic which is changeable or from which dissociation is possible, so long as neither option requires renunciation of basic human rights' (1991: 161).

Being a member of a taxi cooperative, according to the *Acosta* judgment, was membership of a social group Acosta could abandon without requiring a renunciation of his basic human rights. However, the abandonment of homosexual practices and the association with other homosexuals as suggested in the Golchin and Binbasi cases, could, in the Acosta formulation, be conceived as amounting to a renunciation of the basic human rights afforded to Dudgeon before the European Court.

In the case of *Canada (Attorney General)* v. *Ward* (1993), the provisions made in the *Acosta* decision in the USA were evident in the determination of 'particular persecuted social group' status. In the Ward case, Judge La Forrest presented a comprehensive definition in the form of three possible categories for determining 'particular persecuted social group' status. These were: (1) groups defined by an innate or unchangeable characteristic; (2) groups whose members voluntarily associate for reasons so fundamental to their human dignity that they should not be forced to forsake the association; (3) groups associated by a former voluntary status, unalterable due to historical permanence. According to La Forrest J.'s categorisations above:

> The first category would embrace individuals fearing persecution on such bases as gender, linguistic background and sexual orientation, while the second would encompass, for example, human rights activists. The third branch is included more because of historical intentions, although it is also relevant to the anti-discrimination influences, in that one's past is an immutable part of the person
>
> (La Forrest J., *Canada (Attorney General)* v. *Ward* 1993)

The Ward decision made by the Canadian Supreme Court was important both for its comprehensiveness and its limitations on what or who could be included in 'particular persecuted social group' status. According to this decision, it was interpreted that the drafters of the Convention (1951) intended the 'particular social group' category as a cover for any possible lacuna left by the other four categories within the Convention definition. However, the Ward decision clarified the intention of the drafters as not just including 'any association bound by some common thread' (*Canada (Attorney General)* v. *Ward* 1993: 732), as in the Acosta decision where being a member of a taxi cooperative was deemed not 'immutable' enough. The Ward definition of social group status was to limit the interpretation and determination of this category to anti-discrimination notions inherent in civil and political rights (*Canada (Attorney General)* v. *Ward* 1993: 734, 739), thus consolidating the Acosta decision and the subsequent intersection of refugee law and human rights law.

Both the United States Board of Immigration Appeals decision in *A Matter of Acosta* and the Attorney General's decision in *Canada (Attorney General)* v. *Ward* were utilised in the S case 'skeleton argument' prepared for the Court of Appeal in 1996. However, the case that was the most supportive or encouraging to the S case and the preparations for its presentation to the Court of Appeal was that of an Iranian homosexual's application for refugee status in the case of New Zealand *Re: GJ* (1995). In this case the immutability criteria instituted in the Acosta and Ward judgments were utilised before the New Zealand Refugee Status Appeals Authority and resulted in the applicant being granted refugee status based on his homosexual identity. The success of this case, following Acosta and Ward, was the result of establishing a connection or a nexus between refugee determination procedures and prevailing human rights standards.

> The Acosta *ejusdem generis* interpretation of 'particular social group' firmly weds the social group category to the principle of the avoidance of civil and political discrimination. In this way, the potential breadth of the social group category is purposefully restricted to claimants who can establish a nexus between who they are or what they believe and the risk of serious harm ... for the nexus criterion to be satisfied, there must be an internal defining characteristic shared by members of the particular social group. In the Acosta formulation, this occurs when the members of the group share a characteristic that is beyond their power to change, or when the characteristic is so fundamental to their identity or conscience that it ought not to be required to be changed.
>
> (*Re: GJ* 1995: 57)

Hathaway reminds us that, more than any other gauge, international conventions such as the International Bill of Rights and the European Convention on Human Rights, are essential to an understanding of 'the minimum duty owed by a state to its nationals' (1991: 106). The international community has recognised that there are 'certain basic rights ... which all states are bound to respect as a minimum condition of legitimacy' (Hathaway 1991: 106). According to the New Zealand judgment in *Re: GJ* (1995):

> Sexual orientation presents little difficulty ... sexual orientation is a characteristic which is either innate or unchangeable or so fundamental to identity or to human dignity that the individual should not be forced to forsake or change the characteristic. Sexual orientation can, therefore, in an appropriate fact situation, be accepted as a

basis for finding a social group for the purposes of the Refugee Convention.

(*Re: GJ* 1995: 57)

The nexus criteria found in the New Zealand case connected an authenticated homosexual identity to both human rights standards and Iranian human rights abuses. This was aligned to the Acosta decision, which counteracted the practices within refugee procedures evident in Golchin and Binbasi, cases where the appellants were required to avoid persecution by their own actions. The immutability criteria in the New Zealand case ruled that appellants should not be forced to forsake or change themselves to avoid persecution.

On the basis of the Acosta, Ward and New Zealand (*Re: GJ*) cases, Mr S's lawyers submitted their 'skeleton argument' before the Court of Appeal in the UK. However, this extremely strong case never reached the Court of Appeal. Mr S was granted full refugee status prior to his appearance in court. This decision was based on his membership of an Iranian political organisation called the Mojahedin and not on his homosexuality.

Malcolm Bryant (Mr S's lawyer) describes this decision in a letter to the author as a strategy whereby the Home Office avoided making an authoritative judgement on the issue of the inclusion of homosexuals within the Convention definition: 'my personal opinion is that this was a decision taken at the highest level of the Home Office to avoid an authoritative judgement on this issue' (Bryant, 15 January 1997).

In a subsequent letter sent to the author, Bryant described the tactic of including political activities or religious persecution with an application based on homosexuality as becoming a matter of routine. He describes this tactic as a means of giving homosexual clients two chances for obtaining refugee status. As a result the setting of a legal precedent on the issue of homosexuality alone is postponed (Bryant, 26 August 1998).

However, in 1998, a 28-year-old Romanian man, Sorin Mihai, was granted refugee status on the grounds of his homosexuality. In a letter sent to Mr Mihai from the Immigration and Nationality Directorate on 7 September 1998, he was informed that he was being granted indefinite leave to remain in the UK as a refugee recognised under the United Nations Convention relating to the status of refugees of 28 July 1951 and its protocol of 1967. The granting of refugee status to Mr Mihai was on the basis of his application that he had been a practising homosexual in Romania and that as such he was a member of a particular social group with a well-founded fear of being persecuted if returned to Romania. The tribunal authenticated Mr Mihai's homosexual identity and then proceeded to assess the evidence concerning the validity of his fear. Mr Mihai's fear of persecution was accepted by the tribunal as being an objective fear in proportion to the state discrimination towards homosexuals in Romania. According to Mr Gata-Aura (Mr Mihai's legal representative), recent changes in law in

Romania in respect to the criminalisation of homosexuality left it just as oppressive as before.[8] The more recent legislation included a definition of 'causing a public scandal' that was frequently invoked to prosecute homosexuals to the point of persecution (Mr Gata-Aura 1998, letter to the Immigration and Nationality Directorate). According to a spokesperson from the gay and lesbian lobbying group, Stonewall, Mr Mihai's case was a welcome climax to a long struggle 'for gay men to be recognised as refugees if they were facing human rights abuses in their native countries' (*Yorkshire Post*, 9 September 1998: 6).

Following on from this decision, in a case heard in 1999 in the UK regarding the social group membership of women in Pakistan, the situation of homosexuals in refugee law in the UK was clarified. In the case of *R* v. *IAT ex parte Shah*, the practice of focusing on the characteristics and behaviour of the individual was once and for all shifted to focusing, in an appropriate evidence situation, on the position and treatment of groups of people in certain countries. In this case Steyn LJ quoted the Acosta, Ward and *Re: GJ* decisions concerning immutability in his assessment of who should, and in what circumstances, be included in the Convention social group definition. In particular, Steyn LJ accepted the reasoning in *Re: GJ* as correct: 'Subject to the qualification that everything depends on the state of the evidence in regard to the position of homosexuals in a particular country, I would in principle accept the reasoning in Re: GJ as correct' (Steyn LJ *R* v. *IAT ex parte Shah*, All England Law Reports 12 May 1999, 555 h).

The reason Steyn LJ included homosexuals in his deliberation was to challenge the restrictive view in international refugee law that members of a social group should be a 'cohesive group' that emerged in 1986 in the USA in the case of *Sanchez-Trujillo* v. *Immigration and Naturalisation Service*. According to Steyn LJ, the test of immutability that emerged in the Acosta case, and that was demonstrated most forcefully in the *Re: GJ* case in New Zealand, was less restrictive than the 'cohesive group' perspective that emerged in the Sanchez-Trujillo case. According to Steyn LJ, the 'cohesive group' perspective failed to include 'homosexuals, who are, of course, not a cohesive group' (Steyn LJ *R* v. *IAT ex parte Shah*, All England Law Reports 12 May 1999, 555 h).[9]

Reformulations, reconceptualisations and resistance

What I have attempted to do in this chapter is to describe a variety of legal politics initiated by specific legal intellectuals/practitioners whereby the exclusion of non-traditional social groups was to be resisted. As demonstrated in Chapter 2, and in this chapter, clients and legal representatives must play a specific game of truth in order for them to enter stage one of this game. In order to progress into the institutional process whereby refugee status is determined, a homosexual applicant must furnish his tribunal with sufficient evidence to corroborate his self-declaration of being a homosexual. The authentication of a homosexual identity will facilitate the assessment of whether such an identity is synonymous for Convention purposes with membership of a particular social group. This social group membership is subsequently assessed as to the degree of persecution the members of this social group are alleged to suffer at the hands of the state in their countries of origin. The inclusion of homosexuals in the social group category was achieved through the disruption of the institutional discourses that had excluded them from this category. Thus, for authenticated homosexuals to be included within the Convention social group category, they must engage in an institutional politics whereby the preconceptualisation and substitution of 'social group' as meaning traditional minority group within refugee procedures (such as in the Golchin case) must be unsettled.

This can be described as a politics of connection. In the procedure whereby homosexuals are authenticated by immigration authorities, the former's self-declared homosexuality must be connected to (or, in the Vraciu case, disconnected from) the facts made available to law from the evidence provided to the tribunal. The second level of connection must be achieved by connecting the applicant's authenticated homosexual identity and homosexual social group membership with objective proof of the existence of the persecutory intent towards this group in the country of origin. This facilitates a third level of connection in the form of the comparison of the country in question's alleged persecutory intent with that of the host country's legal standards and the standards of the international human rights conventions. Thus, the country of origin's legal interaction is connected with homosexuals as a social group, which is in turn connected to human rights standards. As a result of this last connection, refugee procedures are connected to human rights law. This legal (and political) 'work' in the form of resistance to the exclusion of non-traditional social groups from refugee status by the forging of these connections and legal intersections was achieved by a number of legal practitioners. I refer to these legal 'workers' as specific intellectuals in Foucault's formulation, because they were employed in, and were part of, a specific institutional setting, and the operations of practices in this context.

According to Foucault, this type of intellectual performs essential critical work, in institutions and the practices of institutions, and 'through this they have undoubtedly gained a much more concrete awareness of struggles' (Foucault 1979a: 142). These specific intellectuals/practitioners occupy a 'specific position', that is, 'a specificity linked to the general functioning of an apparatus of truth in a society like ours' (Foucault 1979: 46). These practitioner-intellectuals were not attempting to demolish these institutions but were performing 'a work of examination that consists of suspending as far as possible the system of values to which one refers when testing and assessing it' (Foucault 1988: 107).

The critical and specific intellectual legal practitioners and academics who have contributed to the shifting of social group status away from individual characteristics and restrictive models have all been employed in this enterprise of 'suspending the system'. This 'suspension of the system' involves a multi-layered imbricated institutional politics of law. This politics of connection and disruption encompasses a variety of 'legal' regimes. For example, international human rights standards, refugee case law, and the comparison of the country of origin's criminal law with that of the host country. All these legal regimes are varieties of 'law', used, compared and deployed in order to disrupt and change the preconceptions of this particular 'system' so as to include non-traditional social groups within the Convention (1951) definition of a 'particular persecuted social group'. It is important to note that the success in the New Zealand case, and ultimately in the UK in the case of Sorin Mihai, was the result of this 'critical work' of examining and suspending 'the system'. This was not achieved by the extra-legal mobilisation of homosexuals as a group attempting to be recognised as legitimate subjects who should be protected from persecution alongside other credible refugees.

This was an institutional, specifically legal politics of knowledge. The deployment of an identity political or minoritarian legitimacy claim to counter or resist the exclusion of homosexuals from 'particular persecuted social group' status would have been fundamentally misplaced in this context. The reason for this is that it was the dissimilarity of homosexuals from 'true' minorities that was the primary reason for the exclusion of homosexuals from social group status in the first place. Minoritarian characteristics, for example recognisable social and cultural difference, a transhistorical essence and a procreative ability, were absent in homosexual applicants who were characterised as members of a 'group' who were presented as being voluntary, invisible, clandestine, inconspicuous members of a not particularly cohesive group. What is of academic importance for gay and lesbian and queer studies in the area of 'homosexual' refugee law, and non-traditional 'social group' refugee case law in general, is the particular variety of 'legal' politics that emerges within these events. This is a politics motivated by a resistance to exclusion from refugee social group status that actually initiates what amounts to a diversion or disruption of the 'usual' way of perceiving, comprehending and thinking 'particular persecuted social group' cases. This politics can be described as 'a project of frame-breaking' (Berlant 1997: 14).

Chapter 1 described, with regard to the introduction of passing policies in the armed forces, how the production of 'the homosexual' as incompatible with that context was disrupted and eventually re-imagined by the MoD in terms of circumstantial compatibility. In this chapter a similar process is evident: homosexuality is re-invented in terms of a particular immutability, disrupting the dominant discourse of homosexuality as voluntary. In both cases this frame-breaking or frame-expansion to include alternative perspectives and alternative, subjugated knowledges was achieved not through minoritarian politics but through a subtle blend of 'discursive politics'. The frame-breaking politics evident in contemporary homosexual refugee cases was not perpetuated in terms of an identity politics, founded on a homosexual essence (Fuss 1989), a unitary minority (Seidman 1995, 1996, 1997) who are seeking recognition (Taylor 1994) and legitimacy (Epstein 1987). This politics of resistance to exclusion in homosexual refugee cases was founded not on what homosexuals are and what they were demanding, alone. This was a politics based on a particular conceptualisation of immutability that bears very little resemblance to the 'queer immutability studies' carried out by various established lesbian, gay and queer legal academics.[10] In other words, the issue in this chapter was not about how gays and lesbians could best represent themselves strategically to counter discrimination and inequality before the law and in the legal complex. The political tactic employed became a matter of how homosexuals can be best placed within a nexus or connection of specific legal criteria. This particular example of resistance to exclusion becomes, in the light of the nature of the statuses involved (refugee, homosexual), an anti-foundational or multi-foundational form of political activity: a politics where 'roots' are replaced by 'options' and options in themselves become roots (Santos 1998: 249).[11]

Conclusion

My primary ambition in this chapter was to present the process whereby non-traditional, yet persecuted, groups in societies, such as homosexuals, became recognised in refugee determination processes as being members of a particular persecuted social group. One could say that this process amounted to a specific legal politics that was motivated by resisting the exclusionary practices within international refugee law and its institutional settings. In many ways this was a politics that centred on meaning, on knowledge and the reciprocity of power and knowledge. This political process can be described in terms of an attempt to divert or disrupt the 'usual' or dominant way of perceiving, comprehending and thinking social group membership. The form of resistance analysed in this chapter was made possible by the creation of a space in the conceptualisation procedures for determining social group membership, by 'specific intellectual' legal practitioners and academics in various countries, at various times. The focus of all this specific intellectual work was on the definitional exclusivity of 'particular persecuted social group' membership as defined in the UN Convention (1951). The space created by these specific intellectuals exposed inadequacies and absences in the refugee determination procedure which they attempted to fill with a contextualised reconceptualisation of non-traditional minority groups in relation to state interaction with such social groups and prevailing human rights standards. By so doing they created an interface between international refugee law and human rights law. The resistance to the exclusion of homosexuals and other non-traditional social groups from refugee status was achieved through establishing specific 'nexus criteria' within the multiple spheres of law, or, more accurately, facilitating an interface between intersecting legal systems. The attempt to contextualise non-traditional social group applicants, such as homosexuals, within the comparative nexus criteria, was therefore an attempt to initiate a modification of 'meaning-making' within the determination procedures in international refugee law. This modification – what Foucault would describe as the 'suspension of the system' – caused a re-signification or an opening up of the framework of the meaning of 'the refugee' in order to allow 'the homosexual' to be included in this definition alongside traditional minority groups. This was achieved by disrupting the exclusive (and limited) way the Convention social group category was conceptualised.

In this chapter, I demonstrated the vulnerability of homosexual identity in law, nationally and internationally. This was achieved by the deployment of identity as being significant to homosexuality in five significant ways. First, this chapter presented identity in terms of the process of identification whereby the national 'heterosexual' 'normative' identity was constructed in relation to its others. This is evident in the state's official eradication of homosexuality in nations such as Iran, Romania and Cyprus. The criminalisation and persecution of homosexuals by these states demonstrates the official constitutive outsideness or abjection of homosexuality from the national identity. The second presentation of identity concerns homosexual identity itself: as a process of accommodation to a social world this identity attempts to survive within hostile social, legal and national environments.[12] The third presentation of identity was that of the 'true' or genuine refugee, the 'real' traditional minority social group members deployed in refugee procedures to the exclusion of non-traditional refugee applicants such as homosexuals from the social group category. The fourth presentation of identity results from homosexuals basing their claim for the benefit of refugee status on a homosexual identity that must be authenticated officially. This latter form of identity, as described in Chapter 2, must be presented to immigration and asylum officials in terms of appropriate evidence that must objectively connect the identity claimed to the persecutory intent of the state in question. Thus, this fourth variety of identity must be connected to and supported by facts that provide evidence of the official or 'national identity shaping' strategies for persecuting and eradicating homosexuals in such states. The fifth form of identity is the inclusion of homosexual identity under the protection of human rights standards, as deserving national protection and not national eradication. This is an institutionalised and discursively produced identity conflated with rights. This fifth form of homosexual identity, as protected in the human rights discourse of the European Convention in particular 'restrictive' circumstances (age, number, 'in privacy'), will be expanded upon in Chapter 4. In Chapter 4, for example, the recognition of an adolescent male's homosexual identity by the European Commission in the *Sutherland* v. *United Kingdom* case in 1997 will be analysed. The inclusion of both homosexual refugees and homosexual adolescents within human rights discourse, discussed in this chapter and in Chapter 4 respectively, can be described as a means of connecting these 'groups' of homosexuals to the recognition and to the protections which were previously denied to them. Human rights law, therefore, is presented here and will be further presented in Chapter 4 as a supra-national site for the de-subjugation of alternative knowledges concerning homosexuality, which are currently subjugated and silenced by legal institutional practices at the national level. As well as being a potential mechanism for de-subjugation, human rights law is also produced here as a tactical site for the co-optation of these alternative knowledges into the dominant discourse in order to effect legal, political and social change.

In relation to the five productions of identity in this chapter, I also develop themes first introduced in Chapter 1: the particularity of homosexual identity, difference and social positioning, especially in relation to the heterosexual norm within 'the nation' or specific institutions such as the armed forces. In Chapter 1 I demonstrated that the production of homosexuals as incompatible to armed service by the MoD was simultaneous with the compatible presence of gays and lesbians as 'assumed heterosexuals' in the armed services. In the chapter above I also isolated this ability of homosexuals to remain undetected and unrecognisable as such through the particularity of their difference from the heterosexual norm. I described this tactical ability as arising from homosexuals being both insiders and outsiders, that is, organic strangers, who can hide their outsiderness, their strangeness, by presenting themselves socially as 'appropriate insiders'. I demonstrate how this is an essential survival tactic from a critical perspective which demonstrates that the criminal justice systems in Iran, Romania and Cyprus are used to punish and eradicate homosexual difference to a degree which results in gays and lesbians attempting to pass as insiders or non-homosexuals in an endeavour to avoid official reprisals.

The theme of homosexuals as organic strangers, and outsiders inside, will be developed further in Chapter 4. However, in Chapter 4, organic strangeness will not be developed in terms of the ability of homosexuals to hide their difference by accommodating to a heteronormatively organised social and legal environment.[13] In Chapter 4 my central thesis will consist in developing the presentation within juridical and parliamentary discourse of the organic strangeness of homosexuality in terms of a project of preventing young males from 'becoming' homosexuals. I shall demonstrate that the juridical and parliamentary discourses surrounding the age of consent for homosexual relations between men during the period 1957–2000 can be described as a political project whereby heterosexuality, 'the family', national identity and the national future were to be protected.

4 The fear of 'homosexual spread'

Legislating the heteronormativity of protection 1957–2000

> National heterosexuality is the mechanism by which core national culture can be imagined as a sanitised space of sentimental feeling and immaculate behaviour, a space of pure citizenship.
>
> (Berlant and Warner 1998: 549)

Introduction

In 1967, the British Parliament passed the Sexual Offences Act. It was with the passing of this legislation that homosexual acts between men were decriminalised in specific circumstances: when such acts were committed with consent, 'in private', with no more than two adults over the age of 21 years present. This legislation had its origins in the work of a committee appointed in 1954 to consider the law and practice relating to homosexuality and prostitution. This committee has become known as the Wolfenden Committee. The Wolfenden Committee's final report was published in 1957 as the *Report of the Departmental Committee on Homosexual Offences and Prostitution*, commonly known as the Wolfenden Report.

In this chapter the particular focus of analysis is on the lawful age of homosexual relations between men, that is, the homosexual age of consent. In terms of this analysis, the chapter engages in two main projects, first, the exploration of the relationship between homosexuality, heterosexuality and the criminal law; second, an analysis of the meaning and significance of the Wolfenden Report and its recommendations in the context of the late 1950s and into the 1960s, especially the strategic role the homosexual age of consent was to play in the decriminalisation of homosexual offences in 1967. The central enterprise of this chapter is therefore an exploration of the heteronormativity of legal and political discourses in relation to the Wolfenden Report and the parliamentary debates that would proceed from it, from 1957 to the present. In many ways, therefore, this is an examination of the privileged status of heterosexualities relative to homosexualities in parliamentary and judicial discourse. This chapter can be described as performing a critical re-reading of specific archival material in an attempt to demonstrate that the social, cultural and legal negation of homosexuality in societies is in direct proportion to its cultural significance to those societies (Dollimore 1992: 23). In order to achieve this, the chapter has as much (if not more) to say about heterosexuality as it has to say about homosexuality in legal discourse.

Of particular importance to this enterprise is the distinctive production of both homosexuality and heterosexuality in the Wolfenden Report. Following Alfred Kinsey, the Wolfenden Committee depicted male sexuality as being best conceived as a continuum of practices neither exclusively homosexual nor heterosexual. As a result of this conceptualisation of non-polarised sexualities in the Wolfenden Report, the interdependency of heterosexuality and homosexuality, a theme developed in previous chapters, is further explored.

Many of the claims and theoretical advances produced in this chapter are primarily achieved by paying particular attention to some of the Wolfenden Committee's 'over-looked' (academically speaking) and unimplemented recommendations for the introduction of rehabilitation programmes for the 'treatment' of homosexuals (as an alternative to prison). It is through the re-discovery of these suggestions for treatment programmes and their scientific origin and the deployment of male sexuality as being non-exclusive, that an exploration of the state-organised heteronormativity of these events is possible. More importantly, however, it is through the committee's recommendations for the rehabilitation of homosexuals that it is possible to isolate the particular purposes behind the necessity of initiating a minimum age for lawful homosexual relations in the first place. By bringing as many young men who had committed 'homosexual offences' as possible into the net of the criminal justice system, the committee hoped these young men could be 'saved' from a life of homosexuality through specific rectificational programmes. However, with the implementation of the Sexual Offences Act of 1967, the protection of young people from the advances of homosexuals and the prevention of their indulgence in homosexual acts themselves, had become synonymous with criminalisation (rather than 'rehabilitation'). In the last section of the chapter the issue of 'protection' through criminalisation will be analysed in the context of contemporary homosexual age of consent reform strategies, especially in the last half of 1990s and into the twenty-first century.

The context

The Wolfenden Committee was appointed in 1954 to consider the law and practice relating to homosexuality and prostitution. The final report was published three years later in 1957. The committee consisted of various professionals including psychiatrists, solicitors, and ministers of religion, academics, Members of Parliament, and university vice-chancellors (see Appendix I for a complete list of committee members). In many ways the appointment of the Wolfenden Committee was a response to the liberal backlash against the 'controversial' policing of homosexual offences in the early 1950s (West 1977: 282). Repressive police policy had, at that time, the enthusiastic support of the then Home Secretary Sir David Maxwell Fife, the metropolitan Police Commissioner Sir John Nott-Bower[1] and the devout Catholic Director of Public Prosecutions Sir Theobald Mathew (West 1977: 282). In the 1950s the policing of homosexuality was carried out with considerable zeal. However, the pursuit of convictions of homosexuals at that time led to some sordid prosecutions. According to West, 'gross violations of privacy, the use of compromising letters unearthed in the searches of doubtful legality, and dependence upon guilty persons prepared to give evidence against their friends in return for immunity from prosecution began to alienate public opinion' (West 1977: 282).

Certain notorious and high-profile trials in 1953 and 1954, especially one involving a member of the aristocracy, Lord Montagu (see Higgins 1996) also provoked strong comment in the national press, much of it critical of the authorities (West 1977: 282). As a result, the Home Secretary, bowing to popular demand, agreed to set up a departmental committee to look into the law and practice relating to both homosexual offences and prostitution. In this chapter, the analysis will be limited to homosexual offences.

Blurred boundaries: Wolfendenesque sexual mutability

In this section I will pay special attention to the distinctive quasi-scientific conceptualisation of homosexualities and heterosexualities in the Wolfenden Report. Particular attention will also be paid to the influence Kinsey's research on male sexual behaviour was to have on the Wolfenden Committee. Following Alfred Kinsey's model, from his study entitled *The Sexual Behaviour of the Human Male*, human male sexuality is formulated in terms of a heterosexual–homosexual continuum on a 7-point scale. Kinsey's research can be described as challenging the conception of male homosexuals as being 'fundamentally pathological and belong[ing] to a separate and small group' (Terry 1995: 155). Kinsey's work obliterated the idea of a clear-cut homosexual type (Terry 1995: 156). The Wolfenden Committee's interpretation of Kinsey's research was as follows:

> Homosexuality as a propensity is not an 'all or none' condition, and this view has been abundantly confirmed by the evidence submitted to us. All gradations can exist from apparently exclusive homosexuality without any conscious capacity for arousal by heterosexual stimuli to apparently exclusive heterosexuality, though in the latter case there may be transient and minor homosexual inclinations, for instance in adolescence. According to the psychoanalytic school, that all individuals pass through a homosexual phase in development is very common and should usually cause neither surprise nor concern.
>
> (Wolfenden Report 1957: para 22)

The recognition of the existence of this heterosexual–homosexual non-exclusivity was important to the committee for two reasons:

> first, it leads to the conclusion that homosexuals cannot reasonably be regarded as quite separate from the rest of mankind. Secondly, as will be discussed below, it has some relevance in connection with claims made for the success of various forms of treatment.
>
> (Wolfenden Report 1957: para 22)

The Wolfenden Committee was at pains to present homosexuality as a propensity which was woven into the fabric of society and at all levels of society, in all classes from the most professional and intelligent to the dullest oafs (Wolfenden Report 1957: para 36). The committee concluded that homosexual acts were, or could be, indulged in by 'those whose main sexual propensity was for persons of the opposite sex' (Wolfenden Report 1957: para 19). The Wolfenden Committee evoked the hydraulic model of male sexuality (Weeks 1989: 9) to explain heterosexual males indulging in homosexual acts. As in the 'naval scenario' depicted in Chapter 1, the committee categorised such activities 'in special circumstances that prohibit contact with the opposite sex' (Wolfenden Report 1957: para 19). The men involved were thought to revert to heterosexual behaviour when the opportunity afforded itself (Wolfenden Report 1957: para 19). The committee also presented financial gain as a motivation for the indulgence in homosexual acts by heterosexuals. Thus, men who were heterosexual, that is, men who had a sexual propensity for members of the opposite sex, according to the committee, could indulge in homosexual activities in specific circumstances whilst maintaining their primary sexual orientation and identity as heterosexuals.

What the committee attempted to produce in these examples of mutable sexualities was that there was a distinction between the condition of homosexuality (which relates to the direction of sexual preference) and the acts or behaviour resulting from this preference (Wolfenden Report 1957: para 23). Of considerable interest to the committee was the 'habit' of indulging in homosexual activities by young men whose sexualities remained in a transitional state; this 'homosexual habit' was produced in terms of its susceptibility to 'treatment'.

The committee presented its views on 'the condition of homosexuality' in terms of a chronological immutability reserved only for adults whose sexualities had become more fixed with age. The Wolfenden Committee's discourses of the non-exclusivity and potential mutability of homosexualities and heterosexualities was not simply a plea for greater toleration. This discourse was integral to a specific project of both changing the activities of adult offenders whose homosexual condition was more or less fixed, and eradicating or 'treating' the habit of indulging in homosexual activities by younger men whose sexual path, it was assumed, was still transitional.

The committee's usage of the word 'treatment' was as an inclusive term that covered the diverse ways in which convicted offenders were dealt with by the courts, as well as other institutional, medical and psychiatric 'treatments'. The committee members were especially interested in the various institutional settings and punishment-treatment methods recommended by the English courts in the 1950s for dealing with young men who had been convicted of homosexual offences.[2]

The committee's interest in these various treatments for young offenders focused on the potential they held for diverting young men from indulging in homosexual activities. This was achieved by the attempted installation of mechanisms of self-control and responsibility in the young offender, as well as emphasising the criminality of such acts and behaviours. At the same time, these treatments also included reorientation components that were designed to facilitate the integration of these young offenders 'back' into society. However, the committee wanted to promote the probational rather than the residential scope of these 'treatments' and, importantly, they wanted to modify these probational treatments to include both young and adult homosexual offenders.

According to the committee, the primary objectives for 'treating' or bringing about the homosexual offender's adjustment to society, should be one of three possible outcomes. These are 'a change in the direction of the sexual preference; ... [or] secondly, a better adaptation to life in general; and thirdly, greater continence or self-control.' The committee believed that success in achieving one of these objectives may in turn help in achieving another (para 192, 66). The total reorientation from 'complete homosexuality' to 'complete heterosexuality' was, according to the committee, very unlikely indeed in adult homosexuals (Wolfenden Report 1957: para 193). Another factor which persuaded the committee that a complete reorientation from homosexuality to heterosexuality in adults was unlikely, was the lack of medical reference to such a complete change (Wolfenden Report 1957: para 193). Therefore, the committee promoted the last two objectives as being practical forms of treatment for adult homosexual offenders. What the committee was proposing in these objectives for treatment was the initiation of therapeutic technologies for the transformation of indiscreet and offensive homosexual offenders into discreet and well-behaved homosexuals as a result of a probation-treatment programme.

The Wolfenden Committee's recommendations can be described as offering three primary groups of recommendations for the reforming of the criminal law: first, the decriminalisation of homosexual activities in specific circumstances, resulting in the creation of a 'realm of privacy' in which two men over the age of consent could indulge in homosexual acts;[3] second, the promotion of a specific homosexual subject who, regardless of the criminalisation or decriminalisation of homosexuals, would be well-adapted to society and be discreet in his 'private' practices; finally, those homosexuals who were convicted of a homosexual offence, and therefore were not 'private', discreet or controlled enough, were not to be sent to prison, but sentenced to a probation-treatment regime which would train them in the art of self-discipline.

The committee can be described as attempting to manipulate the space between what Gayle Rubin (1992), in her essay 'Thinking Sex', has described as the two poles of 'good' and 'bad' sex in order to create the specifically packaged homosexual subject's place in society. According to Rubin, heterosexual, married, reproductive, monogamous relations are the best example of 'good' or 'normal,' 'natural' sex (Rubin 1992: 279). By contrast, under the heading 'bad' or 'abnormal, unnatural, sick, sinful, "way out" sex', Rubin catalogues the ensuing group of deviants: transvestites, transsexuals, fetishists, sadomasochists, those engaging in cross-generational sex, as well as those involved in prostitution (Rubin 1992: 279). According to Bristow's reading of Rubin:

> In between these two poles, she designates the 'major area of contest' where one finds sexual behaviours and lifestyles that signal how attitudes are shifting across the moral terrain. In this liminal in-between zone, we find the following: unmarried heterosexual couples; promiscuous heterosexuals; masturbation; and long-term, stable same-sex relationships. Located somewhere closer to 'bad' sex are lesbians in the bar and promiscuous gay men in public places.
>
> (Bristow 1997: 201)

It was in this liminal in-between zone, between the poles of good and bad sex, that the Wolfenden Committee was trying to shift the moral terrain in favour of their recommendations relating to the decriminalisation of homosexuality.

The committee's promotion of the decriminalisation of well-behaved homosexuals and their private sexual activities, as well as the therapeutic manipulation of indiscreet and uncontrolled homosexuals, can be described in terms of what Anna Marie Smith refers to as the promotion of 'the good homosexual subject' (Smith 1994: 207). Smith's isolation of the promotion of this good homosexual subject at the heart of various pieces of legislation since the 1960s was organised around a differentiation between 'private' and 'public' homosexual activities and accompanying lifestyles and identities. 'Private' homosexuals were identified as self-regulating, harmless and assimilable, whereas 'public' homosexuality and homosexuals were identified as flaunting, dangerous, contagious and unassimilable (Smith 1994: 207). According to Smith, in parliamentary and juridical discourses in England there is a consistent differentiation between varieties of good and bad homosexualities. The good varieties were to be promoted in their private self-eradication and the bad varieties were to be regulated and controlled by the social practices of law. Legal indifference to homosexual activities, according to Smith, was possible when homosexuals knew their 'proper place' on the secret and discreet fringes of mainstream society (Smith 1994: 18). Knowing one's proper place amounted to discreet and controlled homo-sexuals existing non-offensively in the narrowly defined realm of privacy created for them in the Wolfenden Report, which was subsequently written into law in the form of the Sexual Offences Act of 1967. What it was hoped would happen by creating this realm of privacy was the 'juridical eradica-tion' (Moran 1996b, 326) of self-controlled and self-disciplined homosexuals from the business of law.[4] The discreet homosexual and his activities was to 'disappear into a narrowly defined private space' (Moran 1996a: 198), deep in the closeted darkness of the Wolfenden Committee's 'private' realm.

This delimitation of the 'proper place' of 'legal' homosexuality, intro-duced in the Wolfenden Report and implemented in the Sexual Offences Act of 1967, can be described as the legal enforcement of homosexual invisi-bility (Moran 1996a: 64), or as the attempted control of the public visibility of homosexuality (Sinfield 1994a: 9). Either way, the reform of the law related to homosexuality introduced by the Sexual Offences Act of 1967 was in keeping with what Minson describes as the 'keep-it-off the streets atti-tude found in the Wolfenden Report' (Minson 1981: 34). It was hoped that by creating a narrowly defined realm of legality for homosexuals, the government would be 'killing two birds with one stone': (a) the affront of homosexual activities would be removed from the public eye;[5] and (b) homosexuals, many of whom, according to the Wolfenden Report, were already conducting themselves with discretion, would further self-regulate and take this opportunity to disappear altogether from the 'public' and hence, legal realm.[6] In relation to the latter point, the committee was already aware that the vast majority of homosexuals were already discreet and controlled and aimed to exist below the awareness of the law and the general public. Not only were these homosexuals discreet and well-behaved, but they were also described by the committee as well-socialised members of the community:

> It has to be borne in mind that there are many homosexuals whose behaviour never comes to the notice of the police or the courts, and it is probable that the police and the courts see only the worst cases; the more anti-social type of person is more likely to attract the attention of the police than the discreet person with a well-developed social sense.
> (Wolfenden Report 1957: para 80)

In a note attached to the Wolfenden Report, two psychiatrists, Dr Curran and Dr Whitby, who were members of the committee, described five vari-eties of homosexualities they had encountered in their professional lives. One of these types of homosexualities was presented by the two psychiatrists as: 'homosexuality in relatively intact personalities' which they described in a similar fashion to the main report as being 'otherwise well socialised'. According to Dr Curran and Dr Whitby, many of the homosexuals so categorised were valuable and efficient members of the community, quite unlike the common conception of 'the homosexual' as being necessarily, or probably, vicious, criminal, effete or depraved (Dr Curran, Dr Whitby, Wolfenden Report 1957: para 3, 73). However, Dr Curran and Dr Whitby also described four other varieties of homosexual offenders, as met with in medical and psychiatric practice, alongside this description of 'homosexuality in relatively intact personalities'. These other categories were homosexuality in 'the adolescent and in mentally immature adult', 'in severely damaged personalities', 'latent and relatively well-compensated homosexuals', and 'a homosexual predisposition co-existing with serious mental disabilities'.

Of importance to the committee's recommended probation-treatment programme, which Dr Whitby and Dr Curran supported, were their descriptions of homosexuality in adolescence and in immature adults as well as homosexuality in severely damaged personalities. They described these varieties of homosexualities as those of:

> 'the adolescent and mentally immature adult', many of who are still in the transitional stage of psycho-sexual development. Quite often they mistake the part for the whole and erroneously suppose that the recognition of a homosexual component indicates that they are irretrievably homosexual. 'Latent heterosexuality' can exist just as much as can 'latent homosexuality'. Such individuals can and do react with shame and misery, or over-compensate by bravado. They can meet an attractive girl, fall in love and all's well.
>
> 'Severely damaged personalities'. Examples are obviously effeminate and flaunting exhibitionistic individuals (these, contrary to popular belief, are quite rare); grossly inadequate, passive, weak-willed persons; or deeply resentful anti-social types.
> (Note by Dr Curran, Dr Whitby, Wolfenden Report 1957: para 3, 73)

The objective of presenting these categories of homosexualities was, according to Dr Curran and Dr Whitby, an attempt to present models of clinical varieties of homosexualities so that individuals who had been convicted of homosexual offences could be dealt with adequately (Wolfenden Report 1957: para 3, 72).

For the two psychiatrists it became a matter of assessing the significance of homosexuality in the individual offender so as to decide on the best form of treatment for the individual involved (Wolfenden Report 1957: para 3, 72). In relation to the five clinical varieties of homosexuality in offenders, the two psychiatrists stipulated the following: 'the same criminal act may be committed as a piece of adolescent experimentation; or be the result of temporary or permanent mental or physical disorder or disease; or it may be part of the individual's lifestyle' (Wolfenden Report 1957: para 3, 72).

Curran and Whitby suggested that an informed medical report would often be of help to the court in matching treatments with types of homosexualities and offenders. Curran and Whitby endorsed the committee's suggestions that oestrogen therapy[7] should be made available to homosexual offenders on a voluntary basis. It was not made clear by Dr Curran and Dr Whitby which varieties of homosexual offenders should be exposed to oestrogen treatment. However, this use of oestrogen treatment, to curb 'desire', could be implicated in the assumption, borne out by the absence of legislation of homosexual relations between women, that women in the absence of men do not possess an autonomous female sexuality in juridical and parliamentary discourse (Smith 1994: 209). Thus, oestrogen treatment may have been an attempt to pacify, moderate and render non-assertive (Smith 1994: 209), that is, 'feminise', the 'excessive' desires of indiscreet and uncontrolled male homosexual offenders. The recommendations in the Wolfenden Report in relation to oestrogen therapy were indeed far reaching. Oestrogen therapy, which was banned in 1950 by the Labour government under Clement Attlee, was (re-)implemented in 1958 by Richard Austen Butler, the then Home Secretary. Butler justified this re-implementation on the grounds of the 'clear recommendation of the Wolfenden Committee' (Richardson 2000: 19).[8]

The adolescent or immature adult homosexual offender was of special importance to Dr Curran and Dr Whitby. The two psychiatrists placed special emphasis on the prognosis of the successful treatment of adolescent or immature adult homosexual offenders. They stated that the encouraging fact in relation to this variety of homosexual offender was that many young men passed through a homosexual phase satisfactorily and without medical help (Wolfenden Report 1957: para 4, 71). It is clear from Dr Curran's and Dr Whitby's commentary, and the Wolfenden Report in general, that all episodes of homosexuality in adolescents were assumed to be transitory and retrievable. In this conception the existence of the condition of homosexuality in male adolescents was disavowed; these young men were viewed as potential heterosexuals, curable and reorientatable 'transitional homosexuals'. In fact, the Wolfenden Committee actually described the potential effective and successful treatment of adolescents in a transitory homosexual phase as one of the reasons they decided to leave homosexual behaviour by persons under 21 years as a criminal offence (Wolfenden Report 1957: para 187). By doing so, the committee hoped to retrieve as many young offenders as possible from homosexuality and return them to heterosexuality in their recommended probation-treatment programme. The committee documented this strategy in the following passage:

> As we have said earlier, we do not contemplate that all such cases should come before the courts. If our recommendations are accepted, persons under 21 will be charged with homosexual offences only where their homosexual behaviour has been accompanied by conduct of a patently criminal or vicious nature, or where it is apparent that the offender would benefit from being placed on probation with a view either to

treatment or to supervision of a more general kind. In these cases, it is likely that the conduct or environment of the offender will have been such as to suggest some maladjustment, which a course of treatment opportunely undertaken might remedy, and in any event a talk with an experienced doctor may well be salutary. We accordingly recommend that a court by which a person under 21 is found guilty of a homosexual offence should be required by law, before passing sentence on that person, to obtain and consider a psychiatric report.

(Wolfenden Report 1957: para 187)

However, in the drafting of the various Sexual Offences Bills between 1965 and 1967, the Wolfenden Committee's recommendations for the rectification and adjustment both of young homosexual offenders under the age of 21 and of adult homosexual offenders were absent. Wolfenden's recommendations in relation to 'treatment', 'probation' and 'continence' were disregarded in the drafting of the Sexual Offences Bills in favour of the more mainstream recommendations in the report related to 'privacy', 'decriminalisation' and to the 'protection' of 'the young and vulnerable'.

The protection of latent heterosexuality

The Wolfenden Committee stated that 'we believe that it is part of the function of the law to safeguard those who need protection by reason of their youth or some mental defect, and we do not wish to see any change in the law that would weaken this protection' (Wolfenden Report 1957: para 48).

The committee was extremely eager to promote in their report that the protection of immature, young males was one of their central concerns. However, the discussions surrounding the lawful age of homosexual relations between men, in the form of deterring young men from indulging their own homosexual tendencies and isolating these youths from sexual contact with proselytising homosexual adults, was of a contradictory nature in the Wolfenden Report. For example, in paragraph 98, the committee disputed the 'widely held' views among police and legal witnesses, which Higgins has described as 'the vampire theory' (Higgins 1996: 24): that seduction in youth was the decisive factor in the production of homosexuality 'as a condition'. According to Higgins, the view that there was 'a moment' when the corruption from heterosexuality to homosexuality 'took root' 'was widely held, and shaped the policy of many members of the legal establishment' (Higgins 1996: 24). The Wolfenden Committee's response to this was dismissive. The committee stated that with regards to the question of how homosexuals are produced: 'seduction has little effect in inducing a settled pattern of homosexual behaviour' (Wolfenden Report 1957: para 98).

However, earlier, at paragraph 71 of the report, the committee proceeded to promote 21 years of age as the recommended lawful age of homosexual relations between men. Central to this decision was the greater protection this higher age of 21, relative to 16 or 18 years, would bring to young men who might be the object of predatory 'attentions of an undesirable kind':

> Some of us feel, on various grounds, that the age of adulthood should be fixed at eighteen. Nevertheless, most of us would prefer to see the age fixed at twenty-one, not because we think that to fix the age at eighteen would result in any greater readiness on the part of the young men between eighteen and twenty-one to lend themselves to homosexual practices than exists in the present, but because to fix it at eighteen would lay them open to attentions and pressures of an undesirable kind from which the adoption of the later age would help to protect them, and from which they ought, in the view of their special vulnerability, to be protected. We therefore recommend that for the purpose of the amendment of the law that we have proposed, the age at which a man is deemed to be an adult should be twenty-one.
>
> (Wolfenden Report 1957: para 71)

When the paragraphs immediately preceding this recommendation are analysed, the explicit social function of the law in the Wolfenden Committee's recommendations is exposed. The criminal law becomes, in this analysis, a mechanism for an attempt to secure heterosexualisation (Moran 1997: 257). The primary function of the law in this mechanism was to prevent, by criminalisation, the indulgence in homosexual activities by young men, and to deter adult homosexuals from attempting to exploit the unfixed nature of young male sexualities by seducing them into indulging in homosexual activities.

According to the committee, 'adulthood', for the purposes of deciding on the minimum age of lawful homosexual relations between men, was to be calibrated in terms of a 'precise chronological age'. The age of consent for homosexual men was to reflect both 'the need to protect young and immature persons' (Wolfenden Report 1957: para 66) and 'the age at which the pattern of a man's sexual development can be said to be fixed' (Wolfenden Report 1957: para 66). It was to be calibrated in terms of a reification of chronological sexual development and the immunisation from undesirable temptations (see Moran 1997).

On the issue of the age at which lawful homosexual relations between men should be set, relative to the heterosexual age of consent, the committee found it hard to believe that young men needed to be protected from 'would be seducers' more carefully than girls did (Wolfenden Report 1957: para 67). However, the committee emphasised the difference between heterosexual and homosexual genital activities as being a matter of the gravity of the act in question. For example, a girl engaging in heterosexual activity at the age of 16, would not, according to the committee, be engaging in activities which could 'set her apart from the rest of society'. However, boys indulging in homosexual activities were produced as being 'incapable, at the age of 16, of forming a mature judgement about actions of a kind which might have the effect of setting [them] apart from the rest of society' (Wolfenden Report 1957: para 71).

The committee's decision to recommend 21 as the minimum age of lawful homosexual relations between men was also based in part on the age of contractual legality, which, at the time, was 21. The age of 21 years and more was when 'a man was deemed to be capable of entering into legal contracts, including the contract of marriage' (Wolfenden Report 1957: para 69). Therefore 21 years and more was regarded by the committee as the age at which a man was 'maturely responsible for his actions' (Wolfenden Report 1957: para 69). The committee accepted the unanimous view of their medical witnesses that an individual's 'main sexual pattern' was laid down in the early years of life, and usually fixed by the age of 16 or earlier (Wolfenden Report 1957: para 68). However, certain circumstances that young men could find themselves in became of special interest to the committee. For example, young men who, for reasons of education, employment or national service, found themselves 'at or about the age of 18' away from home and were thus 'launched into the world in circumstances which render them particularly vulnerable to advances of this sort' (Wolfenden Report 1957: para 71). The committee encountered 'several cases' involving young men who, while away from the stability and order of 'the family' and 'the home' were induced to engage in homosexual activities by 'means of gifts of money or hospitality' offered by older men (Wolfenden Report 1957: para 71). As a result of this evidence the committee 'felt obliged' to fix the age of 'adulthood' at 21 to compensate for this particular period of 'special vulnerability' (Wolfenden Report 1957: para 71).

The committee's description of this 'special vulnerability' can also be described as a simultaneous production of the 'special mutability' of male sexualities. The committee stipulated that they recommended that any homosexual act committed by these vulnerable young men under the age of 21 should continue to be an offence. However, in the spirit of their rehabilitation-treatment programme, they suggested that cases of this sort should seldom reach the courts (except in patently vicious circumstances). Instead, the committee advocated that the young offenders should be placed on 'probation with a view either to treatment or to supervision of a more general kind' (Wolfenden Report 1957: para 72, 27, 28).

The fear of homosexual spread: parliamentary debates (1958–65)

After the publication of the Wolfenden Committee's report in 1957, the committee's conceptualisation of male sexuality and its suggestion that a probation-treatment programme should be introduced for young 'homosexual' offenders came to the forefront in, especially, two significant parliamentary debates. These parliamentary debates occurred in 1958 (in the House of Commons) and in 1965 (in the House of Lords).

In the first of these parliamentary debates the primary focus was on the issues of homosexuality spreading in society and the number of men practising 'homosexual acts' increasing as a result of the suggested decriminalisation of homosexual offences in the Wolfenden Report. These concerns were expressed to the House of Commons by Mrs Mann (MP for Coatbridge and Airdrie) and Mr Renton (the Joint Under-Secretary of State for the Home Department). Mann and Renton presented their fears concerning the potential spread and increase of homosexuality in society in terms of the Wolfenden Committee's formulation of the non-exclusive nature of male heterosexualities and homosexualities. Mann's and Renton's statements to the Commons took the form of a prediction of an impending 'crisis' within the nation's male population if homosexuality was decriminalised as recommended by the Wolfenden Committee. Mann and Renton introduced this discourse to the House of Commons in terms of the manifestation of homosexuality and homosexual activities in two distinct ways and within two distinct groups of males. That is, Mann and Renton, consistent with the Wolfenden Committee's presentation of male sexualities, described two varieties of homosexualities that were to be found in society. The first of these homosexualities they described in terms of a small core group of exclusive or genuine (immutable) homosexuals. However, surrounding these 'genuine' homosexuals, according to Mann and Renton, there existed a larger, more diverse group of 'homosexuals' comprising a range of men and adolescents who, for various reasons, were indulging in homosexual acts with other men, but could not be described as being genuinely homosexual by orientation.

Both Renton and Mann were sympathetic to the Wolfenden Committee's recommendations concerning the decriminalisation of that minority of homosexuals who were described by Mann as being 'genuinely afflicted' by the condition of their homosexuality (Mann, *Hansard*, Commons, 26 November 1958: col. 459). Similarly, Renton described this group as 'a small minority of men whose affections were exclusively homosexual throughout their lives after their adolescence' (Renton, *Hansard*, Commons, 26 November 1958: col. 501). However, the majority of men indulging in homosexual activities, according to Renton, consisted of a 'wide range of others' besides the men with 'unalterable impulses'. Renton described this group of non-exclusive homosexuals in terms of their potential, or latent, heterosexuality. According to Renton, these non-exclusive 'homosexuals' indulged in homosexual activities for reasons as diverse as opportunistic prostitution, or being psychopathic perverts (col. 501). Renton's primary concern was that the number of these non-exclusive, opportunistic 'homosexuals' would increase with decriminalisation, as would the number of practising homosexuals from the ranks of those homosexuals who, during the period of criminalisation, customarily controlled their homosexual tendencies (cols 501–2).

Mann's fears concerning the link between decriminalisation and the spread of homosexuality also produced the potential growth of male 'homosexual' prostitution as a source of 'homosexual spread'. However, her main emphasis was on the increased temptation to indulge in homosexual activities placed on adolescents away from the 'family home' as presented in the Wolfenden Committee's conceptualisation of 'the home' as a safe, homosexual-free zone.

According to Mann, young males would be particularly vulnerable in boarding schools and university hostels if homosexual activities were decriminalised. As a result of decriminalisation, young people would not be deterred from indulging in what she describes as 'fashionable' homosexual activities (Mann, *Hansard*, Commons, 26 November 1958: col. 459). Mann presented decriminalisation as a social signal, and a potential tool used by 'tempters' who could say 'that it [homosexuality] is all right, Parliament has approved it' (col. 460). The result of this parliamentary assent, according to Mann, would be that 'the tempted' would no longer be able to deflect temptation by saying 'that is illegal', that it 'is a crime as well as a sin' (col. 45960).

Mann voiced another concern, again related to the spread of 'homosexual practices' in society associated with the recommended decriminalisation of homosexuality. In this allied concern Mann proceeded to problematise the decriminalisation of homosexuality as recommended by the Wolfenden Committee in terms of decreasing the motivation for homosexuals to seek treatment for their condition. According to Mann, 'those tempted to seek treatment for their condition would find they did not need to bother any further about taking treatment, as they were never likely to be impugned by the law' (Mann, *Hansard*, Commons, 26 November 1958: col. 460).

This tension between 'penal leniency' (Wolfenden's recommendations for decriminalisation), and the necessity of ensuring the heterosexuality of 'that majority' of 'potential homosexuals', became crystallised around two central concerns: (a) that decriminalisation would result in an increase in the number of men who would become involved in homosexual activities; and (b) that decriminalisation would result in a decrease in the number of men indulging in homosexual activities who would seek treatment for this condition. As to the latter concern, the 'treatment' of homosexuals remained a contentious issue in the Wolfenden Report itself and in the parliamentary debates which occurred during the decade between its publication and the implementation of some of its recommendations in the form of the Sexual Offences Act of 1967.[9]

In another parliamentary debate seven years later, in 1965, during the House of Lords debate on homosexual offences, the then Archbishop of Canterbury brought the Wolfenden Committee's programme of probation-treatment for homosexuals to the foreground of parliamentary debate in his speech. According to the Archbishop, the Wolfenden Committee's suggestions 'constituted a big field for the possible bringing of deliverance, or, if not deliverance, at least considerable help to homosexuals' (*Hansard*, Lords,

12 May 1965: col. 81). The aims of probation-treatment, according to the Archbishop, provided the point of entry of 'moral responsibility' into the matter. The Archbishop presented the strength of the Wolfenden Report in terms of its emphasis on the varieties of states and causes of the condition of homosexuality and homosexual activities, and the fact that the committee refused to label these variations with a singular clinical formula (col. 81). As a result, homosexual offences committed by different people could be viewed, from the Wolfenden Committee's perspective, as displaying variations in the degree of culpability, 'with varieties of causes of the trouble and categories of the trouble, psychological and sociological' (col. 80). The Archbishop presented a statement made by the Homosexual Law Reform Society (HLRS)[10] as attempting, contrary to the Wolfenden Report, to over-simplify the problem: 'homosexuality is an involuntary emotional condition which in the present state of medical knowledge can only be cured in a tiny minority of cases' (col. 80). Of course, the HLRS was attempting to affirm an involuntary, if not, immutable condition of homosexuality, where a homosexual condition or identity corresponded with same-sex sexual practices, within a heteronormatively organised discursive context which presented homosexuality (and not heterosexuality) as mutable and curable. At this time, oestrogen and various other 'aversion' therapies had been officially sanctioned by the Home Secretary (under specific conditions).[11] This 'over-simplification' on the part of the HLRS, according to the Archbishop (consistent with the Wolfenden formulation of homosexuality), ignored 'the variety of states and the variety of causes in the condition of the persons known to perform homosexual acts' (col. 80), that is, that homosexual acts and homosexuality as a condition did not necessarily correspond.

The HLRS can be described as attempting to affirm homosexual identity in a 'traditional' or 'first-stage' identity politics strategy (Danielsen and Engle 1995: xiv). This political strategy can be seen, from the perspective of the early twenty-first century, as being particularly mismatched to the discursive context of non-exclusive and treatable sexualities. In this discursive context, 'the homosexual' (and 'the heterosexual') as particular types of person, following the publication of Kinsey's research, were under challenge (Terry 1995: 154). In 'first-stage' identity politics, individuals identify with and affirm identities that consist of 'general characteristics' such as race, gender and sexuality, in order to contend that discriminatory distinctions should not be made on the basis of these categories (Danielsen and Engle 1995: xiv). Therefore, politically, the HLRS seemed to have been engaging in a political strategy that was both inappropriate and dismissable in the post-Wolfenden political context. The Wolfenden–Kinsey production of male sexualities had made the attempt to affirm and mobilise around a distinctive homosexual identity problematic whilst simultaneously recommending legislative reform which would shore up and protect the potential heterosexual identities of young men. Moreover, in this discursive context it was not the 'established' 'condition of homosexuality' in adults (as in the members of the HLRS) that was of primary concern. Instead, rectifying 'the habit' of homosexual practices in young men in a transitional stage of sexual development was the focus of the Wolfenden Committee and of the Archbishop of Canterbury's speech to the House of Lords.

The Archbishop, in support of the Wolfenden Committee's 'total' package of recommendations (decriminalisation and probation-treatment programmes), was especially interested in the committee's concerns and recommendations relating to the prosecution of offenders under the age of 21 years. The committee's attempts to initiate a system whereby prosecutions and sentences could take into account 'the great variety of mental and moral states which can lie behind offences' (*Hansard*, Lords, 12 May 1965: col. 83) was a particularly important component of the committee's recommendations, for the Archbishop. This system, according to the Archbishop, would be a means of customising a young offender's treatment with a view to the committee's probation-treatment aims of reorientation, adaptation and greater continence. Thus, the Wolfenden probation-treatment recommendations held special potential for the distribution of offenders into categories with specific 'treatment' requirements. The mental and moral states that lay behind the offences could be comprehended by creating, in every case of a young offender, a detailed psychiatric profile. These psychiatric assessments could then allow distinction between varieties of homosexualities, for example, those 'who were merely immature, those who have been severely damaged and are resentful, anti-social personalities, those whose disorder of personality is very superficial and those who are deeply on the wrong lines' (col. 83).

The Archbishop concluded his speech in the House of Lords with a significant comment, which exposed the specific heteronormative social project behind his commendation and support of the Wolfenden Committee's recommendations: that the recommendations would provide, especially for young men under the age of 21, 'greater possibilities for some to find their way from the wrong uses of sex and be helped towards better uses of their energies' (Archbishop of Canterbury, *Hansard*, Lords, 12 May 1965: col. 84).

This statement, which emerged from the Archbishop's careful scrutiny of the Wolfenden Report, encapsulated a central metaphor which emanated from the report: that adolescent sexualities and sexual activities are conceived of, not in terms of concrete and immutable categories, but in terms of fluidity, movement, paths and pathways. Homosexuality and/or perversion have always been associated with movement, or, more accurately, deviation. Jonathan Dollimore describes this particular heteronormative perspective in the following passage:

> Illicit desire is especially prone to being conceptualised as aberrant movement ... the idea of deviation – itself the conceptual heart of the

idea of perversion – is about a movement which is dangerous or subversive: to deviate = to go astray.

(Dollimore 1998: xvii)

Thus, the Archbishop's interpretation of the Wolfenden Committee's conceptualisation of the sexual pathways of male sexuality was organised from a perspective which viewed the normative heterosexual path as 'the natural' or 'right' path. This conceptualisation can be described as reproducing a familiar metaphysics of nature (and hence 'the natural') based on what Dollimore describes as the mechanisms of essence/teleology/universality (Dollimore 1992: 19): that is, that 'an essential sexuality moves along a teleologically defined path of psychosexual development to the universal goal: heterosexual union' (Dollimore 1992: 19). To deviate, to indulge in 'unnatural' practices, and therefore, to be 'unnatural' is conceived from this perspective as:

> Erring, straying, or deviating from a path, destiny or objective which is understood as natural or right – right because natural ... [where] the natural/unnatural opposition has been one of the most violent of all hierarchies.

(Dollimore 1992: 10, 11)

Following Kinsey, sexualities, both heterosexualities and homosexualities, in the Wolfenden Report, were conceived in terms of continuums, up and down which males could roam, go astray and settle. At the same time, the Wolfenden Report presented all young males as having potentially manipulable sexualities and lifestyles which could be moulded and shaped to coincide with the circumstantial realm of privacy the Committee recommended should be created for them. However, and most important of all, the sexualities of young males, and especially young male 'homosexual' offenders within the Wolfenden Committee's recommendations (and in the Archbishop of Canterbury's speech to the House of Lords) were conceived primarily in terms of a particular heteronormativity. That is, all such 'movement' was conceptualised in terms of keeping young men on the correct 'heterosexual' path, or bringing them back to it.

Decriminalisation and the protection of male heterosexuality (1965–7)

In this section the analysis will focus on the three most significant parliamentary events, in terms of Private Member's Bills and Standing Committees, that led up to the decriminalisation of homosexual offences with the passing into law of the Sexual Offences Act of 1967. The reason it took so long to re-introduce the Wolfenden recommendations for the reform of the criminal law in relation to homosexuality was variously explained by the division of public opinion over the issues, and the controversial nature of the reforms (West 1977).

However, on 12 May 1965, the Earl of Arran introduced a Private Member's Bill to the House of Lords in an attempt to incorporate the Wolfenden Committee's proposals into the English criminal law.

In the introductory remarks to the presentation of this Bill to the Lords, Lord Arran declared: 'we must all have anxieties is about the corruption of youth. It is the nub of the business' (*Hansard*, Lords, 12 May 1965: col. 74). Lord Arran supported the Wolfenden Committee's proposals that homosexuality should be decriminalised in certain circumstances: if it occurred 'in private' with one other consenting adult over the age of 21 years. In Lord Arran's presentation to the House of Lords he produced the age of 21 years as a 'reasonable' chronological age for assuming that an individual's sexual orientation had become fixed and therefore was 'beyond seduction' and hence diversion from a heterosexual orientation. Lord Arran reiterated the Wolfenden Committee's chronological immutability discourse by declaring that 21 was a point in time where homosexuality was as fixed as heterosexuality:

> If it were demonstrably proved that a man over twenty-one is likely to be diverted from his normal sexual instincts and turned homosexual permanently, then I do not think that many of your Lordships would support a change in the law. Fortunately, I repeat, I do not think that we are faced with this difficulty. For myself, I believe firmly that nothing or nobody is going to change a man's basic desires, his erotic make-up. If a man is basically homosexual he will continue to be homosexual; if he is heterosexual, the same applies.
>
> (Arran: col. 74)

In Lord Arran's conceptualisation, the terms 'man' and 'adult', following the Wolfenden Committee, designated both a chronological age and an age of sexual immunity: an age where a male person has become immune to being diverted or corrupted from a fixed sexual orientation.[12] Lord Arran further supported his attempt to alleviate the Lords' fears about male youths being corrupted by adult homosexuals by evoking the dissuading power or function of the criminal law for prohibiting the preying on of 'the young' by adult homosexuals:

> If any doubt still lingers in your Lordships' minds regarding the corruption of youth, may I here make a practical point, with great emphasis? Assuming the threat of prison to be a deterrent of predatory homosexuals, are they not far more likely, if the law is changed, to seek their adventures among the over 21s and to leave the boys alone? Surely this is obvious.
>
> (Lord Arran, *Hansard*, Lords, 12 May 1965: col. 74)

From the above, we can see that Lord Arran's support of the Wolfenden Committee's proposals for decriminalising homosexual practices in private was rendered palatable to Parliament through the deployment of a punitive paradigm for the protection of 'the young' from homosexuality. This strategy was imitated in 1966 when Leo Abse (MP for Pontypool) took up Lord Arran's Private Member's Bill and introduced it in the House of Commons in the form of the Sexual Offences Bill (No. 2):

> In seeking leave to introduce a Bill of this kind it is important to emphasise that the recommendations made in the Wolfenden Report, as in my proposed Bill, would result in a penalty for a homosexual offence against any boy under the age of 16 which could be up to life imprisonment; that it would mean, under the Bill as under Wolfenden, that any indecent assault upon a boy could result in a period of ten years' imprisonment; and that any public act of indecency, as now, could result in two years' imprisonment and that, further, under the Bill and by way of the recommendations of Wolfenden, in the case of any act of gross indecency against a youth between the ages of 16 and 21 it would result in the present penalty of two years' imprisonment being increased to one of five years' imprisonment.
>
> (Abse, *Hansard*, Commons, 5 July 1966: col. 259)

The attempted implementation of the Wolfenden proposals in the form of Sexual Offences Bills by both Lord Arran in the Lords and by Leo Abse in the Commons can be described as being part of a bifurcated reform strategy. First, they advocated the protection of young men from homosexuality and homosexual practices; second, they supported Wolfenden's 'progressive' suggestions for the partial decriminalisation of homosexual acts in general.

Abse's Bill was eventually passed into law subject to amendments. These amendments and the debates which surrounded them were recorded in the 1967 House of Commons Official Report of the Standing Committee (F) of the Sexual Offences Bill (No. 2). This Standing Committee Report is of special significance as it was here that Leo Abse clarified both his and the Wolfenden Committee's specific focus on the protection of male adolescents, particularly between the ages of 16 to 21. Abse's reading of the Wolfenden Report reproduced the committee's concerns over the period of instability and vulnerability experienced by young males who found themselves away from the safety of 'the family' and 'the home' at the same time as they were in their late adolescent transitory 'sexual phase'. Abse urged the Standing Committee to accept 21 years as the age of lawful homosexual relations as recommended by the Wolfenden Committee. He contextualised the urgency of this particular recommendation in terms of Parliament avoiding the situation in which it was seen to be legally sanctioning the circumstances in which a transitory adolescent homosexual phase was allowed to become fixated (Abse, *Hansard*, Commons Standing Committee F, 19 April 1967: col. 31). Thus, by installing a legal deterrent, Abse hoped to save some immature (potential) heterosexuals from having a homosexual incident in their transitory adolescent phase that might become fixed in their sexual identity and become 'part of their lifestyle later' (col. 31). Here, yet again, heterosexuality, or, more specifically, 'normative (hetero) masculinity' (Collier 1998a: 44) was presented in parliamentary discourse as being both insecure and extremely vulnerable.

It was obvious in the report of the Standing Committee on the Sexual Offences Act in 1967, that the Wolfenden Committee's probation-treatment aims, especially those relating to adolescents, had been excluded from the Sexual Offences Bill which would eventually pass into law. The probation-treatment recommendations were replaced by the nebulous concepts and phrases emanating from the Wolfenden Report, such as 'protection' and 'special vulnerability', and homosexuals being 'set apart from the rest of society'. The wish to protect the especially vulnerable and ensure the development of heterosexuality in young men became, with the passing into law of the Sexual Offences Act of 1967, a matter of prosecution involving the deterrence of legal sanction.

Heteronormativity, permeability and vulnerability (back to the future)

The discursive shift that occurred between the publication of the Wolfenden Report in 1957 and the passing into law of the Sexual Offences Act of 1967 is fundamentally important. It is this discursive shift from probation-treatment to the punitive paradigm implemented in the Sexual Offences Act of 1967 that has characterised the parliamentary debates and reform strategies in relation to the homosexual age of consent since. The shift from the 'Wolfenden' rehabilitation-therapy discourse to the punitive paradigms introduced by parliamentarians who were interpreting the Wolfenden Report's recommendations between 1958 and 1965, and then in 1966–7, exposes the central irony captured in the analysis so far: that debates concerning the legal status of homosexualities turned into the public articulation of anxieties about the vulnerability of male heterosexualities. What this analysis exposes is that, although sexual categories, especially in the male adolescent, seem to be 'scientifically' unsustainable, they simultaneously appear to be, especially in males, socially critical.

This social and legal necessity of maintaining and nurturing adolescent male heterosexuality can be conceptualised in the following terms: 'heterosexuality secures its self-identity and shores up its ontological boundaries by protecting itself from what it sees as the continual predatory encroachment of its contaminated other, homosexuality' (Fuss 1991: 2). This necessity of attempting to protect 'the young' from 'homosexuality' by means of, for example, a higher age of consent for homosexual men, is a matter of 'hetero-sexuality' attempting to protect itself from its own indispensable interior exclusion: homosexuality. What has been exposed in this analysis so far is the particular 'anxious heteronormativity' that permeates the necessity of maintaining the unequal lawful age of homosexual activity between men relative to the heterosexual age of consent in the Wolfenden Report and in parliamentary debates. This variety of heteronormativity can be described as veering between two positions, that is, from the superiority and normativity of heterosexuality to the inherent 'provisionality' and vulnerability of heterosexuality. This can be described as a narrative of how the criminal law has been, and still is, employed in the protection primarily of the privileged status of heterosexuality, and not necessarily of protecting 'the young and vulnerable' whether heterosexual, bisexual or homosexual. The contradictory nature of the particular 'protection' afforded to young men by maintaining a higher age of homosexual consent has been the subject of a number of parlia-mentary debates and committees in recent decades. Most notably, the reduction of the age of consent for homosexual males was the subject of the Policy Advisory Committee on Sexual Offences on the Age of Consent (PACSO) report published in 1981. The findings of this report played a central role in the parliamentary debate over the Criminal Justice and Public Order Bill that became an Act of Parliament in 1994. The result of these debates was that the age of consent for homosexual men was reduced from 21 to 18, but not 16, which would have equalised the homosexual and heterosexual ages of consent.[13]

Fourteen years after the passing into law of the Sexual Offences Act of 1967, the Policy Advisory Committee on Sexual Offences (PACSO) 1981 published its *Report on the Age of Consent in Relation to Sexual Offences*.[14] In this report, the majority of members suggested that the minimum age for homo-sexual relations between males should be reduced from 21 to 18, with the minority of members favouring a further reduction to 16 (PACSO 1981: 1). The PACSO report can be described as being a legal artefact, alongside the Wolfenden Report, that became a site where the heteronormative function of law, in relation to young males and homosexual activities, became cryst-allised. The PACSO report can also be described as being the site where a politics of evidence, similar to the economy of legal exclusivity encountered in the case of Mr Vraciu in Chapter 2, was played out within a heteronorma-tive agenda.

The PACSO report used similar terminology to describe the role of law, and the necessity of fixing an age of consent for heterosexual relations, as it does for the minimum age for homosexual relations between men. Terms such as protection, maturity, deterrence, exposure to physical, emotional and social 'harm' (PACSO 1981: para 11, 7) were deployed in conjunction with both the homosexual and the heterosexual ages of lawful sexual relations. The committee even invoked the authoritative discourses of the British Medical Association (BMA), the Royal College of

Psychiatrists and six teaching associations as a means of supporting their recommendation that the age of (heterosexual) consent should remain fixed at 16. The committee concluded, in answer to arguments submitted to it, that the greater maturity of girls in the late twentieth century should be reflected in the lowering of the age of consent, which was set at 16 in 1885, to 14:

> Although there had been a gradual fall in the average age at which the menarche occurred in girls, a trend which has now stopped, there has been no significant increase in recent times in the level of psychological maturity in girls under sixteen.
>
> (PACSO 1981: para 17, 7)

The issue of maturity, this time in relation to males and the fixing of the minimum age of homosexual relations between males, will be returned to below. First I want to address the different terminologies used by the committee to denote the age of lawful heterosexual and homosexual relations. 'Age of consent' was not used by the committee to describe homosexual relations between males. The term 'age of consent', according to the committee, was to be used only to describe heterosexual sexual relations. The age at which lawful homosexual relations between men could occur was described by the term 'minimum age'. The reason the committee gave for the use of these two different terms was that the activities of under-age girls and under-age boys were subjected to differing degrees of criminal liability. It would be unlikely that the girl would be found to be criminally liable, but in the case of under-age males engaging in homosexual acts, both parties would be liable (PACSO 1981: para 27, 12). Moreover, the different use of the terms 'age of consent' and 'minimum age' were employed in order to produce the two different terms as reflecting the fact 'that homosexual and heterosexual acts do differ' (PACSO 1981: para 27, 12). Moran describes the committee's use of the term 'minimum age' in distinction to the term 'age of consent' as being heteronormatively organised. In other words, this distinction was a vehicle whereby the male genital body and its genital relations with other male bodies might be represented as a body that was not only different from, but also less privileged than, the genital body involved in cross-sex relations (Moran 1996a: 192). Thus, even the terms deployed by the PACSO report to name and denote the lawful age of homosexual relations between males was presented so as to reflect the organisation of the social, sexual and legal order.

The primary issue the PACSO report was set up to investigate was at what age, other than 21, should the minimum age of homosexual relations between men be fixed. The two ages that were proposed and adopted by the majority and minority factions of the committee were 18 and 16 respectively. The means whereby the PACSO report presented these two potential minimum ages was by way of distinguishing the variety and type of organisation or person that supported the different ages. The primary means of distinguishing the supporters of the majority and minority recommendations of 18 and 16 was by means of the 'respectability' and social standing of the supporters of that particular minimum age. The report demonstrated that the primary source of support for the minority recommendation of 16 came primarily from organisations representing homosexuals, whereas the majority recommendation was supported by a wide range of authoritative and respected organisations from the ranks of the legal and medical professions, the police and religious organisations. The committee presented these two groups thus:

> The comments which we received on the provisional conclusions in our working paper that the minimum age should be reduced to eighteen ... fell into two groups. The first consisted of various organisations representing homosexuals. Nearly all these favoured the reduction in the minimum age to sixteen. The second group of comments came from the legal and medical professions, the police, the churches, women's organisations, bodies concerned with probation and after-care and societies interested generally in legislation on sexual offences. A majority of these favoured a reduction in the age to eighteen, some having been converted from their original support for 21 after having read our working paper.
>
> (PACSO 1981: 12)

The outcome of the committee's assessment of all the submissions and comments they received from these organisations and groups was that the majority of the committee recommended that the minimum age of homosexual relations between men should be reduced to 18. This recommendation was made in the light of all the submissions and comments they received in response to their working papers. Of all the comments and submissions received by the PACSO committee, the evidence provided by the British Medical Association (BMA) was the most consulted and considered in the report. The BMA's statement to the committee described the physical development of males as being in general about two years behind that of females (PACSO 1981: para 42, 16). The committee actually used the BMA's opinion relating to the maturation of young males as a vehicle for defusing the assertion made to the committee by various homosexual groups that the issue of reducing the minimum age of homosexual relations for males was a matter of 'sexual equality'. The committee understood the term 'sexual equality' to mean 'the equal treatment of heterosexual and homosexual acts' (PACSO 1981: para 42, 16). In other words, according to organisations representing homosexuals, sexual equality would be achieved when the minimum age for homosexual relations between men was made equal to the heterosexual age of consent set at 16 for heterosexual relations. In answer to this, the committee deployed the BMA's opinion concerning the differential maturation rate of males relative to females as a means to render the equality argument irrelevant, biologically:

> It is reasonable ... to assume that emotional and psychological development do not significantly outstrip physical growth. They [the BMA] consider it incumbent on those who assert that boys and girls of the same age possess much the same degree of emotional and psychological maturity to adduce evidence in support of their claim. In their opinion satisfactory evidence has not been forthcoming.
>
> (PACSO 1981: para 42, 16)

It was the BMA's discourse concerning the difference in the rate of male and female maturation that defused the calls for sexual equality. However, it was clear that the BMA's evidence concerning maturation was organised so as to reflect the dominant social and sexual order. This perspective was also evident in the committee's concern that young men under the age of 18 who participated in homosexual activities would not be sufficiently mature to cope with the consequences of their actions (PACSO 1981: para 42, 16). This discourse of male immaturity was deployed to justify the prohibition of sexual activities involving young men and other men and not the sexual activities of young men with females.

> This last line of argument could suggest that boys under eighteen should be protected from heterosexual intercourse as well as homosexual relations. However, we feel that it is far easier for them to cope with the usual complexities of youthful heterosexual relationships, which are accepted by parents, friends and society, than the greater complexity of homosexual relationships with all the difficulties and pressures involved.
>
> (PACSO 1981: para 43, 17)

The rationale behind the committee's recommendation that the minimum age of lawful homosexual relations between men should be fixed at 18 and not 16 was that the higher age would promote the 'proper expression of human sexuality'. This was to be found in 'heterosexual relationships' (PACSO 1981: para 38, 15). As in the Wolfenden Committee, one of the central themes and objectives found in the PACSO report's recommendations was the role law should play in the diversion of young males from 'the homosexual path'. This entailed, in both the PACSO and Wolfenden reports the politicisation of the age of male maturation, which was translated into law as the minimum age at which a young male was deemed to be irretrievably set on the path to 'normal' and 'natural' heterosexuality. As a result of this conceptualisation, adolescent homosexuals were, therefore, in both the Wolfenden and the PACSO reports, unacknowledged, or only acknowledged in terms of their re-orientatability to heterosexuality.

The PACSO report's recommendation that the minimum age of

homosexual relations between men should be reduced from 21 to 18 was in recognition of the Wolfenden Committee's reliance on the then current legal age of contractual responsibility. However, since the passing of the Sexual Offences Act of 1967 which implemented the Wolfenden age of adulthood at 21, there had been a reduction of the legal age of contractual responsibility from 21 to 18. In 1967 it was recommended in the Latey Report that the legal age of contractual responsibility, for certain purposes, including the capacity to marry without parental consent and to enter into contractual relations, should be reduced from 21 to 18 (PACSO 1981: para 36, 14). This recommendation was passed into law as the Family Law Reform Act of 1969. Subsequently the voting age was also reduced to 18 by the Representation of the People Act 1969, and the minimum age of jury service was also reduced to 18 by the Criminal Justice Act 1972 (PACSO 1981: para 36, 14). The PACSO report concluded that the legal age of contractual responsibility should also become the minimum age at which a young man should no longer need the 'protection' of law from pressures of homosexual 'attentions'. The age of 18 was when he 'should be expected to stand on his own two feet' (PACSO 1981: para 36, 15).

In 1994, thirteen years after the publication of the PACSO report, a clause which would amend the age of lawful relations between men was tabled in the Criminal Justice and Public Order Bill by Mrs Currie (MP for Derbyshire South). Mrs Currie referred to the tabling of this debate as 'historic', as it was the first time in over a quarter of a century that the age of consent for homosexuals[15] had been discussed by the House of Commons (Mrs Currie, *Hansard*, Commons, 21 February 1994: cols 74–5). This debate over the lawful age of homosexual relations between men followed a very similar pattern to that between the majority and minority members in the PACSO report along the lines of support for the reduction of this age to either 16 or 18. However, the difference between the Criminal Justice and Public Order debate in the Commons and the PACSO report was that the supporters of 16 became, in 1994, the 'faction' that was supported by many authoritative and respected organisations, including the BMA. What is more, the BMA, in a report published in 1994, revised their opinion relating to male immaturity that was so crucial to the PACSO recommendations, especially to the PACSO report's use of male immaturity as making calls for equality irrelevant. Therefore, the analysis here of the Criminal Justice and Public Order parliamentary debates of 1994 will focus on these shifts in discourse especially related to maturation and equality. However, I shall also demonstrate that the need to protect and secure heterosexual masculinity was reiterated by the then Home Secretary, Mr Howard, in his evocation of the majority recommendation in the PACSO report.

The revision of the BMA's opinion in 1994 was summarised by Edwina Currie in her speech to the House of Commons. According to Currie, the BMA report stated that 'there is no convincing medical reason against reducing the age of consent for male homosexuals to sixteen years, and to do so may yield positive health benefits' (BMA, cited by Mrs Currie, *Hansard*, Commons, 21 February 1994: col. 78). As a result of this shift in medical opinion, 'sexual equality' was re-introduced into parliamentary discourse as a relevant issue. According to Mr Kinnock, this shift was also evident in the Royal College of Psychiatrists in its statement that: 'there was no developmental reason to treat young men and young women differently' (Mr Kinnock, *Hansard*, Commons, 21 February 1994: col. 82). These authoritative and respected organisations and the reliable and responsible evidence they produced on the issue, according to Mr Kinnock, persuaded him

> that it would be wrong to continue to discriminate in the law between men who are homosexual and those who are heterosexual. It would also be wrong to continue to discriminate in the law between young men who are homosexual and young women who are heterosexual.
>
> (Kinnock, *Hansard*, Commons, 21 January 1994: 82)

During this parliamentary debate, it became clear that concerns about sexual health were to play a major role in the shift in the opinions and positions of authoritative bodies on the matter of the age at which lawful homosexual relations between men should be set. The higher age of lawful relations between men, fixed at 21 in 1967, and the recommended reduction of the age to 18 by the PACSO report did not take account of the emergence of HIV and AIDS and the issues of 'protection' these would introduce. The shift in medical opinion was particularly influenced by concerns about criminalisation having an adverse effect upon the distribution of information regarding 'safer sex' practices to young men under the age of homosexual consent. Mrs Currie captured the ambivalence over criminalisation as fostering both protection and non-protection, thus

> How can we advise young gay men about the dangers of AIDS, how can we talk to them straight about safer sex, when what they are doing is supposed to be strictly against the law?
>
> (Mrs Currie, *Hansard*, Commons, 21 February 1994: col. 78)

Mrs Currie also quoted such authoritative bodies as the World Health Organisation and *The Lancet*[16] in support of her argument that there had emerged with HIV and AIDS a social problem unanticipated by the Wolfenden–PACSO discourse of protection. The setting of the age of lawful homosexual relations between men, in the context of the mid-1990s, was implicated in the non-protection of young men (from sexual health risks). Mrs Currie and Mr Kinnock joined forces across the House on the issue of the detrimental effects caused by the Wolfenden and PACSO brand of protection through criminalisation. According to Mrs Currie:

we are all genuinely worried about protecting vulnerable youngsters. It is a concern shared by all Hon. Members. But a law that keeps people silent and means that they are unable to lodge a complaint is not a protective shield. It is an enforcer of their silence. It is a gag, and it is likely to leave them that much more open to abuse.

(Mrs Currie, *Hansard*, Commons, 21 February 1994: col. 78)

Obviously this gagging and exclusion was compounded by the introduction of section 28 of the Local Government Act of 1988.[17] Although not directly related to the central focus of this chapter (age, consent and decriminalisation), section 28 can be contextualised within the Wolfenden–PACSO discursive formation related to the 'protection' of young people from homosexuality. Section 28 was premised on similar assumptions as those of the Wolfenden–PACSO tradition: that human sexuality was malleable and vulnerable, especially in adolescence, and that the law must play a role in preventing young people, especially males, from being diverted from, or deprived of, a heterosexual orientation, identity and lifestyle by the promotion of, or corruption into, homosexual activities. Section 28, therefore, alongside the criminalisation–protection ethos of the Sexual Offences Act of 1967, can be seen as an apparatus that assumes that all young people can be protected from being recruited into a lifestyle of homosexuality by legal deterrence. The introduction of section 28 can be described in terms of a politics of 'the family' (Rutherford 1990: 12) which was being fought over by the central Conservative government and Labour local authorities.[18] The New Right was attempting to guard 'the family' from 'homosexuality' by preventing the 'leftist' dissemination agencies from alerting 'the young' to alternative, non-heterosexual, sexual paths and lifestyles. According to Rutherford, the New Right mobilised 'the family' and 'the nation' as central themes of its hegemonic identity (1990: 12). Rutherford contextualised this thesis with Mrs Thatcher's (now Baroness Thatcher) views on 'the family': 'the family and its maintenance, really is the most important thing not only in your personal life but in the life of any community, because this is the unit on which the whole nation is built' (Mrs Thatcher, in Rutherford 1990: 12).[19]

Section 28 has been described as a piece of legislation that attempted to regain some control over what 1960s liberalisation had produced (Smith 1994). Through it, the New Right attempted to gain some control over the 'phenomenon' of post-1967 (Sexual Offences Act) homosexuals, who were not conducting themselves quite as discreetly and privately as expected by the Wolfenden Committee. The drafting of section 28 as a particular piece of legislation can be described as an example of the materialisation of the fear of 'homosexual spread'. This 'fear' coincided with Thatcherism's promise of 'strong defences and well-policed frontiers against the progressive threat and displacements of difference' (Rutherford 1990: 11). Section 28 has been described as having an overall 'chilling effect' and as constituting a 'perceived constraint' on local authority policy-making (Cooper and Herman 1991: 73).

The prohibitions within section 28 and the discourses of age, homosexuality and criminalisation within the Wolfenden–PACSO formation all deny the arguments that Mrs Currie and Mr Kinnock presented to the House of Commons in the parliamentary debates during the Criminal Justice and Public Order Bill of 1994: that there are adolescent homosexual males who were being harmed by legislation that had been implemented under misguided conceptions of 'protection'.

It was the then Home Secretary Mr Howard who invoked the discourses of adolescent male vulnerability and the role law should play in securing the heterosexualisation of these young men, in the Wolfenden–PACSO tradition, in his speech to the Commons during the debates on the Criminal Justice and Public Order Bill of 1994. In this speech, Howard isolated what was in his opinion the key issue in relation to fixing the age of lawful homosexual relations between men: that this age should be fixed at a time when these young men are 'mature enough to take a decision on these matters for themselves' (Howard, *Hansard*, Commons, 21 February 1994: col. 93).

Howard invoked the Wolfenden and PACSO reports' concerns that the participation in homosexual activities would have grave consequences for a young man, in the form of setting him apart from the rest of society: 'I believe that those arguments still hold good. It is still true that in following a homosexual way of life a young man sets himself apart from the majority' (Howard, *Hansard*, Commons, 21 February 1994: col. 93). The assumption behind this statement was justified and expanded through the vehicle of 'parental expectations' by Howard:

> The PACSO Committee concluded that the majority of parents would surely wish their children to grow up with the desire and possibility of marriage and children. It is a fact that the way of life we are currently discussing involves an abandonment of those possibilities which sets those people who choose it apart and which requires the criminal law to give all the protection that it can to the young and vulnerable before they are confirmed in that orientation and before they take that decision.
>
> (Howard, *Hansard*, Commons, 21 February 1994: col. 97)

The then Home Secretary thus maintained that the role of the criminal law with regard to male sexuality should safeguard the parental expectation that the nation's children should not be deprived of, nor abandon the possibility of, heterosexuality. Heterosexuality was expressed here, as in the PACSO report, as the 'nation's official sexuality' (Berlant 1997: 19). Homosexuality in 'the nation's sons' was presented from the perspective of the 'heterofamilial norm' as a potential crisis which must be prevented from 'harming' the 'national future' (Berlant 1997: 18). In Howard's speeches to the Commons, discourses of 'the family', 'the nation' and parental expectations intersect with discourses of vulnerability and protection as was expressed in the armed forces' *in loco parentis* argument for the exclusion of homosexuals from armed service in Chapter 1. However, the legal strategy evident in Howard's production of the function of the law in this issue, was not primarily concerned with keeping homosexuals 'out' as in the armed forces exclusion policy. Howard was attempting, through the vehicle of the criminal law, to inhibit or deter a 'confirmed' homosexual orientation and identity from emerging 'within' the nation's young men in the first place.

This use of the criminal law, advocated by Mr Howard, can be described as being an attempt to regulate and deter the emergence of homosexuality as an interior possibility in that mutable and transitional sexual group, the nation's teenage sons. Protection, in Howard's description of the function of the criminal law, can be described as an attempt to inhibit by criminalisation, homosexual interiority (Fuss 1991: 3). The 'threat' here comes less from the 'continual predatory encroachment' (Fuss 1991: 2) of homosexuality from a position outside adolescence. The perceived threat here is associated with the emergence of homosexuality in the sexual transitionality and experimentation of male adolescence. This has obvious parallels with the concerns voiced by Mrs Mann and Mr Renton in the House of Commons in 1958 regarding the fear of homosexual spread. The conceptualisation of the mutability and non-absoluteness of heterosexualities and homosexualities, especially in male adolescents, was presented by Howard in 1994 in terms of a 'threat to the nation and its values' (Stychin 1998: 1). The maturation of male adolescents into active and assertive heterosexual 'sexual beings' within the context of the familial possibilities of heterosexual relations, was, in Mr Howard's speech to the Commons, an outcome that must be supported by the deterrence of criminalisation.

Howard actually side-stepped the issue of male and female maturation rates, so central to the PACSO report, in the light of the shift in medical opinion on the matter. The key question, according to Mr Howard, which the Wolfenden Report and the Majority of the PACSO report made regarding the appropriateness of a different age of consent for heterosexual girls and homosexual boys, was one of consequence: it is 'not simply that one matures later than the other, but because of the consequences of homosexual activities'. According to Howard, this was the point at issue (Howard, *Hansard*, Commons, 21 February 1994: 95). In Howard's formulation, the function of the criminal law in relation to age and homosexuality was to ensure that as many young men as possible reached the 'normalcy', 'naturalness' and fulfilment of a heterosexual lifestyle. As a result, Mr Howard recommended that the age of 18 should be the minimum age of lawful homosexual relations between men.

Howard described this recommendation in terms of a technology of temporality, a technology of giving 'extra time' to ensure heterosexuality, which would allow adolescent sexual transitionality to 'settle down' (cols

93–4). Homosexuality, and the two major social consequences of its emergence – setting the young man apart from society and putting his parents' expectations of him getting married and having children at risk – necessitated, according to Mr Howard, the 'legitimate and important function of the criminal law to protect the young and the vulnerable before that orientation is fixed and determined' (col. 97).

The 'extra time' afforded to young males between 16 and 18, by setting the age of lawful homosexual relations between males at 18, was, according to Howard, the means whereby the criminal law could 'assist … young men' (Mr Howard, *Hansard*, Commons, 21 February 1994: col. 93).

On 21 February 1994 a Commons majority voted that the age at which lawful homosexual relations should be set was 18. This became law with the passing of the Criminal Justice and Public Order Act of 1994.

The reduction of the age of homosexual consent from 18 to 16 has been at the centre of an on-going dispute between the two British Houses of Parliament (the House of Lords and the House of Commons) in the late 1990s. On both the 1998 Crime and Disorder Bill and the 1999 Sexual Offences [Amendment] Bill, a majority in the House of Lords voted to maintain the age of homosexual consent at 18 against the Commons majority which voted to equalise the homosexual and heterosexual ages of consent. These highly publicised and far-reaching parliamentary clashes have extended into the parliamentary clashes between the Lords and the Commons over repealing section 28 of the Local Government Act of 1988 in the readings of the Local Government Bill in both Houses of Parliament in 1999 and 2000.

However, before turning to these high-profile clashes between the English Houses of Parliament, a key moment in this narrative of legislative reform, that occurred in 1997 before the European Commission, will be analysed.

The politics of 16 (1994–8)

The setting of the lawful age of homosexual relations between men at 18 by the Criminal Justice and Public Order Act of 1994 was the subject of a complaint made to the European Commission in 1997. It was a young homosexual male, Euan Sutherland, who brought this complaint before the Commission. The Sutherland case is of strategic importance as the European Commission emphasised what was at stake, politically and legally, in the idea that criminalisation, in the case of the higher homosexual age of consent, could be justified as 'protection'.

The basis of Sutherland's complaint was that the unequal age of lawful homosexual relations between men was discriminatory as it affected Mr Sutherland's enjoyment of his human rights (Article 14)[20] and it was an infringement of his right to respect for a private life (Article 8).[21] Sutherland's complaint was determined as being admissible by the European

Commission in the following terms: 'the very existence of the legislation directly affected his private life: either he respected the law and refrained from engaging in prohibited sexual acts ... or he committed such acts and thereby became liable to criminal prosecution' (*Sutherland* v. *UK* 1997: col. 36).

In the Sutherland case 'the adolescent' and 'the homosexual' were presented as coexistent in one body, and this homosexuality was accepted by the European Commission (majority) as being not of a 'transitory' nature. This acceptance was presented in the form of Sutherland's assertion that he was a homosexual, and in the UK's[22] acceptance (or non-challenge) of this assertion: 'the applicant asserts, and his assertion was undisputed by the government, that he was a homosexual, who had had sexual relations with other males since he attained the age of 16' (*Sutherland* v. *UK* 1997: col. 34).

In order to investigate Sutherland's complaint, the European Commission assessed the House of Commons debates, especially the majority decision in which the homosexual age of consent was reduced from 21 to 18 by the Criminal Justice and Public Order Bill of 1994. Central to the European Commission's investigation of the necessity of maintaining a higher age of consent for homosexuals was Michael Howard's heteronormative reiteration of both the Wolfenden and PACSO concerns about the vulnerability of adolescent male sexualities, and especially his statement (paraphrased from the Wolfenden Report) about the 'grave consequences' of young men participating in homosexual practices and thus finding themselves set apart from the rest of society. However, on this issue, and in direct response to Mr Howard's speech in the House of Commons in 1994, the European Commission ruled that:

> The Commission is unable to accept that it is a proportionate response to the need for protection to expose to criminal sanctions not only the older man who engages in homosexual acts with a person under the age of 18 but the young man himself who is claimed to be in need of such protection. ... As to the second ground relied on – society's claimed entitlement to indicate disapproval of homosexual conduct and its preference for a heterosexual lifestyle – the Commission cannot accept that this could in any event constitute an objective or reasonable justification for inequality of treatment under the criminal law.
>
> (*Sutherland* v. *UK* 1997: col. 65)

Michael Howard's suggested strategy of giving young men the extra time to become heterosexual was dismissed by the European Commission as not being an objective and reasonable justification for the extra two years homosexual males had to wait before their sexual relationships and activities could be lawful. In the Sutherland case, the discursive mechanisms whereby homosexuality and age were comprehensible and put into legal discourse, based on the protection of young men from the danger posed by proselytising homosexual adults, and the 'protection-criminalisation' of young men from their own 'potential' homosexuality, were disrupted. The European Commission concluded in favour of Sutherland by 14 votes to 4 that there had been a violation of Article 8 of the Convention, taken in conjunction with Article 14 (*Sutherland* v. *UK* 1997: col. 66). This decision was reached by the Commission as a result of exposing the illegitimate heteronormative notions of 'protection' behind the unequal homosexual age of consent.

What is of major importance in the Sutherland case is that those who had been subjugated and systematically excluded from the juridical and parliamentary discourses of transitory and correctable sexualities, that is, homosexual adolescents, were made present. The de-subjugation of this 'present absence' in the form of a homosexual male youth bringing his own case to Europe exposed the anomaly at the heart of the intention of 'protecting' young men by fixing the age of homosexual consent higher than the heterosexual age of consent. The anomaly was that this was a circumscribed and illegitimate form of protection in which only one sector of the population, namely heterosexual or potential heterosexual young men, were allegedly being protected, while another sector of the population, namely homosexual or potentially homosexual young men of 16 and 17 were being criminalised.

Thus, the ambiguity of such an abstract concept of 'protection' regarding male adolescents was exposed as protecting no one; its function was a discriminatory and illegitimate one that was, according to the European Commission in the Sutherland case, without objective and reasonable justification. All that remained at this stage of the reform process was a superseded discourse that had been hegemonic for forty years.

Parliamentary clashes (1998–2000)

In response to the ruling from the European Commission in the Sutherland case there have been subsequent attempts to reduce the age of consent for homosexual men in England in 1998, 1999 and 2000 in the House of Commons. On two occasions, in the Crime and Disorder Bill (1998) and in the Sexual Offences [Amendment] Bills in 1999 and 2000 the Commons voted by a majority to reduce the age of homosexual consent from 18 to 16. On both these occasions this reform has been blocked in the House of Lords on the grounds of constitutional issues and principled objections. In terms of the constitutional objections the Lords focused primarily on the matter of the adequacy of the protection for young people in the new legislation. The House of Lords majority concluded that the reduction of the age of consent for homosexuals would leave many vulnerable young men unprotected by the criminal law. The Lords also emphasised that the specific guidelines that were to accompany the reduction of the age of homosexual consent to 16, that the government was proposing for the protection of vulnerable young people, for example, those in care, had been subjected to inadequate parliamentary scrutiny. The principled objections from the Lords demonstrated an overt heteronormative perspective. In the next section the House of Commons debates and the House of Lords debates will be analysed separately.

The House of Commons

On 22 June 1998, an amendment in the Crime and Disorder Bill recommending the reduction of the lawful age of homosexual relations between males from 18 to 16 was introduced to the House of Commons by Mrs Keen (MP for Brentford and Isleworth). The result of this debate was that the House of Commons voted by a majority of 207 (a three to one majority) to reduce the lawful age of homosexual relations between men to 16, thus equalising it with the heterosexual age of consent. The debate in the Commons consisted of speeches calling for equality, citizenship, social inclusion and blatant displays of anti-homosexual prejudice, including the assumption that heterosexual acts are biologically 'normal' and 'natural' and that homosexual activities are synonymous with the spread of disease (from Mr Winterton, the MP for Macclesfield).

Ann Keen opened her speech to the Commons with a call to end discrimination in the name of equality:

> The purpose of the new clause is to make everyone equal under the law ... we must take a positive step forward in creating a culture in which all citizens are given the opportunity to live their lives openly and freely, confident that they will not be discriminated against.
>
> (Keen, *Hansard*, Commons, 22 June 1998: col. 758, 761)

Keen's speech in the Commons reflected the terminology, introduced by Tony Blair three years earlier during the Criminal Justice and Public Order Bill parliamentary debates in 1994:

> Let us be clear about the issue before us tonight. It is not at what age we wish young people to have sex. It is whether the criminal law should discriminate between heterosexual and homosexual acts. It is therefore an issue not of age, but of equality ... it is simply a question whether there are grounds for discrimination.
>
> (Blair, *Hansard*, Commons, 21 February 1994: col. 98)

Blair continued:

> The most basic civilised value is the notion of respect for other people. That is what creates and sustains any decent society. ... A society that has learned, over time, racial and sexual equality, can surely come to terms with equality of sexuality. That is the moral case for change

tonight. It is our chance to welcome people ... into full membership of our society, on equal terms. It is our chance to do good, and we should take it.

(Blair, *Hansard*, Commons, 21 February 1994: cols 100–1)

Keen and Blair produced society, public opinion and law as a social practice in these speeches to the Commons within a civil rights model of ever-increasing inclusion and democratisation. In these speeches, Blair and Keen were attempting to replace the discursive vocabulary of the Wolfenden–PACSO tradition from the heteronormativity of protection to that of a plural Britain, a new Britain, open to, and appreciative of difference, even homosexuality. One could describe the speeches made by Kinnock, Currie and Blair during the debates on the Criminal Justice and Public Order Bill of 1994 and Ann Keen's speech during those on the Crime and Disorder Bill of 1998 as attempting to initiate a specific parliamentary project – a project whereby the hegemonic discourse of the Wolfenden–PACSO tradition was to be made to look 'unfamiliar and uninevitable' (Berlant 1997: 14). Law, the way it had functioned and was functioning, was exposed by Blair and Keen as being illegitimate, as producing an exclusive and excluding representation of 'the nation' and national membership. The Blair–Keen New Labour strategy can be described as an attempt to disrupt this production of the closed and monosexual nation as perpetuated by the criminal law. This was to be done by initiating a strategy for re-imagining 'the nation', and by shifting the criminal law's role away from supporting, producing and promoting only heterosexual relations as the nation's official sexuality. This was to be achieved by attempting to initiate a parliamentary amnesia, whereby the hegemony of the discourses of age and protection, maturation and vulnerability found in the Wolfenden–PACSO discursive formation were to be forgotten and suspended. By so doing, a new discursive formation of human rights, equality, non-discrimination and social inclusion could be substituted, and thus become the new hegemony that would be translated into a re-invigorated criminal law under the Labour government.[23] However, this paradigm shift was to prove a complicated undertaking.

The main source of contention that arose in the 1998 parliamentary debates in the Commons came in the form of Mr Ashton's (MP for Bassetlaw) suggested amendment to the clause tabled by Ann Keen. This amendment proposed that the new clause to reduce the lawful age of homosexual relations to 16 years should be qualified with the following: 'except when one party is in a position of authority, influence or trust in relation to the other, in which case both parties must have attained the age of eighteen' (*Hansard*, Commons, 22 June 1998: col. 754). The Ashton amendment exposed a fundamental contradiction in the Labour government's attempt to remove the age of lawful homosexual relations from the discursive formation of vulnerability and protection. This contradiction came in the attempt by the Labour Party under Blair to try and separate issues of protection from issues of equality, whilst at the same time attempting to legislate both separately. The Labour government had tabled the reduction of the age of lawful homosexual relations between men to 16 while also initiating a working party to investigate an allied concern regarding the protection of young men and women in institutional care from sexual abuse. The working party's recommendations concerning the latter were to be published at the end of 1998.

The contradictory nature of these two undertakings was seized upon in the Commons. It was widely remarked that reducing the age of homosexual consent before the working party had published their final recommendations concerning the protection of young people in institutional care would be irresponsible (*Hansard*, Commons, 22 June 1998: col. 787). The government's response to this suggestion was to stipulate that the new clause to reduce the age of lawful homosexual relations between men to 16 was a separate issue to concerns about the abuse of trust and authority (Mr Michael: col. 778). Furthermore, Mr Ashton's amendment was described as being problematic and simplistic and the potential source of legal anomalies.

The House of Commons voted by a very slender majority to exclude Mr Ashton's amendment from the new clause to reduce the age of lawful homosexual relations from 18 to 16. The slenderness of this majority was significant in terms of demonstrating the persistence of concerns and discourses related to the protective function of law. One can say that the intended shift from legal discourses of age, vulnerability and protection to legal discourses of age as representing equality, anti-discrimination and social inclusion was considerably weakened by the Labour government's failure to separate these two discursive traditions convincingly. Mr Michael's recommendation to the Commons was that they should not vote to include Mr Ashton's 'problematic' amendment, and that the members of the House should vote to include the new clause in the Bill. Attempting to relegate the issues of protection to the political periphery and the 'Conservative' past, yet at the same time recognising the necessity of protecting vulnerable young people, resulted in the Labour government being exposed to criticism in the House of Lords.

The House of Lords

Whereas the House of Commons voted with a majority to equalise the homosexual and heterosexual ages of consent, a month later, on 22 July 1998, the House of Lords voted to keep the lawful age of homosexual relations at 18. This constitutional struggle between the House of Commons and the House of Lords can be described as a dispute over the role of the criminal law in relation to the homosexuality of young men of 16 and 17 years of age. The clash between the House of Commons and the House of

Lords can also be described as a parliamentary clash of discourses, particularly concerning the role of the criminal law in the legislation of heterosexuality as the official sexuality of the nation. The Commons majority was a vote for age as a representation of equality (along with an assurance that 'practical' legislation would follow which would protect young people of both sexes who were vulnerable to abuse). On the other hand, the Lords majority was a vote for age, especially in relation to young men between 16 and 17, as representing the necessity of protection, to facilitate successful establishment of a heterosexual orientation.

The Lords' 'revolt' against the reduction of the homosexual age of consent was led by Baroness Young, the 73-year-old former Tory leader of the House of Lords. Baroness Young's rejection of the Commons vote to reduce the lawful age of homosexual relations between men involved two main issues: a constitutional one and a principled objection. The former consisted of Baroness Young's disapproval of the rushed way the amendment for lowering the age of homosexual relations between men was ushered into the Crime and Disorder Bill (not until its second reading in the Commons), and the contentiousness of the issue. It was the narrowness of the defeat of Mr Ashton's amendment in the Commons (by a small majority of forty votes) that concerned Baroness Young. The narrowness of this margin was significant as it demonstrated that many of the MPs who voted to lower the age of homosexual consent to 16 'were concerned as to the consequences for vulnerable boys and girls being looked after away from home' (Baroness Young, *Hansard*, Lords, 22 July 1998: col. 937). Baroness Young also seized on the disjunction between the acceptance of the amendment in the Commons before the interdepartmental working group had published their findings concerning safeguards and measures to protect 16- and 17-year-olds, who might be vulnerable in particular contexts:

> What I find extraordinary is that the government has accepted an amendment, passed by the House of Commons, to lower the age of consent to 16 and have at the same time immediately recognised that it is seriously flawed and that it is necessary to set up a working party to deal with those young people most at risk. I ask myself, as a simple person: how can they allow this provision to go forward onto the statute books in this unsatisfactory state?
>
> (Baroness Young, *Hansard*, Lords, 22 July 1998: col. 937)

This would create, according to Baroness Young, a two-year gap for the abuse of 16- and 17-year-olds due to the slow process of parliamentary consideration and time-tabling. Baroness Young's constitutional appeal to the Lords thus emphasised the potential risk and non-protection of many young people due to the Commons' desire to rush through the clause to lower the age of lawful homosexual relations between men before Parliament had fully considered all the issues.

The second component of Baroness Young's call for the Lords to vote against the inclusion of the homosexual age of consent clause in the Crime and Disorder Bill was the principle of the matter. It is here, as with the speeches of other key speakers in the House of Lords on this matter, that the intended use of the criminal law to promote heterosexuality as the official sexuality of the nation is made explicit. Baroness Young's initiation of the Lords' rebellion against the reduction of the homosexual age of consent was presented in terms of a concern about the message such legislative reform would send to young people. Her worry was that, by reducing the homosexual age of consent, Parliament would be encouraging homosexuality in the young – that Parliament would be declaring to young people 'that it is just as good to have a homosexual relationship as it is to have a heterosexual one and, moreover, to have one at the age of 16' (Lords, *Hansard*, 22 July 1998: col. 972). Baroness Young added to her principled objection concerning the parliamentary promotion of homosexuality, the Labour government's plans to repeal section 28 of the Local Government Act of 1988:

> I speak as a mother and a grandmother, we are family people.[24] Parents mind very much indeed the prospect of their children being taught about homosexuality. They do not think that it is something which should be taught in schools. If we really have regard for public opinion, that is something we must take into account.
>
> (col. 939)

Baroness Young's view of equality also privileged heterosexuality over homosexuality:

> It is said that this whole issue is one of equality. I do not myself believe that there is a moral equivalence between heterosexual and homosexual relationships. ... I believe that it is a very doubtful argument to bring equality into this issue at all. In many respects it simply does not apply, we are not talking about equal things.
>
> (col. 939)

Along similar lines, George Carey (the Archbishop of Canterbury) writing in *The Times* on the day of the Lords' rejection of the homosexual age clause, framed the necessity of blocking this clause in terms of what he described as 'just discrimination', in the name of 'social protection'. According to Carey, the House of Commons ought to have focused less on questions of human rights, equality, establishing legal uniformity and avoiding an adverse finding by the European Court. Instead, according to Carey, the House of Commons should have looked at this issue 'in the context of an overall vision of what we want a morally healthy society to look like' (Carey, *The Times*, 22 July 1998: 18). Carey can be described as attempting to unsettle the re-framed discourse of age and homosexuality from equality and legislative reform to a question of using the criminal law as a vehicle for repressing homosexuality in society. For the Lords, as for the Archbishop of Canterbury, this was not an issue of human rights or equality. It was an issue of promoting heterosexuality, preferably within the confines of marriage, as the only acceptable context for sexual practices. In order to achieve this conceptualisation, particular members of the House of Lords presented homosexuality as a dangerous, unnatural and morally unhealthy sexual practice – one that it would be morally irresponsible for Parliament to endorse, especially for 16- to 17-year-old 'children' in their formative years. Within this discursive formation 'the child' is constituted from a perspective which is compatible with a 'particular vision of social life and continuous with speculations concerning the future' (Jenks 1996: 2). The conceptualisation of adolescence and childhood in the Wolfenden–PACSO discursive tradition, and in the majority of the speeches in the House of Lords during the debates on the Crime and Disorder Bill of 1998, produces the child-adolescent in terms of both societal and personal risk and danger. According to Jenks, ' "the child" has become a way of speaking about sociality itself. Any assault on what the child is, or rather, what the child will evolve into, threatens to rock the social base' (Jenks 1996: 130).[25]

Baroness Young also described the reduction of the homosexual age of consent as 'the thin edge of the wedge' (Lords, *Hansard*, 22 July 1998: col. 939) – as a potential legitimisation issue and springboard for the creeping inclusion of 'the homosexual other' into the very identity of 'the family people' she purported to represent. Baroness Young's fear was that this legislative reform would not only 'promote' homosexuality in 'the young and vulnerable' but it would also facilitate the creeping inclusion of homosexuality into the core institutions of marriage, family life and public life. The lowering of the age of lawful homosexual relations between men would thus 'lead to a demand for gay and lesbian marriages and for such couples to adopt children' (col. 939). According to Baroness Young, the higher age of lawful homosexual relations between men was one of the last bastions of 'rightness' wherein the superiority of heterosexuality was secured from homosexual infiltration, especially in the realm of 'the family'. The 'family fundamentalism' demonstrated by Baroness Young can be described as a succouring of the heterofamilial 'tradition' by attempting to preserve 'a continuity with the past which would otherwise be lost and doing so as a way of achieving a continuity with the future as well' (Giddens 1994: 48). Giddens defines fundamentalism as nothing other than tradition defended in the traditional way, but where the mode of defence has become widely called into question (1994: 6). Baroness Young did not justify her 'principled' objection in the Lords, but merely asserted her support of heterofamilial traditions. According to Giddens, 'the point about traditions is that you don't really have to justify them: they contain their own truth, a ritual truth, asserted as correct by the believer' (1994: 6). What Baroness

Young refuses to engage with in her monologic belief that she is correct is that 'the family as we have come to know it in ideology and practice is no longer what it was' (Weeks 1999a: 41).[26]

One could say that the danger posed by the homosexuality of male adolescents in this particular legal narrative was articulated in terms of the contingency and vulnerability of 'the normal' as well as in terms of this dangerous other's proximity to hetero-masculinity, 'the home' and 'the family'. In fact 'the family', 'the home' and the associated parental expectations and disappointments which were deployed in the period between the 1950s and the late 1990s are examples of what was, and is, at stake in both the decriminalising of homosexuality and the lowering of the lawful age of homosexual relations between men. This particular identity movement exposes a politics of identity in the form of 'British identity', and heterosexualised 'family identity', which is based on the negative identifications of a group that knows who it is only by what it knows it is not (Cohen 1994: 1).

Rutherford describes this negative process of identification in terms of how 'the centre invests the other with its terrors. It is the threat of the dissolution of the self that ignites and secures its boundaries, that constructs self from non-self' (Rutherford 1990: 11). However, this theory of identification must be contextualised in 'the social', in this case of indiscreet, hybridised constitutive outsiders and insider-outsiders, that is, homosexual organic strangers. In other words, in this legal narrative the heteronormative national and social identity is constructed and shaped by its interaction with that part of its own possibility, its own vulnerability, in the form of an ineradicable 'inner enemy' (Simmel 1950). This politics of identification which primarily focuses on the sexualities of adolescent males is less concerned with *anthropemy*,[27] the ejecting or abjecting of dangerous individuals from the social body, than with preventing the 'dangerous individual' from emerging within itself, its institutions and within the individuals which populate and propagate them.

The deployment of concepts such as 'the home', 'the family' and 'parental expectations' within these debates is reminiscent of Freud's conceptualisation of the 'homely', 'the native' and 'the familiar' in his essay 'The Uncanny'. The uncanny is an inexact English translation of the German word *unheimlich*, meaning 'unhomely', 'unfamiliar', 'that which excites fear' (Freud 1964: 219). I am particularly interested in what Freud had to say about the other term, supposedly the opposite of *unheimlich*, that is, *heimlich*, which can mean 'belonging to the house or the family, not strange, familiar, tame, intimate, friendly' (Freud 1964: 222). However, this same word, *heimlich*, according to Freud, can also mean 'concealed, kept from sight, so that others do not get to know of, or about it, withheld from others ... to do something behind someone's back; to steal away' (1964: 223). Freud demonstrated how this polysemic term *heimlich* was not unambiguous 'but belonged to two sets of ideas that, without being contradictory, were yet very different' (1964: 224–5). So, on the one hand *heimlich* meant 'what was familiar and agreeable, and on the other it meant what was concealed and kept out of sight' (Freud 1964: 224–5).

The mechanisms of 'the home', 'the family' and 'parental expectation' deployed in the parliamentary debates above can be described as producing the adolescent homosexual in similar terms to *heimlich*, as an embodiment of *heimlich*. The adolescent homosexual was deployed as being both familiar and agreeable, indeed organically belonging to, and nurtured, within 'the home' and 'the family'. His homosexual practices, if they occurred, were seen as symptoms of the 'naturally' occurring habits of late adolescent sexuality (as presented in the Wolfenden Report). However, this habit was seen as correctable, this difference was seen as being retrievable, as not yet 'beyond the pale'. Yet the potential permanence and fixity of these sexual habits as a preference, as becoming part of an adolescent's identity were denied and silenced, to become that which 'is concealed and kept out of sight' (Freud 1964: 224–5). According to Freud, *heimlich* also carries the meaning of being obscure, opaque and inaccessible to knowledge, that is, 'withdrawn from knowledge, unconscious' (1964: 226). Instead of considering the obscure and opaque knowledge of *heimlich* – and the concealed and kept-out-of-sight phenomenon of the adolescent homosexual as *heimlich*, in 'the home' and in 'the family' – as being relegated to the depths of the Freudian unconscious, perhaps this practice might be better understood in terms of disavowal. The artificial purity of 'the family' and 'the nation' as perpetuated in the discourses of Thatcherism in the late 1980s (especially in relation to section 28) and in the conservatism of the House of Lords in the late 1990s and early twenty-first century can perhaps be described as disavowal. According to Freud (in his article 'Repression'):

> The objects to which men give most preference, their ideals, proceed from the same perceptions and experience as the objects which they most abhor, and ... they were originally only distinguished from one another through slight modifications ... indeed ... it is possible for the original instinctual representative to be split in two, one part undergoing repression, while the remainder, precisely on account of this intimate connection, undergoes idealisation.
>
> (Freud, in Dollimore 1992: 23)

According to Dollimore, Freud offers a narrative whereby the negation of homosexuality has been in direct proportion to its centrality. It is in this article that Freud also explains why the cultural marginality of homosexuality is in direct proportion to its cultural significance (Dollimore 1992: 23). In addition, this narrative of 'idealisation' and 'repression' also addresses 'why homosexuality is so strangely integral to the self-same heterosexual culture which has so obsessively denounced it' (Dollimore 1992: 23). This is because homosexuality is within the possibility of heterosexuality and homosexuality is within the idealised (heterosexualised) institution of 'the family'. As Dollimore elaborates:

> Deviation originates from within that which it perverts. Literally so: to deviate from something presupposes an antecedent point of congruence with it, either as the identical or (more worrying) the indistinguishable. Typically, this means that perverse deviation discloses something within or about (in proximity to) the normal which the latter must disavow in order to remain itself – a split, a contradiction, a difference; this is one reason why perversion is regarded as dangerous.
>
> (Dollimore 1998: 140)

One could say that production of 'the home', 'the family' and the safety these institutions were alleged to provide from 'homosexuality' and 'homosexuals' is constantly under threat from the close proximity of this perversion/deviation to these institutions. As well as this, both the Wolfenden Committee's discourses, and subsequent parliamentary ones, of adolescent male sexual transitionality and its special vulnerability, can be described in terms of a discursive formation which has worked to conceal, silence and keep out of sight the homosexualities in 'the family's' midst.[28]

However, this mechanism of disavowal has been challenged by a politicisation of the avowal of homosexuals within families. One example of this was the protest held by the lobbying group 'Mothers of gay sons', who marched on the Palace of Westminster waving banners which read 'Equal rights for our gay sons' and 'Equalise the age of consent' on 11 February 1999. This 'army of mothers' as it was referred to in the 'gay press', had mobilised in order to protest against Baroness Young's plans to oppose the passing of the Bill in the House of Lords, which would lower the age of lawful homosexual relations between men for a second time. A few representative parents from the group subsequently met with Baroness Young on 11 February. After this meeting the group's leader Brenda Oakes said:

> the Baroness was terribly sweet and has the best of intentions – but she's just got it all wrong ... we told her how we want our sons to be treated as equals with their straight brothers and sisters, but I don't think we made that much progress.
>
> (quoted in *The Pink Paper*, 12 February 1999: 3)

Another delegate from the group of protesting women, Cath Hall, commented:

> when we were leaving she [Baroness Young] said that mums should stick to what they're good at. But I told her that loving my gay son and helping him cope with his sexuality is part of what I'm good at.
>
> (quoted in *The Pink Paper*, 12 February 1999: 3)

It seems that these particular women and mothers were refusing to take part in the practices whereby the existence of homosexuality has been disavowed within the identity of 'the family'. These particular 'family people' organised their family identity in a less exclusionary way (in contrast to Baroness Young). This perspective problematises the identity of 'the family' in terms of who qualifies to belong in it and to be a part of it. This perspective clearly also extends to an appreciation of equality before the law within families regardless of sexuality. The variety of resistance perpetuated by this group of mothers of gay men is a resistance performed at the very heart of the process of identification which 'structurally aids and abets' (Fuss 1995: 2) the identity of 'the family'. By refusing the self-recognition of the exclusionary (heterosexualised) identity of 'family people' as defined against its alleged antithesis, 'the homosexual', these mothers and the families they represented achieve their 'family identity' by embracing the organic otherness within their midst rather than disavowing it. As a result they radically erase and redraw the frontiers of 'family identity'.

The Sexual Offences (Amendment) Bill of 1999 and 2000

On 24 November 1998, it was announced, in the Queen's Speech that opened the 1998–9 session of Parliament, that a government Bill would be introduced in the next session which would reduce the homosexual age of consent from 18 to 16. This would be the first time ever in the history of 'homosexual' legislation that a Bill would be introduced by a government and not by a private member. However, this government Bill was to include a clause which would restrict the abuse of young people by those in positions of power and authority. The equalisation of the ages of homosexual and heterosexual consent was to become law, but this equality was to be organised around the circumstances of age and vulnerability. The Labour government's paradigm shift from age-protection to age-equality has resulted in the development of an Age of Consent Bill that is a discursive hybrid of both equality and 'practical' protection.

On 25 January 1999 the Sexual Offences (Amendment) Bill was opened for debate in the House of Commons by the Home Secretary Jack Straw. This new Bill, as expected, comprised two 'separate parts'. The first clause comprised the proposed equalisation of the lawful age of homosexual relations between men with that of the heterosexual age of consent at 16. The second clause consisted of the issue of abuse of trust (Straw, *Hansard*, Commons, 25 January 1999: col. 20). According to Straw, the reason for combining these two separate issues was in response to 'the very strongly held views about the vulnerability of sixteen and seventeen-year-olds of both sexes expressed during debates on the equalising of the age of consent held in the House and another place last summer' (col. 20). Straw couched the issue of equalising the ages of consent in terms of 'the question of equality before the law'. Straw also contextualised the legislative reform in terms of the agreement reached between the government and Euan Sutherland whereby the European Commission granted the government the opportunity to vote on this issue (col. 24). According to Straw, the Sutherland case (and the parallel case of Christopher Morris) were current cases before the European Court of Human Rights. The original case was stayed, pending the outcome of the vote in the House of Commons during the summer of 1998. Straw warned the Commons that the hearing before the European Court 'could not be delayed indefinitely, the Court would not permit it' (col. 24).

Straw introduced the revised (from Joe Ashton's problematic amendment of 1998) 'abuse of trust' clause in terms of filling in a legal gap in protection legislation. According to Straw, the 'abuse of trust clause' addresses important issues that 'fall outside the area of the law of sexual abuse as such' (Straw, *Hansard*, Commons, 25 January 1999: col. 24). According to Straw, sexual incidents as a result of the abuse of a position of trust and authority were not adequately covered by criminal legislation in the area of nonconsensual sexual activity (col. 24). However, Straw maintained that, even though the government had always recognised the fact of this particular need for the 'protection' of those young people who could be exploited by those in a position of authority over them, this was not a clause focused on homosexual activity only. Straw stressed 'that the concern is not limited to protecting young boys. Girls of that age are equally, if not more, vulnerable and deserve equal protection' (col. 24). By presenting the issue of protection in this way Straw was careful to deflect the House from reiterating the commonplace discourses of young boys under threat from proselytising homosexual male adults. Straw punctuated this oratorical deflection with the statement: 'Protection is needed against all who might abuse their position of trust, whatever their sexuality' (col. 24).

On 25 January 1999 the House of Commons voted by 313 to 130 to pass this Bill into the statute books. The government made it clear at this time that they would invoke the Parliament Act to force the measure through a year later if they faced further opposition in the House of Lords (Ward 1999: 1).

On 10 February 2000 Britain's lower house of Parliament, the House of Commons, approved the Sexual Offences (Amendment) Bill that would reduce the homosexual age of consent by two years to 16.[29] Straw reiterated many of the themes that had already been expressed in the many hours of parliamentary debates this issue had taken up in the previous two sessions of parliament, and themes explored earlier in this chapter. According to Straw:

> The issue raised in the Bill is one of equality, of seeking to create a society which is free from prejudice, where our relationships with others, including strangers, are based on respect, not fear. When I was a young man, homosexual acts between two men were unlawful, criminal offences attracting a penalty ... of up to life imprisonment. What did

such harsh criminalisation achieve? Let me answer that by saying, first, what the criminal law utterly failed to achieve: it failed to achieve the elimination, or reduction, of gay sex. There were probably as many people who were homosexual then as there are today, but while hetero-sexual people could enjoy sexual relations in peace, those who were homosexual lived in fear, fear of exposure, and of the misery that comes from having to live a lie. Our society suffered too, for it lived a lie as well, and dealt with that lie by institutionalising hypocrisy, pretending that everyone was heterosexual, while knowing that many people were not.

(Straw, *Hansard*, Commons, 10 February, 2000: col. 433–4)

Ann Widdecombe's response to such progressive outpourings was to reit-erate a few familiar themes. Widdecombe stated that in her personal opinion issues of equality should not 'override the imperative to protect young people' (col. 440). Widdecombe, in her speech to the Commons, aligned herself with previous speeches made by Michael Howard (in 1994) and Baroness Young in 1999 and 2000:

It is, in my view, wrong that a young person of sixteen should be free in law to embark on a course of action that might lead to a life style that would separate him, permanently perhaps ... [interruption] perma-nently, from the mainstream life of marriage and family. In particular, I believe that such a person needs protection from older men.

(Widdecombe, *Hansard*, Commons, 10 February, 2000: col. 440–1)

Miss Widdecombe proceeded, like Baroness Young, to speak for 'family people' and parents. According to Widdecombe, 'most parents, I believe, want to see their children grow up and raise a family. Overwhelmingly ... [interruption] Perhaps people do not agree. Overwhelmingly, that is how most children and young people see their future' (col. 441). Yet again, the heterosexualisation of 'the family' and the hetero-familial future is deployed as the core argument against reform. The assertion is that 'straight people "naturally" have access to family, while gay people are destined to move toward a future of solitude and loneliness ... set apart from the rest of humanity' (Weston 1997: 23).

In reply to the discourse of 'familial' opposition to this legislative reform some MPs disrupted Widdecombe's exclusive, heterosexualised 'family iden-tity' and its incompatibility with homosexuality. One such MP was Kali Mountford (Colne Valley), who condemned the psychodynamics of othering homosexuals from the frontiers of family life and family identity in Widdecombe's speech to the Commons. Mountford stated: 'I owe my mother a debt of gratitude for the fact that I am not inflicted with any disability of mind that might make certain people repulsive or repugnant to me' (*Hansard*, Commons, 10 February 2000: col. 464). Mountford proceeded to promote an alternative inclusive 'family' discourse as presented in the speeches of many honourable members of the House of Commons, that is, of families that lesbians and gays are part of: 'Many Hon. Members have discussed the importance of family life and said how many of our sons, brothers, sisters and so on are gay. They are part of our families' (col. 465).

On Tuesday 11 April 2000 the Sexual Offences (Amendment) Bill was read in the House of Lords for a second time. The Attorney General (Lord Williams of Mostyn) opened the debate with the following:

> My Lords, I beg to move that this Bill be now read a second time. Your Lordships will want to know the government's position. First, as far as we are concerned, this is a free vote. If any advice is wanted, and even if it is not, I offer it. I support the principle of the detail of the Bill. I believe that it will improve our law and ensure equality before the criminal law for young homosexuals and heterosexuals. Secondly, should the Bill be once more rejected by your Lordships, we shall use the Parliament Act Procedure.[30]
>
> (Lord Williams of Mostyn, *Hansard*, Lords, 11 April 2000: col. 91)

Between April and November 2000, the Tory-led coalition against the equalisation of the homosexual and heterosexual ages of consent in the House of Lords employed their one remaining strategy to block the reforms, that is, the power of delay. In a similar tactic to that of Michael Howard's calls for legislating the 'extra time' to ensure the establishment of heterosexuality in vulnerable young men in 1994, the Tory-led coalition in the House of Lords can be described as 'playing for time' during this period.

On 30 November 2000, exactly one hundred years to the day after the death of Oscar Wilde, the homosexual age of consent was reduced to 16 (as a result of the government invoking the Parliament Act) and the Act received the Royal assent.

Conclusion

In many ways this chapter has been an exploration of the fragility of the 'normative' position of heterosexuality, especially in males, in parliamentary and judicial discourses.

This fragility is in direct proportion to the alleged social importance of male heterosexuality in parliamentary discourse. Throughout this chapter male sexual fragility during adolescence, and the threat this presents to the heterofamilial vision of the national future, has been central to an explicit project of ensuring heterosexuality in males through the vehicle of the criminal law. The primary means whereby this project was carried out was through fixing the lawful age of homosexual relations between men at 21 years in 1967 and then at 18 years in 1994. Age became the mechanism for legally deterring the possibility of homosexuality emerging in adolescence through contact with already confirmed 'older' homosexuals, and for deflecting, delaying and prohibiting homosexuality occurring and emerging in what the Wolfenden Committee describe as its 'natural occurrence' in adolescence.

In this chapter, the theme of discursive clashes, as explored in previous chapters, was re-addressed. The discursive battle that emerged in this chapter raged around the production of the transitionality and vulnerability of adolescent sexuality in the Wolfenden Report. This particular discourse actively produced the non-homosexuality of adolescents through the categorisation of episodes of adolescent sexualities in terms of correctible 'phases' and rectifiable 'habits'. It was through these assumptions that the homosexual identities of adolescents were silenced and subjugated in juridical and parliamentary discourses. This conceptualisation of homosexuality was challenged by the emergence of adolescent homosexuals in human rights and in parliamentary discourses as a present absence. This was most notable in the form of Euan Sutherland's complaint to the European Commission, the BMA's revised opinion on the issue of the age of consent and in the speeches of mostly Labour MPs in the House of Commons.

This chapter demonstrates that what was at the heart of the debates over the reduction of the homosexual age of consent was the role the criminal law should legitimately play in shaping particular visions of society.

Conclusion
Accommodation trouble, queer legal theory and politics

The realm of sexuality also has its own internal politics, inequities, and modes of oppression. As with other aspects of human behaviour, the concrete institutional forms of sexuality at any given time and place are products of human activity. They are imbued with conflicts of interest and political manoeuvring, both deliberate and incidental. In that sense, sex is always political. But there are also historical periods in which sexuality is more sharply contested and more overtly politicised. In such periods, the domain of erotic life is, in effect, renegotiated.

(Rubin 1992: 267)

Each case study included in this book can be described as a genealogy of specific renegotiations within the social and legal realms and 'the realm of sexuality'. In this conclusion the case studies and the overall approach of the book will be re-examined in an attempt to distil the particular contribution these case studies make to queer studies and queer legal studies. In order to achieve this, this chapter includes a literature review of the work of five contemporary authors working within the field of queer legal theory. The reason for including a literature review of this type relatively late in the book is for the specific purpose of comparing and contrasting the approach found within *Homosexuality, Law and Resistance* with the queer approaches evident in the work of these queer legal theorists.

Before contextualising the contribution made in this book to the wider queer socio-legal studies movement, I would like to say a little about the distinctive bifurcated analysis (of 'the social' and 'the discursive') exemplified in the case studies.

The case studies above can be described as demonstrating, amongst other things, the power of discourse, that is, the interdependent relationship between power and discourse in specific institutional practices. In fact one could say that it is the performative effects of discourse that are the case studies' central 'critical resource in the struggle to rearticulate the very terms of symbolic legitimacy and intelligibility' (Butler 1993a: 3). As critical resources, these discursive regimes and, in particular, the identities deployed within them, were used against themselves in the case studies in order to haunt the 'reasoned' exclusion and restriction of homosexuals and homosexualities in and through a justificatory thematised production of them in legal discourse.

However, alongside the targeting of discourse as a crucial 'critical resource' there was another 'resource' or aspect of legal practice that emerged and demanded attention as the primary means of disrupting and haunting legal discourse in the case studies included in this book. This other resource prompted a micro-sociological analysis alongside the analysis of legal discourse and institutional practices. This complementary level of analysis facilitated the means of documenting the clash of hierarchical identities with alternative identities within the legal struggles under analysis. It was by paying special attention to the episodes of resistance, and the presentation of alternative discourses from the outset of this research, that the theoretical, methodological and political questions that inform these studies were allowed to surface. These new questions have relevance and resonance for the study of law and legal practices in general, and have particular relevance for lesbian and gay studies and, especially, queer studies. The methodological, political and theoretical focus of this book has been 'queer' in the queer theory tradition (see Introduction). However, the particular approaches demonstrated in this book have been critical of, and dissatisfied with, many aspects of queer theory. It is hoped that the case studies included above go some way towards diverting queer studies away from many of the stereo-typical and problematic enterprises associated with 'early' queer theory, particularly those where the potential in queer approaches is subsumed by abstract, reductive and decontextualised politics in and through troubling binary oppositions. In the next section, specific examples of queer legal theories will be reviewed in order to provide points of contrast between them and the approach to the study of law and legal politics in the case studies.

Queer legal theory

Queer legal theory is a relatively recent development within gay and lesbian legal studies and critical legal studies. Queer legal theory, in the specific examples included below, combines a critical legal studies problematisation of liberal legalism with queer theoretical insights into the organisation and power at work within law and society. In this section I shall focus initially on the work of two queer legal theorists: Carl Stychin and Wayne Morgan. I shall also include a discussion of two contemporary authors whose approaches attempt to develop a queer politics of law (and of the state): Duggan's model for 'Queering the State' and Bower's attempt to bring a queer style of subversive 'street' politics into law in order to disrupt legal categorisation and diacritics which privilege heterosexuality. The section will conclude with a discussion of Didi Herman's contribution to queer legal theory in the form of her critique of the heteronormative organisation of human rights procedures.

Wayne Morgan,[1] in his article 'Queer Law: Identity, Culture, Diversity, Law', introduces what he describes as a 'postmodern' queer legal politics premised on the deconstruction of the heterosexual/homosexual binary opposition. According to Morgan, the heterosexual/homosexual binary opposition is 'a fundamental dichotomy permeating through many areas of law' (1995: 12). Morgan presents 'the real queer threat' (1995: 31) to the privileging of heterosexuality and the heteronormativity in legal practices as lying within queer's 'claim to "transcend" identity' (1995: 31). The political efficacy of queer, according to Morgan, lies in its ability to make boundaries between identity categories unstable and fluid; by so doing queer can destabilise the heteronormative organisation of the legal system:

> Queer seeks to destabilise boundaries, hence categories, and hence the system (including law) which is based on these categories. Queer is fluidity.
>
> (Morgan 1995: 31)

Morgan sees the homosexual subject of 'gay liberation' movements as the primary obstacle to this 'queer threat'. According to Morgan, gay liberation movements collude with and perpetuate 'the homosexual' category as an 'interior exclusion' within an interdependent relationship with the normativity of 'the heterosexual' category. He also criticises 'gay reformism' as accepting:

> The basic binary opposition of hetero/homo and attempts to show that the latter is *as good as* the former. It accepts the assumptions which have themselves oppressed lesbian and gay men. Gay liberation seeks to establish that gay men and lesbians are 'good citizens', 'good parents' and 'good soldiers', without questioning the values which lie behind these institutions. Queer particularly reacts against the gay liberation designation of sexuality as a private matter.[2]
>
> (Morgan 1995: 29)

According to Morgan, gay reformism and liberation movements

> view law as one of the major sites of conflict in achieving social change: a battle that is worth fighting in the cause of equality. An important part of its project is to utilise law to achieve change, to demand the 'same rights' enjoyed by others. Not only does this legal reform agenda legitimate dominant (hetero) world views, it also contributes to the suppression of diversity within gay and lesbian communities. ... For gay liberation to achieve legal change, it must speak the language of universal truths and essentialised identities, because this is what the law

understands. The law seeks reduction to categories which name, define and control.

(1995: 29)

Gay reformism and liberation, according to Morgan, depend upon concepts of fixed identity (1995: 33); this is problematic and complicitous with the existing sexual and legal order which privileges heterosexuality just as it demonises homosexuality. Morgan thus advocates a questioning of identity politics and the development of a queer 'posture' which must be employed when approaching legal institutions and analysing legal discourse (1995: 36). Following Terry's (1991) suggestion, Morgan advocates the adoption of a 'deviant' standpoint, a 'vengeful counter-surveillant' subject position (1995: 37). From this deviant counter-surveillant position the queer legal theorist can perform a specific 'reading' role with the objective of exposing:

> the partiality of the dominant account and thus destabilis[ing] it ...
> [this role is] generated from this position of the 'deviant'. By centring
> this deviant subjectivity in our readings of legal texts, we can map the
> techniques by which homosexuality has been marked as different and
> pathological and then locate subjective resistances to this homophobia.
>
> (Morgan 1995: 37)

Thus, Morgan's conceptualisation of a queer legal theory and politics foregrounds the complicity of affirmative homosexual identity politics with the perpetuation of the privileging of heterosexuality. His article demonstrates the political predicament of approaching law from a fixed identity and points to potential ways of overcoming this. His primary suggestion is the re-direction of gay and lesbian political energies away from foundational identity politics. According to Morgan, queer politics must move away from trying to reform legal practices in order to develop queer strategies based on the transgressive reading of 'the corpus of legal knowledge: its texts and other forms of discourse' (1995: 37). The political strategy advocated by Morgan exemplifies the 'early' queer politics of supplementarity (see Introduction). Carl Stychin,[3] in his essay 'Towards a Queer Legal Theory',[4] presents a model of queer legal theory very similar to that of Morgan. Identity fluidity and identity trouble is theoretically, methodologically and politically also central to Stychin's queer legal theory.

According to Stychin, queerness is 'a provisional identity category' (1995a: 155), which requires a 'new elasticity' in our conception of lesbian and gay (1995a: 141). The objective of this introduction of queerness by Stychin is similar to Morgan's contribution to a queer politics within the legal arena, that is:

> to undermine and destabilise sexual (and other) identities as the basis of
> both activism and theory, rather than reinforcing them through the

assertion of categories that have historically been deployed in an oppressive manner.

(Stychin 1995a: 142)

By undermining identity, according to Stychin, identity categories become politically indeterminate and a product of an ongoing contestation over social meanings and definitions (1995a: 144).

[Queerness] thus becomes principally based upon how the subject sees herself in relation to dominant background norms of sexuality, rather than how the subject slots into any particular sexual identity category as it has been historically constituted.

(Stychin 1995a: 146)

Like Morgan's 'queer', Stychin's 'queerness' becomes an undefined subjectivity 'associated with transgressiveness' (Stychin 1995a: 152). 'Thus, queers', according to Stychin, 'rejoice in deviance as a strategy of defiance' (1995a: 152).

Stychin described the decision of the US Supreme Court in *Bowers* v. *Hardwick* (1986) as providing the point of departure for the rise of 'queer politics' in North America (1995a: 149). In the *Bowers* v. *Hardwick* Supreme Court majority decision it was held that regarding homosexuality 'there [was] ... no general, constitutionally imposed zone of privacy for private, consensual sexual activity' (Stychin 1995a: 149). All homosexual activity was therefore illegal. As a result of this, many gay and lesbian legal theorists working in North America gave up on law as a vehicle for emancipation. Thus, 'the emergence of queerness as a political stance, then, in part was a resistance to these developments and the perceived failure of the language of liberal rights as a means to realise social change' (Stychin 1995a: 151). In response to the *Bowers* v. *Hardwick* judgment, which resulted in gays being defined in terms of a set of sexual practices, queers, according to Stychin, 'appropriated that discourse and threw those sexual practices back in their faces' (1995a: 151). The result was that, rather than presenting themselves as a minority group based on more than just sex, as in gay and lesbian minoritism, queers embraced sexual 'deviancy' as there was no other possibility available in certain states in the USA. However, as was explored in the case studies in Chapters 1–4, this is not the case for homosexuals in the United Kingdom. The circumstantial zone of privacy which was implemented in the Sexual Offences Act of 1967 is absent in many states in the United States since the time of *Bowers* v. *Hardwick* (Mahoney 1990: 74). In the United Kingdom, homosexuals who conduct themselves within delimited circumstances set out in the Sexual Offences Act of 1967 have their privacy protected by the European Convention on Human Rights (19). This protection has been demonstrated in the *Dudgeon* v. *United Kingdom* (1981), *Norris* v. *Ireland* (1989) and *Mondinos* v. *Cyprus* (1993) cases. Thus, one could say that queer reform strategies (specifically within the constraints of a right to a private life) in the United Kingdom and the rulings of the European Commission and Court represent 'less of a failure' than the US situation, despite the heteronormative 'othering' of homosexualities within liberal legality. As a result, British and European legal theorists should be careful not to follow their North American queer colleagues too religiously, especially in their rejection of law and human rights standards as an avenue of political contestation.[5]

Both Stychin's and Morgan's queer legal theories can be described as path-breaking, and, in Stychin's case, extremely influential; however, both theories suffer from the political limitations of all 'early' queer theories and politics. In fact, both these theorists seem to appreciate the specific limitations in their theories. For example, Morgan concludes (after 39 pages of 'revolutionary queer') that:

> Queer may not work as a suitable political movement or even a sustainable analytical method but the critique of gay liberation's legal rights agenda it presents has wider resonances and may not disappear quite so easily. Of course no one actually advocates giving up the project of legal reform.
>
> (Morgan 1995: 39)

Stychin goes so far as to call our attention to the 'idealistic' impossibility of queerness in practice: 'queerness as a stance and an identity cannot possibly live up to this idealistic billing in practice' (Stychin 1995a: 147).

Thus, Morgan's and Stychin's queer legal theories can be depicted as suffering from what Wilson (1997) describes as the difficulty of translating, or negotiating between, 'the often exclusive practice of theorising and the inclusive potential of political action' (Wilson 1997: 99). Following Foucault, what I consider to be 'dangerous'[6] in queer studies is theory for theory's sake. Attempting to overcome the limitations in queer theory is what the case studies included in this book have been attempting to do.

Lisa C. Bower is another academic who attempts, in her article 'Queer Acts and the Politics of "Direct Address": Rethinking Law, Culture and Community' (1994), to develop a queer approach to law. However, Bower's work is distinct from Morgan's and Stychin's queer legal theories, as her approach is closely allied not only to queer theory but also to the 'new styles of politics' being developed within queer cultural (or street) politics (1994: 1029). Bower attempts to develop a queer politics in law that is based on the political styles of groups such as Queer Nation in the USA. Queer Nationals use tactics of cultural subversion to 'destabilise the traditional meanings of sex and sexual orientation for the political purposes of undermining and reconstructing dominant forms of (hetero)sexuality' (Bower 1994: 1016). Like Stychin, Bower describes this particular queer approach as being a direct response to the *Bowers* v. *Hardwick* judgment, especially the reduction of homosexuality to 'fixed sodomitical essence' in this ruling (Halley 1991: 354).[7] The result of the Hardwick ruling was the diacritical consolidation and purification of heterosexual America: 'the Hardwick decision was a hegemonic move for heterosexual America because it reduced homosexual identity to a unitary essence based on a single behaviour, [and,] in so doing, stabilised heterosexual identity' (Bower 1994: 1016). As a result of these processes of categorisation and the exposure of fixed homosexual identities in the US courts (and within the gay and lesbian reform movement) queer cultural–street political groups developed practices which had as their aim the disruption of the boundaries between homosexual and heterosexual identities. The primary aim of these tactics was to 'queer' or destabilise heterosexuality. This was to be achieved by affirming less around homosexual difference and more around homosexuality as heterosexuality's interior exclusion (Fuss 1991: 3). According to Bower, the aim of the 'queer acts' found within Queer Nation and the Queer Shopping Network movements was the initiation of social and cultural transformation through the destabilisation of discrete sexual identity categories. A central feature of Queer Nation's political programme was as follows: 'it isn't enough to become parallel to straights – we want to obliterate such dichotomies altogether. And the best way to erase a boundary is to occupy it' (Solomon, in Bower 1994: 1018).

Bower's intention was to attempt to see whether these new styles of post-Hardwick queer cultural politics, in North America, could be incorporated into a new queer legal politics. Her approach was premised on the trouble non-identities or ensemble identities may pose for legal categorisation. Thus, just as queers within the new queer cultural politics were attempting to occupy and trouble the boundary between gay and straight and homosexual and heterosexual, Bower, in her article, attempted to see if these tactics and styles of resistance could be incorporated into legal strategies. The politics Bower hoped to initiate here was aimed at law's power to define and categorise homosexuals, and thereby diacritically 'shore up' heterosexuality. Bower's chosen example of this queer legal politics came in the form of the trouble the case of *Ulane* v. *Eastern Airlines* (1984) caused law. In this case a post-operative transsexual, Karen Ulane, after being fired from her job as a pilot with Eastern Airlines, sued the latter under title vii of the US Civil Rights Act of 1964 (sec. 2000 e- 2a). Title vii deems it an 'unlawful employment practice for an employer to fail or refuse to hire or to discharge any individual because of such an individual's race, colour, religion, sex or national origin' (cited in Bower 1994: 1021). According to Bower, this case resulted in similar confusion and destabilisations in law's attempts to discreetly define what 'sex' actually was under title vii, and whether Karen Ulane's claim fitted this provision. According to Bower, 'Ulane's transsexuality unsettled stereotypical definitions of sex and gender and, by extension, the taxonomies that sustain heterosexuality as the definition of "normal" sex and sexuality' (Bower 1994: 1027). Just as queer cultural politics relied on presentations of identity which were always excessive, never bounded and discreetly recognisable, Bower saw queer potentials in the Ulane case especially in law's inability to discreetly categorise Karen Ulane. Thus, Bower's tentative model for a queer legal politics came in the form of the following:

> The uneasy fit between legal definitions of sex and subjects whose identity is always excessive to those definitions has the potential to effect a re-evaluation of binary thinking. Moreover, in returning to the legal field, a queer reading of law foregrounds the interpretative nature of law and the manner in which legal decision makers create legal fictions that are constituted in relation to fixed definitions of identity.
>
> (Bower 1994: 1029)

Thus, in queer street politics and in Bower's suggestions for a queer legal politics, the focus and resource was the contingency of identities and representations. The ambition of both these varieties of queer politics ('street' and 'legal') was to initiate a reformulation and hopefully a transformation of the sexual order, and thus the heteronormative legal order. This was to be achieved in and by troubling the diacritical system based on discrete identities and categories. However, there is a problem with this legal politics. The Ulane case did indeed trouble the law's ability to categorise and consolidate a heteronormative system based on a coherent relationship of sex, gender and sexuality (Butler 1990). But the queer(ness) of this particular case perhaps cannot be extended to all queer cases.[8] Perhaps Karen Ulane's excessiveness was sufficient to trouble law's power to define, but this would not be the case for many other 'queers' (for example, lesbians, gays and bisexuals) before the law. The law's power to define homosexualities and other non-normative sexualities may ignore subversive attempts to trouble its categorisations. It may categorise homosexuals even if they do not desire to be so categorised. Or, alternatively, as Moran has demonstrated, if a man comes before the law for committing a 'homosexual offence', the alleged conduct which resulted in this particular charge works to conflate the conduct, the crime and the underlying identity of the man so charged (Moran 1996a). Unfortunately, 'we' cannot, without radical surgery, all be as 'queer' and as troublesome to legal categorisation as Karen Ulane.

Lisa Duggan's article 'Queering the State' (1994) is another example of an attempt to develop a queer style of politics. Although not strictly located within law, Duggan's article nevertheless focuses on the role that queer intellectuals/academics should and could play in terms of 'the creative production of strategies at the boundary of queer and nation – strategies specifically for queering the state' (Duggan 1994: 3). The thrust of Duggan's approach is to encourage queer academics to engage in tactical strategies that would highlight the state's relationship with heteronormativity. This is achieved, according to Duggan, by 'high-lighting the embeddedness of heteronormativity in a wide range of state policies, institutions, and practices' (1994: 9). The bringing to light of the collusion between the state and heteronormativity is what Duggan describes as the most effective political task for queer politics and queer academic strategies in general, rather than approaches which promote minority rights and anti-discrimination arguments. Duggan's approach importantly avoids the exclusionary practices of politics based on unitary gay identities, that is, 'we need strategies that do not require us to specify who is and who is not a "member" of our group' (1994: 9). This is an important point for Duggan, who recognises both the exclusivity and normativity of identity categories as well as the 'identity-bashing' tenden-cies within queer theory and politics. Duggan's approach, in contradistinction to the queer approaches advocated by Morgan, Stychin and Bower, 'deconstructs heterosexuality first' (1994: 10) rather than dissolving homosexual distinctiveness in order to deconstruct heterosexu-ality. Yet Duggan's approach shares the 'queer ambition' of these authors in the form of encouraging 'reversal tactics … [to] destabilise heteronor-mativity rather than to naturalise gay identity' (1994: 10). According to Duggan, by highlighting the embeddedness of heteronormativity in the state an agreement on a strategy is facilitated 'without having to resolve our differences' (1984: 10). However, Duggan does recognise both the benefits and the dangers inherent in this approach – that the challenge to and highlighting of the embeddedness of the state and heteronormativity might be ineffectual. Duggan recognises that the strength of potential heteronormative responses could overwhelm tactical trouble at the margins. For example, Duggan warns queer theorists that attempts to trouble heteronormative discourses of 'the family' in state policies could be countered by arguments congruent with a heteronormative hegemony that 'the state must and should promote and prefer heterosexuality as the foun-dation for 'the family' (1994: 11). Duggan also admits that her proposed new direction for queer academic activism is not

> a broad solution but only a local tactic embedded in a larger strategy for destabilising heteronormativity. It is one among many conceivable tactics. It is not meant to replace civil rights strategies, and it would not be appropriate in all situations.
>
> (1994: 11)

Both Bower and Duggan attempt to queer 'the system' in the form of 'the law's' or the state's complicity with heteronormativity. Yet their approaches are different. Even though Bower privileges queer acts, the acts she describes occur in and around identity subversion and excessiveness, and thus her approach is akin to both Morgan's and Stychin's queer legal theories. Duggan, on the other hand, attempts to keep 'identity' out of her strategy. Duggan's approach privileges the activity of queering rather than 'being queer' as in Bower's, Morgan's and Stychin's work. Duggan's approach and strategy, out of the queer approaches discussed above, is the approach that comes closest to the approach in the case studies included in *Homosexuality, Law and Resistance*. Duggan's article, 'Queering the State', rises above the fixation within queer theory and politics with identity: that is, questions of 'who gays and lesbians are' and also the self-erasing, diacritical strategies based on the logic that if 'homosexuals' erase themselves then heterosexual 'superiority' and heteronormativity will collapse as they will have no abjected interior exclusion upon which to constitute themselves. Approaches such as this are examples of queer theory and politics at their most abstract, exuberant and utopian (Butler 1999).

In contrast to this, Duggan delimits her target and devises a strategy that bypasses this stereotypically queer 'relational politics of identity'. She does this in order to engage effectively with what she sees as being central to the devaluing and differential treatment of non-heterosexualities within contemporary America, that is, the state's complicity with heteronormativity.

The primary difference between the approach demonstrated in *Homosexuality, Law and Resistance* and the other queer approaches discussed above, is that my approach can be described as less subversive and less motivated by the hope of a society-wide transformation. The over-emphasis on 'utopian' revolutionary subversion in queer studies might be to the detriment of localised, nuanced analysis of actual episodes of effective resistance. The proffering of transformational, utopian solutions is an 'early' queer practice, that has been bypassed by 'late' queer discursive-sociological approaches which attempt to blend a queer politics of knowledge with localised and contextualised institutional analysis of social practices. The case studies included in this book incorporate and fuse the analysis of discourse with the tracing and teasing-out of the complex blends and effects that resistances to legal exclusion or restriction encounter within each institutional setting. These are textual analyses that break through the text, where discourse and episodes of resistance are given equal emphasis. Moreover, instead of subversion and transformation, these case studies focus on specific examples of local particular resistances that are motivated more by 'survival' than subversion, even though trouble does come with the territory.

Another exemplar of the new legal studies of sexuality is Didi Herman's work, particularly in one of her books, *Rights of Passage: Struggles for Lesbian and Gay Legal Equality* (1994). In this book Herman advances many useful insights into the othering of homosexuals within human rights discourse. For example, according to Herman:

Lesbians and gays are granted legitimacy, not on the basis that there might be something problematic with gender roles and sexual hierarchies, but on the basis that they constitute a fixed group of 'others' who need and deserve protection. Arguably then, human rights frameworks thus regulate new identities in ways that contain their challenge to dominant social relations.

(1994: 44)

Herman's stated aim in her book was 'to present lesbian and gay rights as a "problematic" – a location from which questions arise' (1994: 5). Herman's primary political aim in terms of this problematic was the disarticulation of the constant othering of 'the homosexual' and homosexualities in human rights discourses and practices in relation to normative heterosexualities. This intention prompted Herman to suggest a political model for transforming the heteronormative organisation of law and human rights. Her approach can be described as being similar to that advocated by Stychin and Morgan, above. Herman presented identity and the entrenchment of gay and lesbian identity politics within the heterosexual/homosexual binary opposition as part of the problem, and as the site of a potential solution. Herman's ambition was to try to connect lesbian and gay rights acquisition with the transformation of heteronormative social relations within legal and human rights discourse.

The connection between rights acquisition for lesbians and gay men and the transformation of social relations which produce lesbian, gay, and other identities is not necessarily obvious or inevitable. Such a bridge must be built, not awaited.

(Herman 1994: 9)

Herman advocated a test of the efficiency of gay and lesbian legal and human rights strategies for transforming heteronormative social relations:

For radical gays or lesbian feminists, one test of the 'merits' of lesbian and gay rights reform might be whether such activities lead to the overthrow, or at least the destabilisation of heterosexuality's claim to 'normalcy'.

(Herman 1994: 145)

According to Leo Bersani, this ambition of 'overthrowing' or destabilising heterosexual 'normalcy' is an exhilarating yet alienated theoretical activity. In the following passage Bersani attempts to force queer theorists, such as Herman, Stychin, Morgan and Bower, out of their 'diacritical' and 'denaturalising' preoccupations and abstract strategies which are remote from the materiality of practice:

'they' don't need to be natural in order to rule; to demystify them doesn't render them inoperative ... the dominant heterosexual society doesn't need our belief in its own naturalness in order to continue exercising and enjoying the privileges of dominance.

(Bersani 1995: 4–5)

Echoing the limitations of Stychin's and Morgan's approaches, Herman's solution to the problem of entrenchment within, and thus complicity with, the organisation of the heterosexual/homosexual binary opposition was to problematise minority identities and minority politics. In order to achieve this Herman suggested the disarticulation of the fixity and diacriticality of 'minority' from hegemonic liberal discourse:

A strategy to disarticulate minority from hegemonic liberal discourse might help to challenge dominant understandings of 'minority' as a concept, together with the accompanying 'naturalness' of 'the norm'. If the lesbian and gay minority were represented less in terms of sexual difference, and more in terms of a political opposition, then the meaning of 'minority' in this context might indeed be shifted.

(Herman 1994: 52)

Herman therefore called for the de-sexualisation (contrary to Stychin's and Morgan's 'deviant' sexualisation) of lesbian and gay minority politics as a means of avoiding the othering of these sexualities relative to normative heterosexualities in legal and human rights practices and discourse. However, Herman conceded that this strategy and thus 'the bridge' she attempted to build between gay and lesbian rights acquisition and the disruption and transformation of the heteronormative organisation of human rights discourse and practices which 'other' gays and lesbians, was 'unlikely to happen' (1994: 52).

Homosexuality, law and resistance

The case studies included in this book are demonstrations that queer politics does not begin and end with the troubling of the heterosexual/homosexual binary opposition. These case studies demonstrate that there is more to queer legal studies than reductionist and alienated utopian theoretical enterprises. This book's central contribution comes from the realisation that, in some cases, episodes of local and specific sub-political resistance and disruption are inextricably bound up with the assumptions and 'truths' of dominant discourses. Importantly, this book demonstrates that there are varieties of textual analysis with varying degrees of political engagement. This last statement is an attempt to 'rescue' theoretical and textual analysis from being lumped together as alienated and 'pointless' academic enterprises. For example, Angela McRobbie, describes her despair in relation to 'literary and textual excursions' which she describes as 'cultural studies gone wrong' in the following passage:

> Theory need not always lead so directly to politics. But what has worried me recently in cultural studies is when the theoretical detours become literary and textual excursions and when I begin to lose a sense of why the object of study is constituted as the object of study in the first place. Why do it? What is the point? Who is it for?
>
> (McRobbie 1992: 721)

Homosexuality, Law and Resistance does perform textual analyses; however, these analyses are substantive and substantial. In the textual analyses contained in the case studies included in this book 'the discursive' is not presented as a separate realm from 'the social'. The discursive here is inseparable from the social practices of 'law' as found in legal institutional settings. As well as this, the discursive is presented as being particularly vulnerable to disruption caused by the co-optation of the counter-practices and episodes of resistance evident in the struggles under analysis. What is distinctive about these episodes of resistance is that they were not obtained through ethnographic encounters, but read from the pages of texts, the documents, reports and debates analysed in the case studies. It is from within this particular textual analysis that the power of discourse, the resistant body and certain 'in-social' identities are discernible. It is also through this intersection of the discursive and the micro-sociological that the corporeal accommodation to specific intercorporeal power relations is shown to be interdependent with the queering and 'reshaping from below' (Beck 1994: 22) of law's epistemological claims to know 'the homosexual'.

As well as discourse, resistance and power, another concept that is central or 'haunts' this book is privacy. 'Privacy' is obviously central in all of the case studies above. However, this is a particular type of privacy, in that privacy here is troublesome rather than just assimilationist in motivation. In these case studies the 'homosexual subject of privacy' (Moran 1996a) is accommodating, in that he accommodates to social and institutional positions afforded to him in the legal complex. However, privacy is clearly simultaneous with the disruption of 'the law's' epistemological claims to know 'the homosexual'.

The queer genealogical politics documented in the case studies are examples of political activities characterised by the attempt to 'affect' and/or 'infect' 'law', from within its own discourses and knowledge concerning homosexual identities and behaviours. One of the academic contributions this book presents in this context of genealogical politics is the cartography of the trajectory of de-subjugated alternative knowledges and identities into legal discourse through the processes of discursive co-optation. For example, in Chapter 1, the trajectory of the compatible covert homosexual was mapped from the margins of MoD and parliamentary discourse to the centre of 'passing policy' developments. In Chapters 2 and 3 the trajectory of the privacy and invisibility of homosexuals was mapped from its misrecognition as a reason to refuse refugee status, to an issue of immutability in the face of basic human rights in refugee determination procedures. This was achieved by the creation of an interface (a politics of connection) between International Refugee Law and Human Rights Law by 'specific intellectual-practitioners' in an attempt to prevent the exclusion of homosexuals from the 'social group' refugee category as a result of their 'social invisibility'. Finally, in Chapter 4, the disruption, de-subjugation and co-optation of alternative knowledges of homosexual identities (in the form of adolescent homosexuals) in Human Rights Law and in parliamentary and juridical discourses was mapped from within parliamentary papers, parliamentary debates and European Commission reports. This facilitated the tracing of the trajectory of the politics of disavowal and avowal within the debates concerning the homosexuality of adolescents and the reduction of the age of consent.

In each case, the resistance to an exclusion or restriction was achieved through a particular politics, an invasive institutional and contextualised variety of politics that blended 'the discursive' and 'the social'. These forms of resistance demonstrate that, in many cases, the privatised interiority of the homosexual (within the armed forces, in 'the family') can be described as superseding 'the homosexual' 'constitutive outsider' (in much queer theory) as a figure of political efficacy, especially in terms of co-optational 'effective' disruption and change.

In each case study it was the trajectory of the circumstances and tactics of the material presence and proximity of social agents, that caused the frame through which homosexualities and homosexuals were produced in legal discourse to be bent out of shape. Thus, the case studies included in this book can be described as presenting an alternative queer politics that can perhaps be described as 'subversion trouble'. What is meant by this is that employing tactics of accommodation and privatisation so as to avoid episodes of exclusion, eradication or persecution has been demonstrated to be more (if not just as) efficacious politically as overtly queer subversive antics. This is not to advocate that all queer politics should be accommoda-tional. It is a commentary concerning the specific approach of these studies.

In the case studies included in this book, the dialectics of subjugation and de-subjugation, of discourses and alternative knowledges, of the body as the site of power and the body as the site of resistance are some of the central themes and the primary sites of analysis. These themes and sites of analysis are of particular importance for how legal practices and legal politics are conceptualised and produced. One could say that the case studies contained within this book demonstrate the contemporary political 'shift in focus from an emphasis on social transformation in general towards strategies of "local" resistance in a range of discrete areas' (Ireland and Laleng 1997: 4). Not only are the episodes of resistance documented in this book 'local', they are also, on the whole, complex episodes. The resistances can be said to reproduce, or perhaps modify, the order of a given institutional regime, rather than totally transforming it. As a result the counter-practices documented in the case studies can be described as contradictory amalgamations, of accommodation-trouble, resistant-survival and transgressive-belonging.

In some of the case studies (especially in Chapters 1, 3 and 4) these 'local' struggles take on a rather more international or supra-national character. The involvement in these case studies of international law, specifically United Nation Conventions[9] and international human rights standards, results in the examples of local and discreet resistance and disruption becoming a confluence of both 'the local' and 'the supra-national'. International law and international human rights law is never very far from the 'sub-politics' documented and analysed in the case studies. In Chapters 1, 3 and 4 it was the connection of armed forces policy, international refugee law and criminal law to the human rights standards within the European Convention (1953) that resulted in the breaking of the frames through which heterosexualised and homosexualised identities were presented. As a result, homosexuals were recognised as being inappropriately excluded from armed service, recognised as being members of a persecuted social group, and the homosexuality of adolescents was recognised as a legitimate sexuality (rather than a correctable phase). In this book, 'the treatment' of homosexuals at the level of 'the national', that is, within national institutions, was counteracted, policed and interfered with by the supra-national institutions of the international community. However, international law, for example the European Convention on Human Rights, was presented as not being immune to or independent from the political necessities of the heteronormative social centre. International law and human rights standards do provide opportunities for the unsettling of law's 'truths' and for the disruption, or the questioning, of the interdependency of law's discourses with intolerable power effects perpetuated within nation-states. Success is not guaranteed in every case, however. Although landmark European cases such as *Dudgeon* v. *UK* and *Sutherland* v. *UK* do recognise certain violations in human rights standards perpetrated against homosexual males by the United Kingdom, these violations were presented within the heteronormatively organised recognition of the social necessity of controlling, restricting and privatising homosexual activities between men. In terms of the intersection of the national and the supra-national it will be extremely interesting to see the impact of the Human Rights Act (2000) on the British 'legal complex' in the next few years. It is expected that this impact will be demonstrated most forcefully in the interpretation of the provisions within Article 8 in relation to 'the right to a family life' alongside 'the right to a private life'.

This book therefore illustrates the interconnectedness and complexity of practices and counter-practices within legal institutions and legal events.

The case studies and the resistances and sub-politics demonstrated in them are combinations of the legal and the extra-legal, the discursive and the embodied, the discreet and the local, as well as the supra-national and the national. As a result these case studies have necessarily exhibited a multi-disciplinary perspective, demonstrating an interdisciplinary approach which connects, modifies, explores and utilises various perspectives from different academic 'schools' and movements including critical legal studies, socio-legal studies, gay and lesbian legal studies, queer theory, queer legal theory, cultural studies, sociology and critical discourse analysis. The case studies presented here are 'patently documentary' and the analyses produced in them are the result of an intimate association with the archive of reports and official papers that documented the legal events under analysis. Within this analytic framework the analysis of identity in this book is as concerned with the production of heterosexualised and heteronormative identities (albeit 'anxious' identities) in legal discourse as it is with the production of homo-sexual identities. This approach facilitates not only an interdisciplinary inclusivity but also opens up specific legal practices to scrutiny by laying bare the idiosyncrasy of legal practices. Moreover, the sensuality or the inter-corporeality of 'law' as a social practice, practised and populated by living, embodied beings and affecting other living and embodied in social beings is exposed. Thus this study has incorporated an analysis of the institutional practices of law, the deployment of identities in legal discourse and the social tactics utilised for surviving the juridical effects justified by such discourses. As well as this, this study has demonstrated – and this is its major achievement – how alternative knowledges can disrupt the inter-dependency of power/knowledge in specific institutions in the 'legal complex'.

Appendix
The membership of the Wolfenden Committee

John Wolfenden (Chairman), Vice-Chancellor, Reading University
James Adair, Scottish Solicitor and former Procurator Fiscal of Glasgow
Mary Cohen, Vice-President, Scottish Association of Mixed Clubs and Girls
     Clubs; Vice-President, City of Glasgow Girl Guides
Dr Desmond Curran, Consultant Psychiatrist at St George's Hospital,
     Tooting
Revd Victor Demant, Regius Professor of Moral and Pastoral Theology at
     the University of Oxford and Canon of Christ Church, Oxford
Kenneth Diplock, Barrister, Recorder of Oxford
Sir Hugh Linstead, Conservative MP for Putney, 1942–66; Pharmaceutical
     Chemist and Barrister
The Marquess of Lothian; Junior Minister at the Foreign Office
Kathleen Lovibond, Chairman, Uxbridge Juvenile Courts
Victor Mischon, Solicitor and Labour Leader of the Greater London Council
Goronwy Rees, Principal of the University of Wales at Aberystwyth
Revd R.T. Scott, Scottish Presbyterian Minister
Lady Stopford, Doctor and Magistrate
W.T. Wells, Labour MP for Walsall, Barrister
Dr Joseph Whitby, GP in North London and Psychiatrist

(Higgins 1996: 322)

Notes

Introduction

1 That is, the *Report of the Committee on Homosexual Offences and Prostitution* (1957), commonly known as the Wolfenden Report.
2 The author acknowledges that although lesbians are not directly affected by this particular legislation, they are not immune from criminal prosecution. According to Lynda Hart, the work of Louis Crompton and Ruthann Robson exposes the myth of lesbian impunity. According to Hart, these authors recover much of the 'hidden' history of the non-exemption of female homosexuals from legal prosecution. However, the research carried out by these two theorists does not indicate that male and female homosexuals were subjected to legal prosecution equally. Rather, according to Hart, research:

> shows that gay men and lesbians have not been prosecuted in the same way and for the same offences. The historical relevance of this difference resides largely in the idea that lesbianism remained a secret that could be kept from 'women'.
>
> (Hart 1994: 5)

3 In the case studies included in this book, legal practices and operations are shown to have sensual and corporeal aspects, rather than being purely rational (Bently 1996: 3). 'Law' and legal practice are shown to be 'cognitively open' (Bently 1996: 3); the Cartesian dualisms of mind/body and reason/sensation are blurred by 'law' being practised by living embodied individuals on other living and embodied individuals. In this book, I demonstrate that it is at the level of the cognitive, especially 'the visual', that 'law' knows and affects homosexual bodies. Therefore this book contributes to a growing legal scholarship in the area of 'law and the body', for example, Cheah *et al.* (1996), Hyde (1997), Bently and Flynn (1996), Bridgeman and Millin (1995), Collier (1998a), Moran (1996a) especially Chapter 7, and Moran and McGhee (1998).
4 Following de Certeau, passing is a tactical social practice demonstrates that, alongside the 'monotheistic' apparatus of the panopticon, and the over-theorisation of power in Foucault's *Discipline and Punish*, a 'polytheism of scattered practices survives' (de Certeau 1984: 48).
5 According to Giddens, Goffman was above all 'the theorist of co-presence' (1988: 255) and this concentration on co-presence drew attention 'to the body, its dispositions and display' (1988: 257). The significance of Goffman's work to the intercorporeality of legal practices comes from his focus on everyday 'encounters' in which he illuminated the 'interaction order' wherein and whereby we send and receive embodied communication, which 'calls forth a

monitoring by each individual of the other and the others' responses in relation to their own' (1988: 258).

6 This analysis is supported by the works of sociologists such as Goffman, Plummer and Simmel, and in the works of social theorists such as de Certeau, and queer theorists such as Edelman and Butler.

7 Anthologies such as Beemyn and Eliason's *Queer Studies* (1996) have attempted to address 'the gaps' within existing queer studies texts. Beemyn and Eliason describe their anthology as comprising essays 'that deal with areas that have often been excluded, marginalised, or ignored by queer studies in the past: race, gender, transgender, bisexuality, and s/m' (1996: 2–3).

8 This work on the developments in queer theory and politics began to surface from the mid-1990s. Whereas much 'early' queer theory was focused on redirecting what Cohen describes as 'our' political emotion' (1991: 71) from gay and lesbian identity and minoritarian politics to a queer 'politics of knowledge', 'late' queer academics can be described as attempting to refine queer politics and theory, in order to expose its limitations and consolidate its strengths. The major points of tension were the abstract textualism and elitism of early queer theory, its distance from 'real' social identities, politics and institutional contexts, and the problematic translation of queer theory into political action (Phelan 1997; Wilson 1997).

9 The limits of deconstruction have been recognised by feminists (especially in criminology and socio-legal studies), for example Naffine (1997), Cain (1995), Daly (1997). For example:

> the preoccupation with the limit of textual meaning could well be regarded as a limit to deconstruction itself, for the concern seems always to be one of unravelling, of undoing the concepts that shape and constitute our thought processes. Of lesser concern are the robust economic, political and legal structures that help to keep the traditional meaning in place and make it appear natural and inevitable.
>
> (Naffine 1997: 89)

Naffine continues, 'deconstruction may do some of the job of effecting change, but alone it is insufficient to undo the institutional systems that have been built upon, and help to sustain, the economic and political power of men over women' (1997: 89). Feminist criminologists and feminist legal theorists have begun to call for a range of analyses to be employed in order to approach women and law. Alongside deconstruction, feminists are reinvigorating empirical social science research in an attempt to challenge the contemporary hegemony of the humanities (Daly 1997).

10 Throughout the book I use the term 'accommodation'. This term should be qualified and distinguished from the closely allied concept of assimilation. According to Park and Burgess, accommodation

> has been described as a process of adjustment, that is, an organisation of social relations and attitudes to prevent or to reduce conflict, to control competition, and to maintain a basis of security in the social order for persons and groups of divergent interests and types to carry on together their varied life-activities.
>
> (1970: 360)

Assimilation, however, according to Park and Burgess, 'is a process of interpretation and fusion in which persons and groups acquire the memories, sentiments, and attitudes of other persons or groups, and, by sharing their experience and history, are incorporated with them in a common cultural life' (1970: 360).

11 Genealogy, according to Lash, concerns knowledge; it concerns power; it concerns, probably above all, the body (Lash 1993: 256).

12 The documents, reports and transcribed cases I analyse in the case studies are taken to be sedimentations of social practices (May 1997: 157) and 'sedimented understandings' (Spivak 1991: 177). My role as researcher is 'patently documentary' (Foucault 1977c: 139). As documentary researcher I employ an 'illustrative style' (May 1997: 176) whereby I include selective data within my text which 'illustrate general themes which emerge and which can be supported by the use of specific examples' (May 1997: 176) from the documents under consideration.

13 When it comes to theoretical positions and analytic preconceptions, Foucault, according to Sawicki, 'looks for its dangers, its normalising tendencies ... [Foucault] ... asks how it might hinder research' (Sawicki 1991: 55).

14 This points to a contradiction between Foucault as genealogical scholar/political activist with his ambition to initiate 'change' and what Nancy Fraser describes as his intransigent anti-humanism and anti-Enlightenment sentiments at a theoretical level (Fraser 1989: 151). The latter is belied by the argument in *Discipline and Punish*, according to Fraser, which 'even as it indicts humanist reform for complicity in disciplinary power ... depends for its crucial force on the reader's familiarity with and commitment to the modern ideals of autonomy, dignity and human rights' (1989: 57). History, in Foucault's conceptualisation, is an endless play of domination, as a result of this, he can be accused of putting himself in a situation where he could not use such terms like equality, freedom, justice' (Sarup 1993: 84). Habermas, describes Foucault in *Discipline and Punish* as presenting a particularly bleak vision of the carceral society whereby rationalisation in modern societies produce ever more insidious apparatuses of control; this is a vision of rationality which does not recognise the other side of the equation in terms of the gains in liberality, legal security and the expansion of civil rights guarantees (Habermas 1987: 290). According to Habermas, Foucault's generalising theory of panoptic power in modern societies, along with this particular selectivity (of filtering out the gains of modern rationality in terms of increased rights and security), results in Foucault's analysis omitting the consideration of what Habermas describes as the dilemma of the spread of legal regulation in the welfare-state democracies of the West; that is, that it is both regulatory and constitutive of the possibilities of greater freedom. Habermas captures this dilemma in the following passage: 'it is the legal means of securing freedom that themselves endanger the freedom of their presumptive beneficiaries' (1987: 291). In this book a balance will be struck between Foucault's insights concerning disciplinary society and his later conceptualisation of the governmentality in liberal rationality. At the same time, the consideration of law and legal practices will replicate Foucault's own prescriptions for institutional insurrection and disruption. Therefore in this book, Foucault's limitations (as pointed out by Habermas) are engaged with and modified by Foucault's own prescriptions. This is one of the benefits of utilising a theorist such as Foucault, as there are 'many Foucaults' and they are often contradictory. This means that certain parts of the Foucauldian legacy can be utilised to modify and counteract other parts of it.

15 In the case studies, 'the local' and the supra-national can be described as intersecting and colluding in the de-subjugation and resistant co-optation of alternative knowledges through the interference of the mechanisms of the European Convention (in Chapters 1 and 4) as well as international refugee law (in Chapter 3).

1　Military men: queering the homosocial habitus

1　The Special House of Commons report from the Select Committee on the Armed Forces Bill. Henceforth, HC Paper (1995–1996) No. 143. I also refer to previous quinquennial Armed Forces Bill House of Commons Select Committee reports, HC Paper (1990–1991) No. 179, and HC Paper (1985–1986) No. 170.

2　Ministry of Defence, *Report of the Homosexuality Policy Assessment Team*, February 1996. Henceforth, HPAT (1996).

3　*R* v. *Ministry of Defence, ex parte Smith and other applicants* [1995] 4 ALL E.R. Henceforth *R* v. *MoD* [1995].

4　*R* v. *Ministry of Defence, ex parte Smith and other appeals* [1996] 1 ALL E.R. Henceforth *R.* v. *MoD* [1996].

5　My focus is particularly on males and masculinities within the armed forces environment. I take it to be axiomatic that this environment is a male space that includes a relatively small number of women. The issue here, as will be demonstrated below, is male homosexuality. However, this does not mean that female homosexuals are unaffected by the exclusion policy, which will also be addressed below.

6　In a postscript at the end of this chapter I describe the complaint taken to the European Court of Human Rights on 27 September 1999 by these four individuals (in two separate cases) concerning the British armed forces homosexual exclusion policy.

7　This is presented here as a fear of a sexualising 'look' from an embodied homosexual onlooker. However, because this could be described as being an example of scopophobia, a fear of being looked at, perhaps this alleged 'look' could be more accurately described as a gaze, that is, a more spectral, disembodied seeing. Both Kendal Thomas (1993) and Kaja Silverman (1992) make this distinction.

8　The HPAT report lists a number of military environments or situations as being particularly problematic in relation to the eroticisation of 'ordinary' servicemen by homosexuals. These include both actual sexual activity between servicemen and inadvertent collusion in potentially erotic situations when the 'ordinary' serviceman has to touch, lie alongside or constantly brush past a homosexual in confined spaces (HPAT 1996: 120). These are: snow holes (temporary overnight shelters in arctic conditions, shared sleeping bags (simultaneous occupancy to ward off hypothermia or frostbite), bivouacs (improvised tents), trenches, gun pits, observation posts, barracks, and armoured vehicles (especially when closed down), mess decks (especially with triple bunks and with 'hot bunking' (sharing the same bunk at different periods of the watch-keeping day) (HPAT 1996: 120–1).

9　According to Nikolas Rose, many of the major figures of post-war psychology were involved in 'war work' (Rose 1990: 16).

10　This theme, of the relationship between young people, especially male adolescents, and homosexuality as constructed around the potential corruption of young males by older homosexuals, will be investigated further in Chapter 4. The focus of Chapter 4 is the juridical and parliamentary debates surrounding the various lawful ages for homosexual relations between men since the publication of the Wolfenden Report in 1957.

11　One cannot but surmise that the unfixity of sexual orientation of a number of young recruits must result in 'defences' against same-sex sexual expression occurring, especially in the 'special' non-privacy and intimacy of the forces environment referred to above. Perhaps the demonisation of the practice of homosexuality and concentration of this in the articulation of homosexual identity, as in the discussion of homosociality (later in this chapter), is one such mechanism. According to David Morgan, it cannot be denied that this is, indeed, part of the story, 'especially where young men are coming to terms with or to an understanding of their own sexuality away from home and in the company of men' (Morgan 1994: 167).

12 In Chapter 4, I describe how Baroness Young deployed 'the child' in a similar manner as in Mr Wilkinson's speech, in order to block reducing the age of consent for homosexual relations between men from 18 to 16. I use Jenks (1996) and Collier (1998a) to explore this particular deployment of 'the child'.

13 The HPAT's desire to 'know' and identify 'the homosexual' of the armed forces is demonstrated in the following taxonomy of sub-categories of homosexualities. These categories of homosexuality are described as 'potential and actual categories':

> *A Homosexual.* A homosexual is 'a person who is sexually attracted to a member of the same sex' (Armed Forces Policy and Guidelines on Homosexuality, December 1994).
>
> i.   *A Homosexual Activist* would work openly for the expansion of homosexual acceptance and opportunities in the services;
> ii. *A Flamboyant Homosexual* would emphasise his or her sexual orientation so that it was a constant factor in relation with fellow personnel;
> iii. *A Declared Homosexual* would explicitly inform fellow service personnel of his or her orientation in such a way that it became generally known;
> iv. *An Open Homosexual* would, by his or her consistent, expressive behaviour or reported conduct, clearly indicate a homosexual orientation to fellow service personnel, though without necessarily explicitly declaring it;
> v.   *A Strongly Suspected Homosexual* has by his or her expressive behaviour or reported conduct given strong grounds for fellow service personnel to assume a homosexual orientation to fellow personnel;
> vi. *A Suspected Homosexual* has given some indications of homosexual orientation;
> vii. *A Covert Homosexual* has by controlling his or her actions, expressive behaviour or outside conduct prevented the service authorities gaining compelling evidence of a homosexual orientation;
> viii. *A Known Homosexual* has become generally understood by his, or her, fellow service authorities to be homosexual whether or not his, or her, intention was to remain covert;
> ix. *A Celibate or Non-Practising Homosexual* has a homosexual orientation that may be declared but has demonstrated that he or she will not engage in any homosexual activity in either service or civilian contexts.
>
> (HPAT, Feb. 1996: 17–18)

14 I am indebted here to Lauren Berlant's (1993) essay, 'National Brands/National Body: Imitation of Life', in which the material circumstances that contribute to 'successful' racial passing were demonstrated.

15 This works well for male homosexuals in the armed forces but, according to Edmund Hall (1995), less so for lesbians. Within the heterosexual matrix:

> the stereotype of a successful woman in a military environment is that of a tough masculine dyke. A woman who climbs and swings well on an assault course, gives loud and clear orders on a parade ground and wears a uniform is clearly giving off confusing signals when society expects women to present themselves in quite a different way.
>
> (Hall 1995: 34)

Hall also comments on the problems lesbians may face within the overtly 'masculinised and heterosexualised' forces environment: 'the problem for women in the armed forces is complicated even further by the male military sex ethic: "Is she screwable?"' (Hall 1995: 35). Women in the forces, therefore, face the dilemma of lesbian connotations in the refusal of heterosexual advances and the physicality/masculinity of 'the job'. These dilemmas, according to Hall, are manifest in the service police investigators spending a disproportionately large amount of time investigating suspicions of female homosexuality when women only make up a relatively small proportion of the armed forces (Hall 1995: 35).

16 Also, visible abnormalities in how one is perceived to be practising one's gender, in this panoptic heterosexual matrix, are disciplined and punished and subjected to various practices which could be referred to as the 'cultural orthopedics' of gender alignment (or attempted gender realignment.) In this sense, the shaping and making-coherent of a child's gender, or, more accurately, specific children's gender ambiguity, is through modes of punishing. In the 'special' armed forces environment, ambivalent displays of masculinity would be subjected to the similar modes of punishing which would result in a more or less homogeneous institutionalised gendered space.

17 This has been observed by numerous authors; for example Hunt and Wickham: 'it should be noted that his [Foucault's] attention to resistance is never as developed or as full as his analysis of power' (1994: 17). Colin Gordon describes Foucauldian power as composed of three elements: its discourses, its practices and its effects; however, according to Gordon, these three elements never fit together or correspond (1980: 246–55). Therefore, implicit in Foucauldian power, are the conditions for resistance or subversions and 'unintended consequences' (Hunt and Wickham: 1994: 29).

18 According to de Certeau, 'a tactic depends on time' (1984). In this case, the potential invisibility of a sexual orientation gives gays in the armed forces the time to be tactical. What Edelman (1994) refers to as the 'unremarkableness' of homosexuality allows the undetected homosexual the time to internalise and accommodate to the habitus, in order to tactically use it to camouflage his 'inappropriate' sexuality by performing habitus-appropriate 'masculinity' in order to signify 'assumed heterosexuality'.

19 The Rand Report that investigated the US military homosexual exclusion policy also supports this observation. The National Defense Research Institute of the Rand Corporation prepared this report for the US Secretary of Defense in 1993. The Rand researchers also visited the armed forces of other countries, such as Canada, France, Germany, Israel, the Netherlands, Norway and the UK. With the exception of the UK, all the other countries visited by the Rand researchers permit administratively 'known' homosexuals to serve in some capacity in their armed forces. According to the Rand researchers' findings, 'several broad themes' emerged from these visits; these themes had, according to the Rand Report, 'potential implications' for military policy related to homosexuals in the US forces. For example:

> in countries that allow homosexuals to serve, the number of openly homosexual service members was small and was believed to represent only a minority of homosexuals actually serving. Service members who acknowledge their homosexuality were appropriately circumspect in their behavior, while in military situations they did not call attention to themselves in ways that could make their service less pleasant or impede their careers.
>
> (cited in HC Paper (1995–1996) No. 143, at Appendix iii)

20 This 'protection' is theoretical. According to *The Pink Paper* (7 March 1997) the number of gays dismissed from the US armed forces has risen sharply since the introduction of the don't ask, don't tell policy. In 1996, 850 lesbians and gays were discharged compared with 682 in 1993. According to a later report in *The Pink Paper* (29 January 1999) the total number of lesbians and gays discharged from the armed forces in 1998 hit record levels, 92 per cent higher than in 1993

when the don't ask, don't tell policy was first introduced. The total number of discharges was 1,147 from all the US armed services, up 14 per cent on the 1997 figures.

21 According to Halley, the essence of military capability is high standards of morale, good order and discipline, and unit cohesion (1996: 184).

22 According to Halley, homosexual identity was hidden in this policy within a new language of conduct so capacious that virtually any performative gesture, verbal or physical, could be designated as 'homosexual conduct' (1996: 162). For Halley, this has implications for both homosexuals and heterosexuals; as everyone in the US armed services, in theory, was 'vulnerable to act-based discharge' under this policy (1996: 162). Halley describes this aspect of the US policy as 'a code of military conduct that will produce ... its performance in the everyday lives of thousands of service members' (1996: 162). Thus, the don't ask, don't tell policy could be described as a policy which attempted to formalise the panoptic surveillance, and resulting self-surveillance and homogenised (heterosexualised) comportment within the informal homosocial habitus.

23 According to Butler, this discerner of homosexual signs, the 'reasonable person' should be read as 'the embodiment of heteronorms' (Butler 1996: 255). The embodied discerner of homosexual signs was also a component in Plummer's description of the process whereby homosexuals became socially recognisable (Plummer 1975: 179). According to Plummer, homosexual recognition depends upon both perception and action: 'somebody must identify a homosexual, and certain actions must be identifiable as homosexual' (Plummer 1975: 179). Thus, homosexual recognition depended on homosexuals 'giving away' information that can be seen by an embodied viewer and discerner of the gestures, behaviour or comportment which may connote a potential propensity of one acting homosexually or being a homosexual.

24 Stonewall's policy proposal was influenced by the existence of an operational uniform code of sexual conduct in the Australian Defence Force (ADF). This ADF code of conduct was concerned with sexual behaviour that was at risk of affecting the maximal operational effectiveness of the force:

> the ADF was concerned with the sexual behaviour of members in terms of its obligation ... [of maximising operational efficiency]. ... Sexual behaviour which was inconsistent with this obligation was termed unacceptable sexual behaviour, that is, any sexual behaviour, activity or attitude that places operational efficiency or effectiveness at risk.
> (HC Paper (1995–1996) No. 143, at Appendix v)

25 According to Stonewall, the main recommendation made by the Rand Report was that policy should be 'conduct-based' and not 'identity or status-based' as in the non-discretionary ban on homosexuals as a 'class' or a 'social group' from armed service. The Report recommended that:

> policy would consider sexual orientation, by itself, as not germane to determining who would serve in the military. The policy would establish clear standards of conduct for all military personnel, to be equally and strictly enforced, in order to maintain the military discipline necessary for effective operations.
> (cited in HC Paper (1995–1996) No. 143, at Appendix iii)

I am indebted to Angela Mason for providing me with both the ADF and Rand unpublished memoranda included in Stonewall's submission to the 1995–1996 Select Committee on the Armed Forces Bill.

26 However, as pointed out by Hall (1995), this cultural unintelligibility and ability to pass is 'easier' for gay men in the armed forces, than it is for lesbians. The passing policies documented in this chapter, can therefore be described as

protecting male homosexuals who can pass as assumed heterosexuals within an environment which provides the material circumstances which makes their presence seem unlikely. However, it is debatable if women in general and female homosexuals in particular will enjoy a similar degree of protection. If passing policies are designed around the significance of the gendered body within the intercorporeal scrutiny of the heterosexual matrix, then clearly gay 'military men' benefit from these policies far more than lesbian 'military women' do.

27 *Lustig-Prean and Beckett* v. *United Kingdom*, 27 September 1999, Application nos. 31417/96 and 32377/96.

28 *Smith and Grady* v. *United Kingdom*, 27 September 1999, Application nos. 33985/96 and 33986/96.

29 Article 8, in so far as it is relevant for this case, reads as follows:

1. Everyone has the right to respect for his private ... life ...

2. There shall be no interference by a public authority with the exercise of this right except such as is in accordance with the law and is necessary in a democratic society in the interest of national security ... for the prevention of disorder ...

30 The court adopted the same reasoning and reached the same conclusion in *Smith and Grady* v. *United Kingdom* as in the case of *Lustig-Prean and Beckett* v. *United Kingdom*, regarding article 8.

31 These post-confession interrogations were reputed to be of a distasteful nature, as recorded by the Rank Outsiders in their submission to the Special Report from the Select Committee on the Armed Forces Bill of 1996. The Rank Outsiders described how people felt 'raped' by Military Police during questioning. Questions such as the following were asked:

How many fingers do you use to masturbate?
Do you molest your child?
Do you have sex with your dog?
What does sperm taste like?

(HC Paper (1995–1996) No. 143, at 197)

32 See earlier in the chapter, under the sub-heading 'Passing policies'.

33 In January 1996 the Army published an Equal Opportunities Directive dealing with racial and sexual harassment and bullying.

34 See note 13 above.

35 Both Lustig-Prean's and Beckett's homosexuality came to the attention of the service authorities through anonymous letters sent to the said authorities.

36 Jeanette Smith, Graeme Grady, Duncan Lustig-Prean and John Beckett were awarded the sum of £324,000 between them by the European Court of Human Rights, as compensation for the emotional and psychological impact of their dismissal from the British armed forces.

2 Authenticity, evasion and the unknowable homosexual

1 Refugee status is a special category within the general class of 'asylum seeker'. Refugee status is determined on the basis of 'objective criteria' established by the United Nations. Refugees are entitled as a 'right' to have their status determined; in contrast, asylum status is granted at the discretion of the state (Hefferon 1993: 187).

2 Note the United Nations Convention assumption concerning the gender of refugees.

3 This background information originates from pages 1–2 of Vraciu's second IAT report, *Vraciu* IAT (11559) (1995, unreported).

4 Not telling (or don't tell) here becomes a problem, whereas in Chapter 1 not telling about one's homosexuality becomes a solution and policy initiative for allowing homosexuals to serve in the armed forces.

5 Vraciu failed to mention the existence of this lover until his second appeal hearing. Simon Russell, his legal representative, did not even know about the existence of Mr Vraciu's lover until this time.

6 Yet, as will be demonstrated below, law does not disregard all other knowledges. In fact it appropriates and requests the expertise of many disciplines, for example medical and psychiatric opinions and examinations. This will be demonstrated both in this chapter and in Chapter 4, where the importance of a particular 'authoritative discourse' (the British Medical Association's discourse on adolescent male sexuality) will be analysed in relation to the lawful age of homosexual relations between men.

7 According to the Wolfenden Report: 'Either method may lead to fallacious results' (Wolfenden Report 1957: para 19, 11).

8 Performed by specific agents, for example, doctors, psychiatrists, judges, prosecutors, adjudicators and juries.

9 This conceptualisation of homosexuals as socially indistinguishable from heterosexuals, contrasts with the MoD's discursive machinery in the form of the HPAT report that attempted to present the opposite of this conceptualisation of homosexuals, that is, as a highly visible and disruptive sexual identity.

10 In Chapter 1, sexual acts between men were, according to MoD discourse, no certain indications of a homosexual identity on the part of the parties involved. The MoD listed episodes such as the sexual activity between two adolescent males as horseplay and not as an indication of a homosexual identity. As well as this, the MoD produced episodes of hydraulic acts of sexual substitution, where heterosexual men perform sexual acts with homosexuals in the absence of female sexual partners, as also being an uncertain indication of a homosexual identity in the parties (men) involved.

11 Hocquenghem drew my attention to the concept of 'anal privacy', relative to 'phallic publicity'. That is: 'whereas the phallus was essentially social, the anus was essentially private. The anus has no social desiring function left because all its functions have become excremental: that is, chiefly private' (Hocquenghem 1980: 82). Our anus is 'truly our own' according to Hocquenghem; it is the 'subsoil' of 'the individual', it is the 'well hidden' secret depths of one's person (1980: 82, 83, 86). Anal privacy comes with social and legal sanctions; according to Hocquenghem, the anus must be 'totally yours ... you must not use it ... [publicly]: keep it to yourself' (1980: 86). The assumption behind calling for an anal examination therefore could be interpreted as being that a 'true' homosexual would have lent his 'anal privacy' to 'public' use by other men.

12 In the UK the most famous legal pronouncement about the recognisability and distinctiveness of 'homosexual' males through 'bodily stigmata' (Collier 1998b: 11) was made by Lord Sumner in 1918. According to Lord Sumner, sodomites were stamped with 'the hallmark of a specialised and extraordinary class as much as if they had carried on their bodies some physical peculiarities' (Radzinowicz, in Weeks 1989: 100).

13 As well as discussing Lombroso's work, Karlen also discusses a medico-legal treatise of 1726 by Paulus Zacchius, which referred to the obliteration of the radial folds around the anus as a sign of sodomy (Karlen 1971: 186).

14 During the (1986/7) Cleveland child abuse 'scandal', the 'forensic anus' was the primary site of legal-medical dispute between paediatricians Doctors Higgs and Wyatt and a senior police surgeon, Dr Urvine, about the reliability of the alleged appearance of the anus in child-abuse cases. This dispute raged around

Dr Higgs's development of Reflex Anal Dilatation (RAD) as a physical sign that a child had been 'anally' abused. Dr Urvine disputed Higgs's diagnoses and described RAD as being 'unreliable'. Urvine's opinion also contradicted the Police Surgeons Association's and British Paediatricians Association's endorsement of RAD as a physical sign of abuse in children. However, these organisations qualified their endorsements of RAD, beleiving it not reliable on its own but only when other evidence, such as an unlikely knowledge of 'adult' sexual activity and practices, supported it (Campbell 1988).

Another example of the medical-legal fascination with the anus, this time as a site of homosexual degradation, arose in the Policy Advisory Committee on Sexual Offences (PACSO) 1980 *Working Paper on the Age of Consent* (report published in 1981). According to Moran (1997), in response to this working paper, evidence from 'certain organisations' was sent to PACSO. Some of these organisations stated that 'the anal sphincter might be read as a sign of the degraded state of homosexuality; the anal sphincter of a man who regularly plays a passive role in buggery may slacken, leading in the course of time to incontinence' (Moran 1997: 264). According to Moran, PACSO rejected the latter 'evidence' on the basis of advice given to them by the Department of Health and Social Security, on the grounds that: 'there had been no surveys of the prevalence of this condition or its causation. Nor was there any evidence that it was a common problem among homosexuals' (Moran 1997: 264).

15 This assumption and this particular practice of truth limited medical examiners to discovering evidence of Vraciu being the 'passive' partner of sodomitic intercourse. Yet it is unclear whether anal examination could accurately place Mr Vraciu in Romania as a practising homosexual. The possibility that Vraciu could have expressed himself alternatively with other men – not engaging in anal intercourse, or perhaps only engaging in anal intercourse as the 'active' partner – were absent considerations here. Perhaps the assumption is that the only homosexual activity that results in potential permanent signs or traces of male-to-male genital activity, especially over a time period of years, is being the 'passive' partner during anal intercourse. Other activities such as being the 'active' partner in anal intercourse or performing oral sex or mutual masturbation certainly would not be evident a few hours never mind a few years after their occurrence; these traces can be washed away easily or a condom could be used. This particular medical authentication is also exclusively aimed at male homosexuals. One can only wonder how a lesbian refugee applicant would be authenticated for these purposes in terms of such idiosyncratic criteria.

16 I requested the independent psychiatric report from Mr Russell at the Refugee Legal Centre, but I was informed that, unlike the IAT hearing and the special adjudicator's report of the tribunal, which are public, the psychiatric report is private and unavailable. I have since written to Russell to try and get him to send me an edited version of this report, or even his own comments on the psychiatric techniques or methods used to determine Vraciu's (homo)sexuality, without revealing any of Vraciu's intimate details. This request was also refused by Mr Russell, who stated in a written reply that: 'our duty of confidentiality is absolute and I am not prepared to ask Vraciu to waive his rights in this respect' (Simon Russell, Refugee Legal Centre, 5 June 1997).

17 The special adjudicator recorded some of Vraciu's answers to questions relating to his relationships and sexual identity, both as a child and an adult. For example, 'his homosexual tendencies developed when he was about eight years of age when he used to play basketball with girls and when girls found men attractive, he also found men attractive', 'he discussed this tendency with his school friend who apparently shared the same emotions. Their sexual relationship started in 1990 and he had no sexual relationship with anyone prior to that'.

Since arriving in the UK 'he picked up people when he felt the need to do so. He knows where he can locate such people' (special adjudicator, *Vraciu* 1995: 5, 6).

18 The Institute of Psychiatry memorandum (HO345/8 XC 2499A) submitted to the Wolfenden Committee did not outline procedures that were utilised by psychiatry to recognise homosexuality. This memorandum's primary concern was to 'understand' homosexual offenders and offences for the criminal law, and the treatment or curing of homosexuals of their homosexuality.

19 Article 200, paragraph 1, of the Romanian penal code prohibits lesbian and gay sex in private between consenting adults if the activity in question comes to the attention of a third person and causes a 'scandal'. Paragraph 5 punishes the expression of a homosexual identity by banning 'the incitement or encouragement' of homosexuality, and any 'propaganda or proselytising' about it.

20 Amnesty International, http://www.raglb.org.uk/campaign, accessed 6 June 1996.

21 In fact, in Part 2 of the UNHCR's handbook, *Procedures for the Determination of Refugee Status*, 'privacy' or 'a right to privacy' seems to be absent, especially in Part 2B, entitled: 'Establishing the Facts'. The process of ascertaining and evaluating the facts is summarised as follows:

(a) The applicant should:

(i) Tell the truth and assist the examiner to the full in establishing the facts of his case.

(ii) Make an effort to support his statements by any available evidence and give a satisfactory explanation for any lack of evidence. If necessary he must make an effort to procure additional evidence.

(iii) Supply all pertinent information concerning himself and his past experience in as much detail as is necessary to enable the examiner to establish the relevant facts. He should be asked to give a coherent explanation of all the reasons invoked in support of his application for refugee status and he should answer any question put to him.

(b) The examiner should:

(i) Ensure that the applicant presents his case as fully as possible and with all available evidence.

(ii) Assess the applicant's credibility and evaluate the evidence (if necessary giving the applicant the benefit of the doubt), in order to establish the objective and the subjective elements of the case.

(iii) Relate these elements to the relevant criteria of the 1951 Convention, in order to arrive at a correct conclusion as to the applicant's refugee status.

(UNHCR 1979: para 205)

22 Without the appropriate 'facts' to support his case, Mr Vraciu's second appeal was dismissed. According to his lawyer, Simon Russell, Ioan Vraciu remains in the UK under the general status of asylum seeker.

3 Persecution and immutable identities: homosexual refugees

1 It is outside the scope of this chapter to look at the types of harm specific to gay and lesbian claimants. 'Homosexual' as used in this chapter, refers to male homosexuals. There is no lesbian refugee case law as yet, in the UK, to include in this analysis; lesbian cases also do not figure centrally in the wider analysis of the growing relationship between international refugee law and human rights law. As a result this chapter does not include any analysis of the experiences of lesbians, or of how the differential construction of gender identity within the interpretation of the 1951 UN Convention might affect women and men to

different degrees. This is not to say that lesbians in the countries in question do not suffer from similar, and in some cases more brutal levels of persecution than male homosexuals. There is a great deal of research needed in the area of the persecution suffered by lesbians and the restrictions women in general experience in many countries, relative to men. The political context of gender identity construction and the problems women who refuse to conform to heterosexual relationships encounter in many countries need to be addressed. For researchers interested in lesbian refugees, a starting point might be Goldberg's (1993) article in which, due to the lack of published and unpublished decisions internationally in relation to lesbian refugee cases, Goldberg resorted to constructing her own 'hypothetical case' of Tatiana, a Romanian lesbian seeking asylum in the USA. Other important resources are the Immigration and Nationality Directorate's 'Country Assessment' sections on homosexuals (including homosexual men and lesbian women).

2 I have agreed with Mr S's lawyers not to use his name, in exchange for being permitted to use all Mr S's Immigration Appeal Tribunal adjudicator's reports.

3 I am extremely grateful for the help provided by Malcolm Bryant of Maurice Cohen and Co. Solicitors, in providing me with all these documents.

4 See Chapter 2 for this definition.

5 I am grateful to Simon Russell of the Refugee Legal Centre for providing me with the Golchin IAT report.

6 This case was concerned with the question of whether women in Pakistan can be described as being a particular social group.

7 Including the UK, as described in the Wolfenden Committee's recommendations for the eradication of homosexuality to a self-policed realm of 'privacy' (see Chapter 4).

8 Article 200.1 of the 1968 penal code had been replaced with legislation in the form of Article 200.1 (1996).

9 Lord Steyn's primary objective here was to promote the Acosta-like immutability test in the Shah case over the 'cohesive group' perspective that also emerged in the USA in the Sanchez-Trujillo case. In the Sanchez-Trujillo case the United States Court of Appeals, Ninth Circuit, held that 'particular social group implies a collection of people closely affiliated with each other' (*Sanchez-Trujillo* v. *Immigration and Naturalisation Service* (1986) 801 f 2d 1571).

10 See Currah (1995), Stychin (1995a) and Halley (1994) for debates about issues such as immutability, 'suspect classes' and ethnic models in gay and lesbian legal politics.

11 In Santos's description 'roots' tend towards unitary, apparently cohesive origins, for example, essentialist immutable identities, whereas 'options' are pluralities, for example, human rights standards. Roots look to the past, options towards the future. Roots are fixed, options are open (Lash *et al.* 1998: 12).

12 This obviously follows on from my analysis of the tactics employed by homosexuals serving in the armed forces to appear to as 'assumed heterosexuals'.

13 Although this theme will be touched on in the next chapter in terms of the Wolfenden Committee's suggestions concerning the partial decriminalisation of homosexual acts in circumscribed and private situations.

4 The fear of 'homosexual spread': legislating the heteronormativity of protection 1957–2000

1 For more details on Sir John Nott-Bower's role in producing a report on homosexual offences in London for the Wolfenden Committee see Moran and McGhee (1998).

2 For example, Borstal training; detention centres; approved schools; care/fostering; corrective training; preventative detention.

3 This decriminalisation through privacy was described in the following terms in the Wolfenden Report:

> there must remain a realm of private morality not the law's business. To say this is not to condone or encourage private immorality. On the contrary, it is to emphasise the personal and private responsibility of the individual for his own actions, and that is a responsibility which a mature agent can properly be expected to carry for himself without the threat of punishment from the law.
>
> (Wolfenden Report: para 61, 24)

4 The Wolfenden philosophy concerning the function of the criminal law was as follows:

> the organs of government should seek only to constrain the external manifestations of morality in 'visible' conduct. A 'private' realm of personal desires and predilections was to be delineated, to be regulated by the force of public opinion, by the pressures of civil society and personal conscience, but not by the coercive powers of the state.
>
> (Rose 1990: 229)

5 The Wolfenden Committee's description of homosexual 'privacy', and this 'private' realm, became a spatial and visual-intercorporeal arrangement between homosexuals and members of the public, between the watchers and the self-policing homosexual 'watched', just as was advocated in the MoD's passing policy in Chapter 1:

> It is our intention that the law should continue to regard as criminal any indecent act committed in a place where members of the public may be likely to see and be offended by it, but where there is no possibility of public offence of this nature it becomes a matter of the private responsibility of the persons concerned and as such, in our opinion, is outside the proper purview of the Criminal Law.
>
> (Wolfenden Report 1957: para. 64, 25)

Thus, a 'homosexual act', according to this definition, would be determined as being 'in private' if it was conducted in a place where it was unlikely to be witnessed by, and thus cause offence to, a member of the general public. Here, the Wolfenden Committee incorporated a definition of homosexual privacy which invoked a panoptic spatial arrangement with the heteronormative gaze of the potential, ever-present overseer, who could be easily offended by the display of homosexual tendencies or the sight of homosexual acts. According to the Wolfenden Committee's formulation: privacy and publicity became embodied phenomena which were discernible through offence or non-offence caused to the eyes of a heteronormative subject, 'a member of the public', who might see and be offended by the corporeal, genital interaction of male bodies. Thus, the Wolfenden conceptualisation of 'in private' evoked 'the public' and 'the private' as a 'lived distinction' in and around 'bodily behaviours' (Young 1990: 140). The decriminalisation and privatisation of homosexuality was thus to be achieved through the self-surveillance and circumspection of homosexual bodies structured by an intercorporeal relationship organised around what Moran describes as 'the paranoid figure of an ever-present third party' (Moran 1996a: 58).

6 On the passing of these Wolfenden Committee recommendations into law in the Sexual Offences Act of 1967, public homosexual activities and indiscreet homosexuals were subject to rigorous policing. This project was described by Weeks as initiating a contradictory series of effects as 'privatisation did not necessarily

involve a diminution of control' and the Wolfenden reforms were 'restrictive in one direction, liberal in the other' (Weeks 1989: 243). So that, following decriminalisation in the form of the Sexual Offences Act of 1967, arrests for homosexual offences 'in public' actually increased.

7 The use of oestrogen therapy to treat homosexual offenders was based on the hypothesis that 'the strength of a man's desire may well be an important factor in his behaviour, and if the strength of the desire can be diminished it is not unreasonable to suppose that the disposition to commit offences will be correspondingly lessened' (Wolfenden Report 1957: para. 209).

8 For a fuller account of the use of oestrogen therapies in England post-1958 see Richardson (2000) and King and Bartlett (1999).

9 A similar concern was published in the Wolfenden Report in Mr Adair's 'Reservations'. According to Adair, if the sanctions of the criminal law were removed, there would also be removed the main motivation for homosexuals to consult medical advisers (Adair, Wolfenden Report 1957: para 8.1). Adair conceded that the number of homosexuals who consulted medical advisers at the time of the report was relatively small, and this consultation was usually only made when homosexuals found themselves in the hands of the police and the courts; 'it appears, therefore, that even the small number who attend for medical examination will be reduced considerably if the proposed change be carried out' (Adair, Wolfenden Report 1957: para. 8.1).

10 The Homosexual Law Reform Society was a homosexual lobbying group set up after the publication of the Wolfenden Report in order to preach 'the gospel' of the Wolfenden Report especially in relation to decriminalisation (West 1977: 283). For a fuller discussion of the HLRS see Grey (1992).

11 According to Richardson, in 1958 the Home Secretary circulated a memo that concluded:

> I therefore recommend that you agree that oestrogen treatment may be given to male prisoners in those cases where: a) the prisoner desires it; and b) the prison medical officer considers that it would be beneficial (either as a treatment *per se* or as an element in other forms of treatment); and c) the prisoner gives his written consent and a written acknowledgement that he understands the risks involved.
>
> (Richardson 2000: 20)

12 According to Moran, the difference between determination of 'adult' and 'the young' by the Wolfenden Committee (and in Lord Arran's formulation above)

> might be understood in terms of a calibration that plots the male body according to the requirements of an economy of physical and psycho-sexual vulnerability and independence. The line which divides them might be a frontier that inscribes the male body by way of an intimacy that is understood as a surplus within the almanac of the psycho-sexual process of heterosexualisation when heterosexualisation is secured.
>
> (Moran 1997: 257)

13 For more on the PACSO report see Moran (1997).

14 This report was published after the publication of two working papers. These working papers were designed to invite comment on the proposed reform of the law in relation to sexual offences. These papers were the Policy Advisory Committee on Sexual Offences, *Working Paper on the Age of Consent in Relation to Sexual Offences* (1980) and the Criminal Law Revision Committee, *Working Paper on Sexual Offences* (1979).

15 During the Criminal Justice and Public Order Bill debate in the Commons the terminology 'age of consent' that the committee reserved for heterosexual relations, was used to describe homosexual relations too.

16 According to Mrs Currie, the World Health Organisation stated that: 'people who hide their sexual orientation for fear of criminalisation or alienation … are placed in situations that are not conducive to safe sexual practices'. *The Lancet* stated on 22 January 1994 that 'all young people need safer sex education but the needs of young homosexuals are not being met. This worrying disparity may arise both directly and indirectly from the current legislation' (cited by Mrs Currie, *Hansard*, Commons, 21 February 1994: col. 78).

17 Section 28 of the Local Government Act states that:

(1) A local authority shall not:

  (a) Intentionally promote homosexuality or publish material with the intention of promoting homosexuality.
  (b) Promote the teaching in any maintained school of the acceptability of homosexuality as a pretended family relationship.

18 Section 28 emerged in a power struggle between municipal socialism, local democracy and the central government's control of local government, see Thomas and Costigan (1990), Colvin (1989), Cooper (1993, 1994), Smith (1994).

19 Jeffrey Weeks (1986) can be described as initiating a body of academic writings from authors such as Cindy Patton, Anna Marie Smith, Didi Herman, etc. who have all identified the rise of reactionary (to the new politics of sexuality) 'heterosexual' identity politics within the New Right. According to Weeks:

the new politics of sexuality may have created new spaces. It has also, however, opened new fissures and generated new hostilities. There is no doubt that one of the contributions to the rise of the 'New Right' in America, with its own moral agenda, was deep hostility to what was seen as the moral and social collapse represented by feminism and lesbian and gay politics.

(Weeks 1986: 106)

20 Article 14 of the European Convention on Human Rights and Fundamental Freedoms:

The enjoyment of the rights and freedoms set forth in this Convention shall be secured without discrimination on any grounds such as sex, race, colour, language, religion, political or other opinion, national or social origin, association with a national minority, property, birth or other status.

21 Article 8 of the European Convention on Human Rights and Fundamental Freedoms:

1. Everyone has the right to respect for his private and family life, his home and his correspondence.
2. There shall be no interference by a public authority with the exercise of this right except such as is in accordance with the law and is necessary in a democratic society in the interests of national security, public safety or the economic well-being of the country, for the prevention of disorder or crime, for the protection of health or morals, or for the protection of the rights and freedoms of others.

22 At that time the Labour government under the leadership of Prime Minister Tony Blair had been in power for two months, having been voted into office in May 1997. Perhaps if the Conservative government had still been in power at the time of the Sutherland case, the UK would have accepted Sutherland's self-assertion that he was a homosexual less readily.

23 In this strategy we see traces of what Giddens (1994) describes as dialogic democracy and Weeks describes as radical pluralism (Weeks 1985, 1992, 1995). According to Weeks:

> the aim of a Radical Pluralism is to realise the possibilities of liberalism by identifying and combating the forces that limit its full potentiality: above all, institutionalised inequalities and structures of domination and subordination. ... Radical Pluralism is an argument for a more open and democratic culture which does not assume any historic inevitability nor any *a priori* justification in 'the nature of humankind'. Its success will not be measured by the attainment of an ideal society but by its ability to respond to individual and collective needs as these evolve and change over time.
>
> (Weeks 1992: 407)

In Giddens's description of dialogic democracies, individuals approach one another as equals in an atmosphere of mutual tolerance (Giddens 1994: 118, 119).

24 Baroness Young uses the term 'family people' here in order to substantiate a particular 'family identity' (Sedgwick 1994: 6). This bringing into being of a sense of identity, of being 'family people', is an example of the process of identification where the achievement of an identity is through the play of difference and similitude in the self–other relationship. For Fuss, 'identification is the detour through the other that defines a self' (Fuss 1995: 2). Baroness Young can be described as drawing the boundaries of the identity she has encapsulated by the term 'family people' so as to include familial or normative heterosexuality as the 'normal' and 'natural' and to exclude 'the homosexual' in its male and female incarnations and familial associations as other to this bounded identity.

25 The employment of 'the child' and the young and vulnerable in the discursive formation of homosexuality, age and protection, from the publication of the Wolfenden Report to the House of Lords debates in the last years of the twentieth century, illustrates what Jenks (1996) describes as the distinction between the concept of 'the child of modernity' and 'the child of postmodernity' (1996). According to Collier, Jenks's description of the child of modernity is of an innocent child dedicated to the future (1998a: 94). In contrast, the child of postmodernity, as highlighted in the Lords' objections to lowering the lawful age of homosexual relations between men

> has become the site for the relocation of a variety of discourses concerned not so much with futurity as with questions of stability, integration and the maintenance of the social bond itself ... within recent debates the postmodern child appears as guarantor of the sociality of the present as well as, given the heavy investment which has been made in this child, a potential threat to that social bond.
>
> (Collier 1997: 95)

26 See also Weeks and Donovan (1999) 'Everyday Experiments: Narratives of Non-Heterosexual Relationships' and, for the 'fragmentation' or the restructuring of the 'heterosexual' family and 'the family' in general, see Smart (1999) *Family Fragments*.

27 From the Greek, *emein*, to vomit (Cohen 1994: 37).

28 An interesting twist to this observation is that two of the central 'players' in the process whereby homosexuality was partially decriminalised in the UK both had close family members who were homosexuals. Sir John Wolfenden's son Jeremy Wolfenden was homosexual (see Sebastian Faulks's triple biography *The Fatal Englishman: Three Short Lives* [1996]) and Lord Arran's elder brother Lord Sudley was also reputed to have taken male lovers. According to Higgins:

> [Lord Arran] never revealed to the House his motive for pursuing the Bill so vigorously, but it was probably his way of atoning for the way that his aristocratic family had treated his elder brother Lord Sudley. ... Sudley regularly brought Guardsmen back to his home in Chelsea, one, a Scot, becoming his companion. The family felt that Sudley was being exploited by the former soldier, who had moved his wife and children into the house. Lord Sudley's family managed to send Sudley away to a home where he remained until his death. It was clear Lord Arran was drawn to the measure because of the tragedy of his brother.
>
> (Higgins 1996: 133)

29 Straw included in his speech the importance of dealing with the unfinished business of this issue. In particular he reminded the House that the Parliament Act might have to be employed. Straw also stated that the legislative reform in Scotland on this issue provided a clear mandate to Parliament. On 19 January 2000 the Scottish Parliament voted by 90 to 16 in favour of the Sexual Offences (Amendment) Bill that would equalise the homosexual and heterosexual ages of consent alongside creating a new criminal offence of breach of trust.

30 Under the Parliament Act, any legislation that has been rejected by the Lords can automatically become law one year later, if it reflects the wishes of the House of Commons.

Conclusion

1 Wayne Morgan is an Australian queer legal theorist and activist, based in Melbourne, Australia.

2 In contradistinction to this queer anti-privacy, I have emphasised the tactical privatisation of homosexuals, through circumspect comportments, in the case studies. In the case studies I demonstrate that homosexual circumspection and privacy is an efficacious political tactic for surviving within heteronormative legal and social environments.

3 Carl Stychin is a Canadian legal academic teaching and residing in the UK.

4 Which can be found in his book *Law's Desire* (1995a).

5 For example, I would dispute, in the context of the UK and the European Union, what Stein, in a similar vein to Stychin and Morgan, describes as one of the hallmarks of queer theory: the 'rejection of civil rights strategies in favour of a politics of carnival, transgression and parody which leads to deconstruction, decentring, revisionist readings, and an anti-assimilationist politics' (1997: 167). In the case studies included in this book, especially in Chapters 1, 3 and 4, I demonstrate the importance of international law and especially the human rights standards within the European Convention for the disruption and altering of legal institutional procedures, most notably in refugee law and the discursive regimes within the criminal law (especially related to adolescent homosexuals). However, the advantage and disadvantage of human rights for legal struggles in and around homosexuality, as demonstrated in the case studies, is that they are 'the raw material of both conservative and of progressive interpretative strategies, following competing conceptions of the good' (Gaete 1993: 161).

6 According to Foucault, 'my point is not everything is bad, but that everything is dangerous. ... If everything is dangerous, then we always have something to do' (1982: 232).

7 Bower describes Janet Halley's work on the Hardwick decision as being part of the first wave of queer legal scholarship (1997: 271). What Halley introduced to North American queer legal theory was the focus not on categories, but on the process of categorisation (Halley 1993: 83). By focusing on the processes of

categorisation, Halley concluded that it was heterosexuality that was called into question in 'sodomy' cases such as Hardwick: 'despite its representation as monolithic in its nonhomosexuality, heterosexuality as it operates in Federal equal protection cases is a highly unstable, default characteristic for people who have not marked themselves or been marked by others as homosexual' (1993: 83). What Halley uncovers in her analysis of the processes of categorisation within 'sodomy' cases such as the Hardwick case is that legal description of homosexuality 'as different' is a means of displacing the anxieties and doubts that sustain the classification 'heterosexual' as a cohesive class or subject position (Bower 1997: 1016).

8 This is a problem for Bower's development of a queer legal politics, even though she does insist on 'local particular interventions' (1994: 1030) as in queer cultural political tactics, her declared ambition was, however, to develop a political approach for queers in general:

> My purpose in the following is to suggest how queers might 'stand before the law' with awareness of law's capacity to enable and constrain claims to identity and, at the same time, how they might deploy a strategic framework which seeks to articulate a subject who is not defined in unitary terms.
>
> (Bower 1994: 1020)

9 For example the United Nations Convention Relating to the Status of Refugees (1951).

Bibliography

Abelman, S. and Foster, K. (1992) Critical Legal Theory: The Power of Law, in I. Grigg-Spall and P. Ireland (eds) *The Critical Lawyers' Handbook*, London: Pluto Press, 39–43.

Ahearne, L. (1995) *Michel de Certeau: Interpretation and its Other*, Cambridge: Polity Press.

Allen, B. (1998) Foucault and Modern Political Philosophy, in J. Moss (ed.) *The Later Foucault*, London: Sage Publications, 164–198.

Altman, A. (1990) *Critical Legal Studies: A Liberal Critique*, Princeton, NJ: Princeton University Press.

Amnesty International (1996) *Campaign for Romanian Lesbian and Gay Human Rights*, http://www.raglb.org.uk/campaign, 06/06/96 13:15, 1–5.

Amnesty International (1997) *Breaking the Silence: Human Rights Violations Based on Sexual Orientation*, Amnesty International: United Kingdom.

Bamforth, N. (1997) *Sexuality, Morals and Justice*, London and Washington: Cassell.

Barker, P. (1993) *Michel Foucault: Subversions of the Subject*, New York: Harvester Wheatsheaf.

Barry, A., Osborne, T. and Rose, N. (eds) (1996) *Foucault and Political Reason: Liberalism, Neo-Liberalism and Rationalities of Government*, London: UCL Press.

Bartky, S.L. (1990) *Feminity and Domination: Studies in the Phenomenology of Oppression*, London and New York: Routledge.

Bartowski, F. (1988) Epistemic Drift in Foucault, in I. Diamind and L. Quinby (eds) *Feminism and Foucault: Reflection on Resistance*, Boston: Northwestern University Press, 43–58.

Bauman, Z. (1988) Strangers: The Social Constructon of Universality and Particularity, *Telos*, 78, winter, 7–42.

Baxter, H. (1996) Bringing Foucault into Law and Law into Foucault, *Stanford Law Review*, 48, January, 449–479.

Beck, U. (1994) The Reinvention of Politics: Towards a Theory of Reflexive Modernization, in U. Beck, A. Giddens and S. Lash (eds) *Reflexive Modernization: Politics, Tradition and Aesthetics in the Modern Social Order*, Cambridge: Polity Press, 1–55.

Beemyn, B. and Eliason, M. (eds) (1996) *Queer Studies*, New York and London: New York University Press.

Bently, L. (1996) Introduction, in L. Bently and L. Flynn (eds) *Law and the Senses: Sensational Jurisprudence*, London and Chicago: Pluto Press, 1–20.

Bently, L. and Flynn, L. (1996) *Law and the Senses: Sensational Jurisprudence*, London and Chicago: Pluto Press.

Berlant, L. (1993) National Brands/National Body: Imitation of Life, in B. Robbin (ed.) *The Phantom Public Sphere*, Minneapolis: University of Minnesota Press, 173–208.

Berlant, L. (1997) *The Queen of America Goes to Washington City*, Durham, NC, and London: Duke University Press.

Berlant, L. and Warner, M. (1998) Sex in Public, *Critical Inquiry*, 24, winter, 547–566.

Bersani, L. (1987) Is the Rectum a Grave? *October*, 43, winter, 197–222.

Bersani, L. (1995) *Homos*, Cambridge, MA: Harvard University Press.

Best, S. and Kellner, D. (1991) *Postmodern Theory: Critical Interrogations*, London: Macmillan.

Bhabha, H. (1994) *The Location of Culture*, London: Routledge.

Bottomley, A. (1992) Feminism: Paradoxes of the Double Bind, in I. Grigg-Spall and P. Ireland (eds) *The Critical Lawyers' Handbook*, London: Pluto Press, 22–29.

Bottomley, A. and Conaghan, J. (1993) Feminist Theory and Legal Strategy, *Journal of Law and Society*, 20(1), 1–5.

Bourdieu, P. (1977) *Outline of a Theory of Practice*, Cambridge: Cambridge University Press.

Bourdieu, P. (1994) Structures, Habitus and Practices, in *The Polity Reader in Social Theory*, Cambridge: Polity, 95–110.

Bower, L. (1994) Queer Acts and the Politics of 'Direct Address': Rethinking Law, Culture, and Community, *Law and Society Review*, 28(5), 1009–1033.

Bower, L. (1997) Queer Problems/Straight Solutions: The Limits of a Politics of 'Official Recognition', in S. Phelan (ed.) *Playing with Fire: Queer Politics, Queer Theories*, London and New York: Routledge, 267–291.

Bowers v. *Hardwick*, 478 U.S. 186, 106 S. Ct. 2841 (1986).

Bridgeman, J. and Millin, S. (eds) (1995) *Law and the Body Politic: Regulating the Female Body*, Aldershot: Dartmouth.

Bristow, J. (1997) *Sexuality*, London and New York: Routledge.

Brown, W. (1998) Genealogical Politics, in J. Moss (ed.) *The Later Foucault*, London: Sage Publications, 33–49.

Burchell, G. (1991) Peculiar Interests: Civil Society and Governing 'The System of Natural Liberty', in G. Burchell, C. Gordon and P. Miller (eds) *The Foucault Effect*, London: Harvester Wheatsheaf, 119–150.

Burchell, G. (1996) Liberal Government and Techniques of the Self, in A. Barry, T. Osborne and N. Rose (eds) *Foucault and Political Reason*, London: UCL Press, 19–36.

Butler, J. (1989) Gendering the Body, in A. Garry (ed.) *Woman, Knowledge and Reality*, London and New York: Routledge, 253–262.

Butler, J. (1990) *Gender Trouble*, London and New York: Routledge.

Butler, J. (1991) Imitation and Gender Insubordination, in D. Fuss (ed.) *Inside/Out*, London and New York: Routledge, 13–31.

Butler, J. (1992) Sexual Inversion, in D. Stanton (ed.) *Discourses of Sexuality*, Michigan: University of Michigan Press, 344–361.

Butler, J. (1993a) *Bodies that Matter*, London and New York: Routledge.

Butler, J. (1993) Critically Queer, *GLQ: A Journal of Lesbian and Gay Studies*, 1(1), 17–32.

Butler, J. (1996) Status, Conduct, Word, and Deed: A Response to Janet Halley, *GLQ: A Journal of Lesbian and Gay Studies* 3(2–3), 253–261.

Butler, J. (1997) *Excitable Speech*, London and New York: Routledge.

Butler, J. (1999) Revisiting Bodies and Pleasures, *Theory, Culture & Society*, 16(2), 11–20.

Cain, M. (1995) Horatio's Mistake: Notes on Some Spaces in an Old Text, *Journal of Law and Society*, 22(1), 68–77.

Campbell, B. (1988) *Unofficial Secrets*, London: Virago.

Canada (Attorney General) v. *Ward* [1993] 4 D.L.R. 103 at 1; [1993] 2 R.C.S: 689.

Carey, G. (1998) We Can't Endorse This Error, *The Times*, 22 July, 18.

Chaney, D. (1996) *Lifestyles*, London and New York: Routledge.

Cheah, P. and Grosz, E. (1996) The Body of Law: Notes Towards a Theory of Corporeal Justice, in P. Cheah, D. Fraser and J. Grbich *Thinking Through the Body of Law*, St Leonards, Australia: Allen and Unwin, 3–25.

Cheah, P., Fraser, D. and Grbich, J. (1996) *Thinking Through the Body of Law*, St Leonards, Australia: Allen and Unwin.

Cohen, E. (1990) Are We (Not) What We Are Becoming? Gay Studies and the Discipline of Knowledge, in J.A. Boone and M. Cadden (eds) *Engendering Men*, London and New York: Routledge, 161–175.

Cohen, E. (1991) Who Are 'We'? Gay 'Identity' as Political (E)motion, in D. Fuss (ed.) *Inside/Out*, London and New York: Routledge, 71–92.

Cohen, R. (1994) *Frontiers of Identity: The British and the Others*, London and New York: Longman.

Collier, R. (1998a) Nutty Professors, Men in Suits and New Entrepreneurs: Corporeality, Subjectivity and Change in the Law School and Legal Practice, *Social and Legal Studies*, 7(1), 27–53.

Collier, R. (1998b) *Masculinities, Crime and Criminology: Men, Heterosexuality and the Criminal(ised) Other*, London: Sage Publications.

Colvin, M. (1989) *Section 28: A Practical Guide to the Law and its Implications*, London: National Council for Civil Liberties.

Cooper, D. (1993) An Engaged State: Sexuality, Governance, and the Potential for Change, *Journal of Law and Society*, 20(3), 257–275.

Cooper, D. (1994) *Sexing the City: Lesbian and Gay Politics Within the Activist State*, London: Rivers Oram Press.

Cooper, D. (1995) *Power in Struggle: Feminism, Sexuality and the State*, New York: New York University Press.

Cooper, D. and Herman, D. (1991) Getting 'the Family Right': Legislating Heterosexuality in Britain, 1986–1991, *Canadian Journal of Family Law*, 10, 41–78.

Cooper, J. (1995) The Last Taboo – Establishing the Right to a Sexual Identity, *Interrright Bulletin*, 9(4), 107–111.

Critchley, S. (1992) *The Ethics of Deconstruction: Derrida and Levinas*, Oxford: Blackwell.

Currah, P. (1995) Searching for Immutability: Race and Rights Discourse, in A.R. Wilson (ed.) *A Simple Matter of Justice? Theorizing Lesbian and Gay Politics*, London and New York: Cassell, 51–90.

Daly, K. (1997) Different Ways of Conceptualising Sex/Gender in Feminist Theory and Their Implications for Criminology, *Theoretical Criminology*, 1(1), 25–51.

Danielsen, D. and Engle, K. (1995) Introduction, in D. Danielsen and K. Engle (eds) *After Identity: A Reader in Law and Culture*, Routledge: London and New York, xiii–xix.

Davies, M. (1996) *Delimiting the Law: 'Postmodernism' and the Politics of Law*, London: Pluto Press.

Davies, P. (1992) The Role of Disclosure in Coming Out Among Gay Men, in K. Plummer (ed.) *Modern Homosexualities: Fragments of Lesbian and Gay Experience*, London and New York: Routledge, 75–83.

de Certeau, M. (1984) *The Practices of Everyday Life*, Berkeley: University of California Press.

de Certeau, M. (1986) *Heterologies*, Manchester: Manchester University Press.

de Lauretis, T. (1987) *Technologies of Gender*, New York: Macmillan.

de Lauretis, T. (1988) Sexual Indifference and Lesbian Representation, *Theatre Journal* 40(2), May, 151–177.

de Lauretis, T. (1991) Queer Theory: Lesbian and Gay Sexualities: An Introduction, *Differences*, 3(2), iii–xviii.

Derrida, J. (1963) *Of Grammatology*, Baltimore, MD: Johns Hopkins University Press.

Derrida, J. (1981) *Positions*, Chicago: Chicago University Press.

Derrida, J. (1982) *Margins of Philosophy*, Chicago, University of Chicago Press.

Devlin, P. (1965) *The Enforcement of Morals*, Oxford: Oxford University Press.

Dollimore, J. (1991) *Sexual Dissidence: Augustine to Wilde, Freud to Foucault*, Oxford: Clarendon Press.

Dollimore, J. (1992) The Cultural Politics of Perversion: Augustine, Shakespeare, Freud, Foucault, in J. Bristow (ed.) *Sexual Sameness: Textual Differences in Lesbian and Gay Writing*, London and New York: Routledge, 9–25.

Dollimore, J. (1998) *Death, Desire and Loss in Western Culture*, London: Allen Lane, Penguin.

Douzinas, C. and Warrington, R. (1992) The Impossible Pedagogical Politics of (the Law of) Postmodernism, in I. Grigg-Spall and P. Ireland (eds) *The Critical Lawyers' Handbook*, London: Pluto Press, 30–38.

Douzinas, C. and Warrington, R. (1994) *Justice Miscarried*, New York and London: Harvester Wheatsheaf.

Dreyfuss, H. and Rabinow, P. (1982) *Michel Foucault: Beyond Structuralism and Hermeneutics*, New York and London: Harvester Wheatsheaf.

Dudgeon v. *United Kingdom*, Series A. No. 59; (1982) 4 E.H.R.R. 149.

Duggan, L. (1992) Making it Perfectly Queer, *Socialist Review* (San Francisco) 22 (part 1), 11–31.

Duggan, L. (1994) Queering the State, *Social Text*, 39, 1–14.

Ebert, T.L. (1995) (Untimely) Critiques for Red Feminism, in M. Zavarzadeh, T. Ebert and D. Morton (eds) *Post-Ality: Marxism and Postmodernism*, Washington, DC: Maisonneuve Press, 113–149.

Edelman, L. (1994) *Homographesis*, New York: Routledge.

Epstein, S. (1987) Gay Politics, Ethnic Identity: The Limits of Social Constructionism, *Socialist Review* (San Francisco), 17 (part 3–4), 9–54.

Epstein, S. (1996) A Queer Encounter: Sociology and the Study of Sexuality, in S. Seidman (ed.) *Queer Theory/Sociology*, Oxford, UK and Cambridge, MA: Blackwell, 145–167.

Escoffier, J. (1998) *American Homo: Community and Perversity*, Berkeley: University of California Press.

Evans, D. (1989/90) Section 28: Law, Myth and Paradox, *Critical Social Policy*, 9(3), 73–95.

Ewald, F. (1990) Norms, Discipline, and the Law, *Representations*, Spring, 138–161.

Faulks, S. (1996) *The Fatal Englishman: Three Short Lives*, Isle of Man: Vintage.

Fine, M. (1994) Dis-Stance and Other Stances: Negations of Power Inside Feminist Research, in A. Gitlin (ed.) *Power and Method: Political Activism and Educational Research*, London and New York: Routledge, 13–35.

Flynn, L. (1996) See What I Mean: The Authority of Law and Visions of Women, in L. Bently and L. Flynn (eds) *Law and the Senses*, London and Chicago: Pluto Press, 139–159.

Fornas, J. (1995) *Cultural Theory and Late Modernity*, London: Sage Publications.

Foucault, M. (1972) *The Archaeology of Knowledge*, New York: Pantheon.

Foucault, M. (1973) *The Birth of the Clinic: An Archaeology of Medical Perception*, London: Tavistock Publications.

Foucault, M. (1974) Human Nature: Justice Versus Power, in F. Elders (ed.) *Reflexive Waters: The Basic Concerns of Mankind*, London: Souvenir, 29–48.

Foucault, M. (1977a) *Discipline and Punish*, Harmondsworth: Penguin.

Foucault, M. (1977b) Intellectuals and Power: A Conversation Between Michel Foucault and Gilles Deleuze, in D.F. Bouchard (ed.) *Language, Counter-Memory, Practice*, Ithaca, NY: Cornell University Press, 205–217.

Foucault, M. (1977c) Nietzsche, Genealogy, History, in D.F. Bouchard (ed.) *Language, Counter-Memory, Practice*, Ithaca, NY: Cornell University Press, 139–164.

Foucault, M. (1978) *The History of Sexuality, Volume 1: An Introduction*, London: Penguin Books.

Foucault, M. (1979a) Truth and Power, in M. Morris and P. Patton (eds) *Michel Foucault: Power, Truth and Strategy*, Sydney: Feral Publications, 29–38.

Foucault, M. (1979b) The Life of Infamous Men, M. Morris and P. Patton (eds) *Michel Foucault: Power, Truth and Strategy*, Sydney: Feral Publications, 74–85.

Foucault, M. (1980a) Two Lectures, in C. Gordon (ed.) *Power/Knowledge: Selected. Interviews and Other Writings 1972–77*, Brighton: Harvester Press, 78–108.

Foucault, M. (1980b) Truth and Power, in C. Gordon (ed.) *Power/Knowledge: Selected. Interviews and Writings 1972–1977*, Brighton: Harvester Press, 109–133.

Foucault, M. (1981) The Order of Discourse, in R. Young (ed.) *Untying the Text*, Boston, London and New York: Routledge and Kegan Paul, 48–78.

Foucault, M. (1982) The Subject and Power, in H. Dreyfuss and P. Rabinow (eds) *Michel Foucault: Beyond Structuralism and Hermeneutics*, London: Harvester Wheatsheaf, 208–226.

Foucault, M. (1985) *The Use of Pleasure: The History of Sexuality, Volume 2*, New York: Pantheon.

Foucault, M. (1987) Questions of Method: An Interview with Michel Foucault, in K. Baynes (ed.) *After Philosophy: End or Transformation?*, Cambridge, MA: MIT Press, 100–117.

Foucault, M. (1988) Practicing Criticism, in L.D. Kritzman (ed.) *Michel Foucault: Politics, Philosophy, Culture,* London and New York: Routledge, 152–156.

Foucault, M. (1991) Governmentality, in G. Burchell, C. Gordon and P. Miller (eds) *The Foucault Effect*, London: Harvester Wheatsheaf, 87–104.

Foucault, M. (1997) The Abnormals, in P. Rabinow (ed.) *Michel Foucault: Ethics, Subjectivity and Truth*, London: Allen Lane, Penguin, 51–59.

Fraser, N. (1989) *Unruly Practices*, Cambridge: Polity Press.

Freud, S. (1964) The Uncanny, in J. Strachey (ed. and trans.) *The Standard Edition of the Complete Psychological Works of Sigmund Freud*, vol. 17, 1917–1919, London: Hogarth Press, 218–256.

Fuss, D. (1989) *Essentially Speaking: Feminism, Nature and Difference*, New York and London: Routledge.

Fuss, D. (1991) Inside/Out (Introduction), in D. Fuss (ed.) *Inside/Out: Lesbian Theories, Gay Theories*, London and New York: Routledge, 1–12.

Fuss, D. (1995) *Identification Papers*, London and New York: Routledge.

Gaete, R. (1993) *Human Rights and the Limits of Critical Reason*, Aldershot: Dartmouth.

Gagliardi, D.P. (1988) The Inadequacy of Cognizable Grounds of Persecution as a Criterion for According Refugee Status, *Stanford Journal of International Studies*, 24, 259–287.

Gandal, K. (1986) Foucault's Intellectual Work and Politics, *Telos*, 6–7, spring, 121–134.

Gashe, R. (1986) *The Tain of the Mirror*, Cambridge, MA: Harvard University Press.

Gay Times (1995) (untitled article), March, 23.

Gibney, M. (1988) A 'Well-Founded' Fear of Persecution, *Human Rights Quarterly*, 10, 109–121.

Giddens, A. (1988) Goffman as a Systematic Social Theorist, in P. Drew and A. Wootton (eds) *Erving Goffman: Exploring the Interaction Order*, Boston: Northeastern University Press, 250–279.

Giddens, A. (1994) *Beyond Left and Right: The Future of Radical Politics*, Cambridge: Polity Press.

Godzich, W. (1986) Foreword, in M. de Certeau, *Heterologies*, Manchester: Manchester University Press, i–xiii.

Goffman, E. (1962) *Asylums*, Chicago: Aldine Publishing Company.

Goffman, E. (1963) *Stigma*, London: Pelican. (Reprinted 1968.)

Goffman, E. (1967) *Interaction Ritual: Essays on Face-to-Face Behaviour*, Garden City, NY: Anchor Books.

Golchin IAT (7623) (1991, unreported).

Goldberg, S.B. (1993) Give me Liberty or Give me Death: Political Asylum and the Global Persecution of Lesbians and Gay Men, *Cornell International Law Journal*, 26, 605–623.

Goodrich, P. (1987) *Legal Discourse*, London: Macmillan.

Goodrich, P. (1990) *Languages of Law*, London: Weidenfeld.

Goodwin-Gill, G.S. (1983) *The Refugee in International Law*, Oxford: Clarendon Press.

Gordon, C. (ed.) (1980) *Michel Foucault: Power/Knowledge*, Brighton: Harvester Press.

Gordon, C. (1987) The Soul of the Citizen: Max Weber and Michel Foucault on Rationality and Government, in S. Whimster and S. Lash (eds) *Max Weber, Rationality and Modernity*, London: Allen and Unwin, 293–317.

Gordon, C. (1991) Governmental Rationality: An Introduction, in G. Burchell, C. Gordon and P. Miller (eds) *The Foucault Effect*, London: Harvester Wheatsheaf, 1–52.

Grahl-Madsen, A. (1966) *The Status of Refugees in International Law, Volume 1: Refugee Character*, Amsterdam: Sijthoff-Leyden.

Grey, A. (1992) *Quest for Justice: Towards Homosexual Emancipation*, London: Sinclair-Stevenson.

Grigg-Spall, I. and Ireland, P. (eds) (1992) Introduction, *The Critical Lawyers' Handbook*, London: Pluto Press

Grosz, E. (1995) *Space, Time and Perversion: Essays on the Politics of the Body*, London and New York: Routledge.

Guttman, H. (1988) Rousseau's Confession: A Technology of the Self, in L.H. Martin *et al.* (eds) *Technologies of the Self: A Seminar with Michel Foucault*, London: Tavistock Publications, 99–120.

Habermas, J. (1987) *The Philosophical Discourse of Modernity: Twelve Lectures*, F. Lawrence, trans., Cambridge: Polity Press.

Haldar, P. (1991) The Evidencer's Eye: Representations of Truth in the Laws of Evidence, *Law and Critique*, 11(2), 172–189.

Haldar, P. (1996) Acoustic Justice, in L. Bently and L. Flynn (eds) *Law and the Senses: Sensational Jurisprudence*, London and Chicago: Pluto Press, 123–136.

Hall, E. (1995) *We Can't Even March Straight*, London: Vintage.

Hall, S. (1980) Reformism and the Legislation of Consent, in National Deviancy Conference (ed.) *Permissiveness and Control: The Fate of Sixties Legislation*, London: Macmillan, 1–43.

Hall, S. (1991) Ethnicity: Identity and Difference, *Radical America*, 13(4), 9–20.

Hall, S. (1996) Introduction: Who Needs 'Identity'? in S. Hall and P. Du Gay (eds) *Questions of Cultural Identity*, London: Sage Publications, 1–17.

Halley, J. (1991) Misreading Sodomy: A Critique of the Classification of 'Homosexual' in Federal Equal Protection Law, in J. Epstein and K. Straub (eds) *Body Guards: The Cultural Politics of Gender Ambiguity*, London and New York: Routledge, 351–378.

Halley, J. (1993) The Construction of Homosexuality, in M. Warner (ed.) *Fear of a Queer Planet*, Minnesota: University of Minnesota Press, 82–106.

Halley, J. (1994) The Politics of the Closet: Towards Equal Protection for Gay, Lesbian and Bisexual Identity, in J. Goldberg (ed.) *Reclaiming Sodom*, London and New York: Routledge, 145–204.

Halley, J. (1996) The Status/Conduct Distinction in the 1993 Revisions to Military Anti-Gay Policy: A Legal Archaeology, *GLQ*, 3(2–3), 159–252.

Halperin, D. (1995) *Saint Foucault: Towards a Gay Hagiography*, Oxford and New York: Oxford University Press.

Hansard (1958) Official Reports, 5th Series, Parliamentary Debates, House of Commons, vol. 596.

Hansard (1965) Official Reports, 5th Series, Parliamentary Debates, House of Lords, vol. CCLXVI.

Hansard (1966) Official Reports, 5th Series, Parliamentary Debates, House of Commons, vol. 731.

Hansard (1967) Official Reports, Standing Committee F, House of Commons, vol. 10.

Hansard (1994) Official Reports, 6th Series, Parliamentary Debates, House of Commons, vol. 238.

Hansard (1996) Official Reports, Standing Committee D, House of Commons, no. 7.

Hansard (1996) Official Reports, 6th Series, Parliamentary Debates, House of Commons, vol. 277.

Hansard (1998) Official Reports, Parliamentary Debates, House of Commons, no. 1793.

Hansard (1998) Official Reports, Parliamentary Debates, House of Lords, no. 1741.

Hansard (1999) Official Reports, Parliamentary Debates, House of Commons, no. 1810.

Hansard (2000a) Official Reports, Parliamentary Debates, House of Commons, http://www.parliament.the-stationery-office.co.uk/pa/cm199900/cmhansard/.../00210-14.ht, 10 February 2000, 15/06/00.

Hansard (2000b) Official Reports, Weekly, Parliamentary Debates, House of Lords, http://www.publications.parliament.co.uk/pa/ld1999697/ldhansard/pdrn/lds00/text/00411-05.htm, 11 April 2000, 15/06/00.

Hart, H.L.A. (1963) *Law, Liberty and Morality*, Oxford: Oxford University Press.

Hart, L. (1994) *Fatal Women*, London and New York: Routledge.

Harvey, C.J. (1998) Taking Human Rights Seriously in the Asylum Context? A Perspective on the Development on Law and Policy, in F. Nicholson and P. Twomey (eds) *Current Issues of UK Asylum Law and Policy*, Aldershot: Ashgate Dartmouth, 213–233.

Hathaway, J.C. (1991) *The Law of Refugee Status*, Toronto and Vancouver: Butterworth.

Healy, M. (1996) *Gay Skins*, London and New York: Cassell.

Hefferon, L. (1993) In Search of a Human Rights Approach to Refugees, in A. Whelan (ed.) *Law and Liberty in Ireland*, Dublin: Oak Tree Press, 184–202.

Hefferon, L. (1994) *Human Rights: A European Perspective*, Dublin: Round Hall Press.

Helton, A.C. (1983) Persecution on Account of Membership in a Social Group as a Basis for Refugee Status, *Columbia Human Rights Law Review*, 15, 39–67.

Herek, G.M. (ed.) (1996) *Out in Force*, Chicago: University of Chicago Press.

Herman, D. (1993) The Politics of Law Reform: Lesbian and Gay Rights Struggles into the 1990s, in J. Bristow and A.R. Wilson (eds) *Activating Theory: Lesbian, Gay and Bisexual Politics*, London: Lawrence and Wishart, 246–263.

Herman, D. (1994) *Rights of Passage: Struggles for Lesbian and Gay Equality*, Toronto: Toronto University Press.

Higgins, P. (1996) *Homosexual Dictatorship*, London: Fourth Estate.

Hindness, B. (1996) Liberalism, Socialism and Democracy: Variations on a Governmental Theme, in A. Barry, T. Osborne and N. Rose (eds) *Foucault and Political Reason*, London, UCL Press, 65–80.

Hocquenghem, G. (1980) *Homosexual Desire*, London: Allison and Busby.

Honeychurch, K.G. (1996) Researching Dissident Subjectivities: Queering the Grounds of Theory and Practice, *Harvard Educational Review*, 66(2), 339–355.

HPAT (Homosexuality Policy Assessment Team) (1996) *Report of the Homosexuality Policy Assessment Team*, February, London: Ministry of Defence.

Hughes, G. (1998) Understanding Crime Prevention: Social Control, Risk and Late Modernity, Buckingham: Open University Press.

Hunt, A. (1987) The Critique of Law: What is Critical about Critical Legal Studies?, in P. Fitzpatrick and A. Hunt (eds) *Critical Legal Studies*, Oxford, UK, and Cambridge, MA: Blackwell, 5–20.

Hunt, A. (1997) Law, Politics and Social Sciences, in D. Owen (ed.) *Sociology after Postmodernism*, London: Sage Publications, 103–123.

Hunt, A. and Wickham, G. (1994) *Foucault and the Law*, London: Pluto Press.

Hyde, A. (1997) *Bodies of Law*, Princeton, NJ: Princeton University Press.

Immigration and Nationality Directorate (2000) Asylum in the UK, http://www.homeoffice.gov.uk/ind/asylum/asylum_home.html, 08/11/00.

Ireland, P. and Laleng, P. (eds) (1997) Introduction, *The Critical Lawyers' Handbook*, 2nd edn, London and Chicago: Pluto Press, 1–9.

Irigaray, L. (1985) *The Speculum of the Other Woman*, Ithaca, NY: Cornell University Press.

Jacobson, P.D. (1996) Sexual Orientation and the Military, in G. M. Herek (ed.) *Out in Force*, Chicago: Chicago University Press, 39–61.

Jacques IAT (11580) (1994, unreported).

Jenks, C. (1996) *Childhood*, London and New York: Routledge.

Kairys, D. (ed.) (1982) Introduction, in *The Politics of Law*, New York: Pantheon Books, 1–10.

Kairys, D. (1992) The Politics of Law: A Progressive Critique, in I. Grigg-Spall and P. Ireland (eds) *The Critical Lawyers' Handbook*, London: Pluto Press: 11–15.

Kaplan, M.B. (1997) *Sexual Justice: Democratic Citizenship and the Politics of Desire*, London and New York: Routledge.

Karlen, A. (1971) *Sexuality and Homosexuality*, London: MacDonald.

Kimmel, M.S. (1994) Masculinity as Homophobia, in H. Brod (ed.) *Theorizing Masculinity*, London: Sage Publications, 119–141.

King, M. and Bartlett, A. (1999) British Psychiatry and Homosexuality, *The Journal of Psychiatry*, 175, 106–113.

Kinsey, A.C., Pomeroy, W.B. and Martin, C.E. (1948) *Sexual Behaviour in the Human Male*, Philadelphia, PA: Saunders.

Kritzman, L.D. (1988) Introduction: Foucault and the Politics of Experience, in L.D. Kritzman (ed.) *Michel Foucault: Politics, Philosophy, Culture*, London and New York: Routledge, ix–xxv.

Laclau, E. and Mouffe, C. (1985) *Hegemony and Socialist Strategy: Towards a Radical Democratic Politics*, London: Verso.

Lash, S. (1993) Genealogy and the Body: Foucault/Deleuze/Nietzsche, in M. Featherstone, M. Hepworth and B.S. Turner (eds) *The Body: Social Process and Cultural Theory*, London: Sage Publications, 256–282.

Lash, S., Quick, A. and Roberts, R. (1998) Introduction: Millenniums and Catastrophic Times, in S. Lash, A. Quick and R. Roberts (eds) *Time and Value*, Oxford: Blackwell.

Levinas, E. (1961) *Totality and Infinity: An Essay on Exteriority*, Pittsburgh: Duquesne University Press.

Lingis, A. (1994) *Foreign Bodies*, New York: Routledge.

Lustig-Prean and Beckett v. *United Kingdom*, 27 September 1999, Application nos 31417/96 and 32377/96.

Lyotard, J.F. (1988) *The Differend: Phrases in Dispute*, Manchester: Manchester University Press.

MacCormick, N. (1982) *Legal Rights and Social Democracy*, Oxford: Clarendon Press.

McIntosh, M. (1968) The Homosexual Role, *Social Problems*, 16, fall, 182–192.

MacManners, H. (1998) Army to Lift Ban on Gay Soldiers, *Sunday Times*, 5 April, p. 1.

MacNay, L. (1996) *Foucault: A Critical Introduction*, Cambridge: Polity Press.

McNay, L. (1999) Gender, Habitus and the Field: Pierre Bourdieu and the Limits of Reflexivity, *Theory, Culture & Society*, 16(1), 95–118.

McRobbie, A. (1992) Post-Marxism and Cultural Studies: A Post-script, in L. Grossberg, G. Nelson and P.A. Treichler (eds) *Cultural Studies*, London and New York: Routledge, 719–730.

Mahoney, P. (1990) Judicial Activism and Judicial Self-Restraint in the European Court of Human Rights; Two Sides of the Same Coin, *Human Rights Review Journal*, 11(1–2), 57–88.

Matter of Acosta, US Board of Immigration Appeals, interim decision 2986, 1 March 1985.

May, T. (1997) *Social Research: Issues, Methods and Process*, 2nd edn, Buckingham: Open University Press.

Miller, D.A. (1988) *The Novel and the Police*, Berkeley: University of California Press.

Miller, D.A. (1991) Anal Rope, in D. Fuss (ed.) *Inside/Out*, London and New York: Routledge, 119–141.

Ministry of Defence (MoD) (2000) *Homosexuality and the Armed Forces: The Armed Forces Code of Social Conduct: Policy Statement*, online www.mod.uk/policy/homo-sexuality/code.htm, accessed 15 June 2000.

Minson, J. (1981) The Assertion of Homosexuality, *m/f*, 5–6, 19–36.

Modinos v. *Cyprus*, Series A No. 259; (1993) 16 E.H.R.R. 485.

Mohr, R.D. (1988) *Gays/Justice: A Study of Ethics, Society and Law*, New York: Columbia University Press.

Moran, L.J. (1991) The Uses of Homosexuality: Homosexuality for National Service, *International Journal of the Sociology of Law*, 19, 149–170.

Moran, L.J. (1996a) *The Homosexual(ity) of Law*, London and New York: Routledge.

Moran, L.J. (1996b) The Homosexualization of Human Rights, in C. Gearty and A. Tomkins (eds) *Understanding Human Rights*, London and New York: Mansell, 313–335.

Moran, L.J. (1997) Enacting Intimacy, *Studies in Law, Politics and Society*, 16, 255–274.

Moran, L.J. and McGhee, D. (1998) Perverting London: The Cartographic Practices of Law, *Law and Critique*, 9(2), 207–224.

Morgan, D.H.J. (1994) Theatre of War, in H. Brod (ed.) *Theorizing Masculinity*, London: Sage Publications.

Morgan, W. (1995) Queer Law: Identity, Culture, Diversity, Law, *Australian Gay and Lesbian Law Journal*, 5, 1–41.

Morris, M. (1988) The Pirate's Fiancé: Feminists and Philosophers, or Maybe Tonight It'll Happen, in I. Diamond and L. Quinby (eds) *Feminism and Foucault: Reflections on Resistance*, Boston, MA: Northeastern University Press, 21–42.

Mort, F. (1994) Essentialism Revisited? In J. Weeks (ed.) *The Lesser Evil and The Greater Good*, London: Rivers Oram, 201–221.

Mosse, G.L. (1985) *Nationalism and Sexuality*, Wisconsin and London: University of Wisconsin Press.

Munoz, J.E. (1996) Ephemera as Evidence: Introductory Notes to Queer Acts, *Women and Performance: A Journal of Feminist Theory*, 8(2), 5–16.

Naffine, N. (1997) *Feminism and Criminology*, Cambridge and Oxford: Polity Press.

Newburn, T. (1992) *Permission and Regulation*, London and New York: Routledge.

Nicholson, L. and Seidman, S. (1995) Introduction, in L. Nicholson and S. Seidman (eds) *Social Postmodernism: Beyond Identity Politics*, Cambridge: Cambridge University Press, 1–38.

Norris v. *Ireland*, Series A No. 142; (1991) 13 E.H.R.R. 186.

Park, R.E. and Burgess, E.W. (1970) *Introduction to the Science of Sociology*, Chicago and London, Chicago University Press.

Parker, A., Russo, M., Sommer, D. and Yaeger, P. (eds) (1992) *Nationalisms and Sexualities*, Wisconsin and London: University of Wisconsin Press.

Patton, C. (1993) Tremble Hetero Swine, in M. Warner (ed.) *Fear of a Queer Planet*, Minneapolis: University of Minnesota Press, 143–176.

Phelan, S. (ed.) (1997) *Playing with Fire: Queer Politics, Queer Theories*, London and New York: Routledge.

Pink Paper (1997) News in Brief, 7 March, 2.

Pink Paper (1999) US Military Don't Ask, Don't Tell Fails, 29 January, 4.

Pink Paper (1999) Mother of All Protests, 12 February, 3.

Plummer, K. (1975) *Sexual Stigma: An Interactionist's Account*, London and Boston: Routledge and Kegan Paul.

Policy Advisory Committee on Sexual Offences (1980) *Working Paper on the Age of Consent in Relation to Sexual Offences*, London: HMSO.

Policy Advisory Committee on Sexual Offences (1981) *Report on the Age of Consent in Relation to Sexual Offences*, Cmnd. 8216, London: HMSO.

PRO HO 345/7, CHP/12, Memorandum from the Admiralty for the Departmental Committee on Homosexual Offences and Prostitution.

PRO HO 345/8, CHP/57, Memorandum Submitted. from the Institution of Psychiatry for the Departmental Committee on Homosexual Offences and Prostitution.

PRO HO 345/9, CHP/95, Memorandum of Evidence Prepared by a Special Committee of the British Medical Association for Submission to the Departmental Committee on Homosexual Offences and Prostitution.

R v. *Immigration Appeal Tribunal ex parte Shah*, All England Law Reports 12 May 1999, 555h.

R. v. *Ministry of Defence, ex parte Smith and other applicants* [1995] 4 All England Law Reports.

R. v. *Ministry of Defence, ex parte Smith and other appeals* [1996] 1 All England Law Reports.

R. v. *Secretary of State for the Home Department ex parte Binbasi* (1989) IMM AR 595.

R. v. *Secretary of State for the Home Department* v. *'S.'* IAT (75394) (1996, unreported).

Rabinow, P. (1984) *The Foucault Reader*, Harmondsworth: Penguin.

Rajchman, J. (1988) Foucault's Art of Seeing, *October*, 44, spring, 89–119.

Ramazanoglu, C. (ed.) (1993) *Up Against Foucault: Explorations of Some Tensions between Foucault and Feminism*, London and New York: Routledge.

Rand for the National Defense Research Institute (1993) *Sexual Orientation and the US Military Personnel Policy: Options and Assessment*, MR–323–OSD.

Re: GJ (1312/93) unreported decision of the New Zealand Refugee Status Appeals Authority, 30 August 1995.

Richardson, C. (2000) 'Mr. Butler's Experiments', *Gay Times*, January, 19–24.

Robson, R. (1992) *Lesbian (Out)law: Survival Under the Rule of Law*, New York: Firebrand Books.

Rose, N. (1987) Beyond the Public/Private Division: Law, Power and the Family, *Journal of Law and Society*, 14(1), 61–76.

Rose, N. (1990) *Governing the Soul*, London and New York: Routledge.

Rose, N. (1996) Governing Advanced Liberal Democracies, in A. Barry, T. Osborne and N. Rose (eds) *Foucault and Political Reason*, London: UCL Press, 37–64.

Rose, N. and Valverde, M. (1998) Governed by Law, *Social and Legal Studies*, 7(4), 541–551.

Ross, S.D. (1985) Foucault's Radical Politics, *Praxis International*, 5, 131–144.

Rubin, G. (1992) Thinking Sex, in C.S. Vance (ed.) *Pleasure and Danger*, London: HarperCollins, 267–319.

Russell, S. (1998) Sexual Orientation and Refugee Claims Based on 'Membership of a Particular Social Group' Under the 1951 Refugee Convention, in F. Nicholson and P. Twomey (eds) *Current Issues of UK Asylum Law and Policy*, Aldershot: Ashgate Dartmouth, 133–151.

Rutherford, J. (1990) A Place Called Home: Identity and the Cultural Politics of Difference, in J. Rutherford (ed.) *Identity, Community, Culture, Difference*, London: Lawrence and Wishart, 9–27.

Sanchez-Trujillo v. *Immigration and Naturalisation Service* (1986) 801 f2d 1571.

Santos, B. de S. (1998) Time, Baroque Codes and Canonization, in S. Lash, A. Quick and R. Roberts *Time and Value*, Oxford, Blackwell, 245–262.

Sarup, M. (1993) Post-Structuralism and Postmodernism, 2nd edn, New York and London: Harvester Wheatsheaf.

Sawicki, J. (1991) *Disciplining Foucault: Feminism, Power and the Body*, London and New York: Routledge.

Schneider, E.M. (1991) The Dialectics of Rights and Politics: Perspectives from the Women's Movement, in M.A. Albertson-Fineman and N.S. Sweet-Thomadsen (eds) *At the Boundaries of Law: Feminism and Legal Theory*, London and New York: Routledge, 301–319.

Secretary of State for the Home Department v. *'S.'*, IAT (75394) (1995, unreported).

Secretary of State for the Home Department v. *Mihai,* IAT (M690375) (1998, unreported).

Sedgwick, E.K. (1985) *Between Men: English Literature and Male Homosexual Desire*, New York: Columbia University Press.

Sedgwick, E.K. (1991) *The Epistemology of the Closet*, London and New York: Routledge.

Sedgwick, E.K. (1994) *Tendencies*, London and New York: Routledge.

Seidman, S. (1995) Deconstructing Queer Theory or the Under-Theorization of the Social and the Ethical, in L. Nicholson and S. Seidman (eds) *Social Postmodernism: Beyond Identity Politics*, Cambridge: Cambridge University Press, 116–141.

Seidman, S. (1996) *Queer Theory/Sociology*, Oxford: Blackwell.

Seidman, S. (1997) *Difference Trouble*, Cambridge: Cambridge University Press.

Shawver, L. (1995) *And the Flag Was Still There: Straight People, Gay People and Sexuality in the US Military*, New York and London: Harrington Park Press.

Shiner, L. (1982) Reading Foucault: Anti-Method and the Genealogy of Power-Knowledge, *History and Theory*, 21, 382–398.

Silva, E.B. and Smart, C. (eds) (1999) *The New Family*, London: Sage.

Silverman, K. (1992) *Male Subjectivity at the Margins*, New York: Routledge.

Simmel, G. (1950) The Stranger, in K.H. Wolf (ed.) *The Sociology of Georg Simmel*, London: Collier-Macmillan Ltd, 402–408.

Simpson, M. (1994) *Male Impersonators*, London: Cassell.

Simpson, M. (ed.) (1996) *Anti-Gay*, London: Freedom Editions.

Sinfield, A. (1994a) *The Wilde Century*, London: Cassell.

Sinfield, A. (1994b) Foreword, in M. Simpson, *Male Impersonators*, London and New York: Cassell, ix–xii.

Smart, C. (1989) *Feminism and the Power of Law*, London and New York: Routledge.

Smart, C. (1991) Feminist Jurisprudence, in P. Fitzpatrick (ed.) *Dangerous Supplements: Resistance and Renewal in Jurisprudence*, London: Pluto Press, 133–158.

Smart, C. (1995) *Law, Crime and Sexuality: Essays in Feminism*, London: Sage Publications.

Smart, C. (1999) *Family Fragments*, Polity Press: Cambridge.

Smith, A.N. (1990) A Symptomology of an Authoritarian Discourse, *New Formations* 10, 41–65.

Smith, A.N. (1994) *New Right Discourse on Race and Sexuality: Britain 1968–1990*, Cambridge: Cambridge University Press.

Spargo, T. (1999) Foucault and Queer Theory, Cambridge: Totem Books.

Special Report from the Select Committee on the Armed Forces Bill (1985–6), House of Commons Paper No. 170.

Special Report from the Select Committee on the Armed Forces Bill (1990–1), House of Commons Paper No. 179.

Special Report from the Select Committee on the Armed Forces Bill (1995–1996), House of Commons Paper No. 143.

Spivak, G.C. (1985) Strategies of Vigilance: An Interview, *Block* 10, 5–9.

Spivak, G.C. (1991) Theory in the Margin, in J. Arac and B. Johnson (eds) *Consequences of Theory*, Baltimore, MD: Johns Hopkins University Press, 154–180.

Stanley, L. (ed.) (1990) *Feminist Praxis*, London and New York: Routledge and Kegan Paul.

Stein, A. (1997) Sex after 'Sexuality': From Sexology to Post-Structuralism, in D. Owen (ed.) *Sociology after Postmodernism*, London: Sage Publications, 158–173.

Stein, A. and Plummer, K. (1996) 'I Can't Even Think Straight': 'Queer' Theory and the Missing Sexual Revolution in Sociology, in S. Seidman (ed.) *Queer Theory/Sociology*, Oxford, UK and Cambridge, MA: Blackwell, 129–144.

Stevens, D. (1998) The Case of UK Asylum Law and Policy: Lessons from History, in F. Nicholson and P. Twomey (eds) *Current Issues of UK Asylum Law and Policy*, Aldershot: Ashgate Dartmouth, 9–33.

Stonewall (1998) *The Case for Equality* (pamphlet) London: Stonewall Lobbying Group Ltd.

Stoufer, S.A. (1949) *Volume 2: The American Soldier: Combat and Its Aftermath*, New York: Wiley.

Stychin, C. (1995a) *Law's Desire*, London and New York: Routledge.

Stychin, C. (1995b) Essential Rights and Contested Identities, *Canadian Journal of Law and Jurisprudence*, 8, 49–66.

Stychin, C. (1996) To Take Him at His Word: Theorizing Law, Sexuality and the US Military Exclusion Policy, *Social and Legal Studies* 5(2), 179–200.

Stychin, C. (1998) *The Nation by Rights*, Philadelphia, PA: Temple University Press.

Sutherland v. *United. Kingdom* (1997), Application No. 25186/94, Report of the Commission.

Taylor, A. (1997) A Queer Geography, in A. Mendhurst and S.A. Munt (eds) *Lesbian and Gay Studies: A Critical Reader*, London and Washington: Cassell, 3–19.

Taylor, C. (1994) The Politics of Recognition, in D. T. Goldberg (ed.) *Multiculturalism: A Critical Reader*, Oxford, UK and Cambridge, MA: Blackwell, 75–106.

Terry, J. (1991) Theorizing Deviant Historiography, *Differences* 3(2), 55–75.

Terry, J. (1995) 'Anxious Slippages' Between 'Us' and 'Them': A Brief History of the Scientific Search for Homosexual Bodies, in J. Terry and J. Urla (eds) *Deviant*

Bodies: Critical Perspectives on Difference in Science and Popular Culture, Bloomington and Indianapolis: Indiana University Press, 129–169.

Theweleit, K. (1989) *Male Fantasies*, vol. 2, Cambridge: Polity Press.

Thomas, K. (1993) Shower/Closet, *Assemblage* 20, 80–81.

Thomas, P. and Costigan, R. (1990) *Promoting Homosexuality: s. 28 of the Local Government Act of 1988*, Cardiff: Cardiff Law School.

Thomson, A. (1992) Foreword: Critical Approaches to Law: Who Needs Legal Theory?, in I. Grigg-Spall and P. Ireland (eds) *The Critical Lawyers' Handbook*, London: Pluto Press, 2–10.

Tuitt, P. (1996) *False Images: The Law's Construction of the Refugee*, London: Pluto Press.

Tuitt, P. (1997) Defining the Refugee by Race: The European Response to the 'New Asylum Seekers', in P. Ireland and P. Laleng (eds) *The Critical Lawyers' Handbook 2*, London and Chicago: Pluto Press, 96–106

Turkel, G. (1990) Michel Foucault: Law, Power, and Knowledge, *Journal of Law and Society*, 17(2), 170–193.

Turner, V. (1977) *The Ritual Process*, Ithaca, NY: Cornell University Press.

UN (United Nations) (1951) United Nations Convention Relating to the Status of Refugees, 189 UNTS.

UNHCR (United Nations High Commissioner for Refugees) (1979) *Handbook on Procedures and Criteria for Determining Refugee Status*, Geneva: UNHCR.

Valdes, F. (1995) Queers, Sissies, Dykes, and Tomboys: Deconstructing the Conflation of 'Sex', 'Gender', and 'Sexual Orientation' in Euro-American Law and Society, *California Law Review*, 38(1), 11–375.

Vraciu IAT (11559) (1994, unreported).

Vraciu IAT (11559) (1995, unreported).

Ward, L. (1999) MPs Back Gay Consent Age of 16 but Face New Clash in Lords, *Guardian*, 26 January, 1.

Ward, L. (2000) Tory Peers Side-Step Battle on Gay Rights, 12 April, http://www.guardianunlimited.co.uk/Archive/Article/0,4273,3985153, 00.html.

Warner, M. (1993) Introduction, in M. Warner (ed.) *Fear of a Queer Planet: Queer Politics and Social Theory*, Minneapolis: University of Minnesota Press, vii–xxxi.

Warner, M. (2000) *The Trouble with Normal: Sex, Politics and the Ethics of Queer Life*, Cambridge, MA: Harvard University Press.

Weeks, J. (1977) *Coming Out*, London: Quartet.

Weeks, J. (1985) *Sexuality and its Discontents: Meanings, Myths and Modern Sexualities*, London and New York: Routledge.

Weeks, J.(1986) *Sexuality*, London and New York: Routledge.

Weeks, J. (1989) *Sex, Politics and Society*, London and New York: Longman.

Weeks, J. (1992) Values in the Age of Uncertainty, in D.C. Stanton (ed.) *Discourses of Sexuality: From Aristotle to AIDS*, Michigan: The University of Michigan Press, 389–412.

Weeks, J. (1995) *Invented Moralities: Sexual Values in the Age of Uncertainty*, Cambridge and Oxford: Polity Press.

Weeks, J. (1999) Sexual Citizenship, *Theory, Culture & Society*, 15 (3–4), 35–52.

Weeks, J. and Donovan, C. (1999) 'Everyday Experiments: Narratives of Non-Heterosexual Relationships', in E. Silva and C. Smart (eds) *The New Family*, London: Sage, 83–99.

West, D.J. (1977) *Homosexuality Re-Examined*, London: Duckworth.

Westbrook, S.D. (1980) The Potential for Military Disintegration, in S.C. Sarkasian, *Conduct Effectiveness: Cohesion, Stress and the Volunteer Military*, Beverly Hills, CA: Sage Publications, 244–278.

Weston, K. (1997) *Families We Choose: Lesbians, Gays, Kinship*, revised edition, New York: Columbia University Press.

Wildeblood, P. (1957) *Against the Law*, London: Penguin.

Williams, P.J. (1993) *The Alchemy of Race and Rights*, London: Virago.

Williams, S.J. and Bendelow, G. (1998) *The Lived. Body: Sociological Themes, Embodied Issues*, London: Routledge.

Wilson, A.R. (1997) Somewhere Over the Rainbow: Queer Translating, in S. Phelan (ed.) *Playing with Fire: Queer Politics, Queer Theories*, London and New York: Routledge, 99–112.

Wintermute, R. (1995) *Sexual Orientation and Human Rights*, Oxford: Clarendon Press.

Wolfenden Report (1957) *Report of the Departmental Committee on Homosexual Offences and Prostitution*, Cmnd. 247: London: HMSO.

Worrall, A. (1990) *Offending Women: Female Lawbreakers and the Criminal Justice System*, London: Routledge.

X v. *Germany* (1976) Application No. 5935/72, 3 D. 7 R., Report of the Commission.

X v. *United. Kingdom* (1978), Application No. 7215/75, European Human Rights Report 63.

Young, A. (1996) *Imagining Crime: Textual Outlaws and Criminal Conversations*, London: Sage Publications.

Young, I.M. (1990) *Justice and the Politics of Difference*, Princeton, NJ: Princeton University Press.

Index